Little America

THE WAR WITHIN THE WAR
FOR AFGHANISTAN

Rajiv Chandrasekaran

BLOOMSBURY

LONDON • NEW DELHI • NEW YORK • SYDNEY

First published in Great Britain 2012

Copyright © 2012 by Rajiv Chandrasekaran

Map by Gene Thorp

The author has asserted his moral rights

Bloomsbury Publishing Plc
50 Bedford Square
London WC1B 3DP

www.bloomsbury.com

Bloomsbury Publishing, London, New Delhi,
New York and Sydney

A CIP catalogue record for this book is
available from the British Library

Hardback ISBN 978 1 4088 3007 9
Trade paperback ISBN 978 1 4088 3180 9

10 9 8 7 6 5 4 3 2 1

Designed by Wesley Gott
Typeset by North Market Street Graphics,
Lancaster, Pennsylvania
Printed in Great Britain by Clays Ltd, St Ives plc

MIX
Paper from
responsible sources
FSC
www.fsc.org   FSC® C018072

For Julie and Max

"You, Miss Maxwell, didn't your government in
     Washington hand you a neatly typed report on
     Kabul? Mean temperature. Dress warmly. Expect
     dysentery."
"Yes," Miss Maxwell laughed.
"And it was all the truth, wasn't it?"
"Yes."
"But did it prepare you for today?"

Caravans
JAMES A. MICHENER
1963

CONTENTS

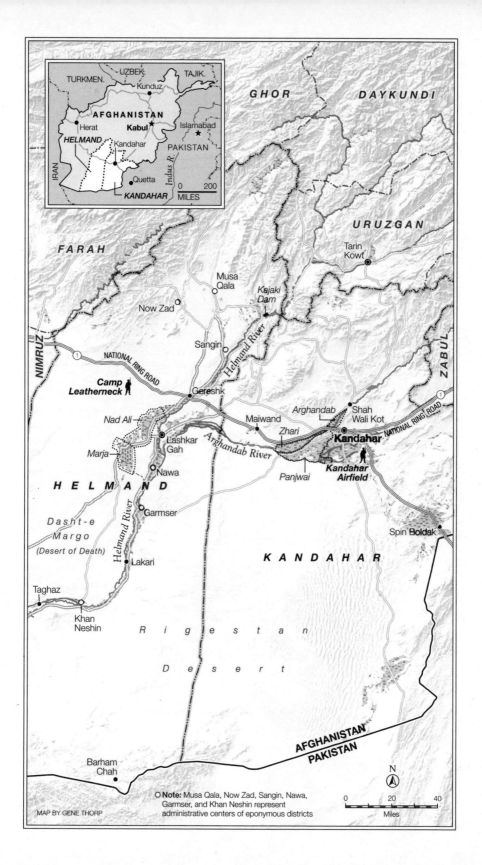

Note: Musa Qala, Now Zad, Sangin, Nawa, Garmser, and Khan Neshin represent administrative centers of eponymous districts

Little America

Prologue

Set atop a dusty plain between two ridgelines, the orchards of Now Zad once yielded pomegranates as large as softballs, luring visitors from across southern Afghanistan during the harvest season. After they gorged on the juicy magenta fruit, most headed home. Others grew so intoxicated by the prospect of farming the fertile soil that they transplanted their lives. Waves of settlers in the 1960s and 1970s transformed Now Zad, which means "newborn" in Persian, into the fourth largest city in Helmand province.

By the fall of 2006, the city looked like old death. The pomegranate fields had been booby-trapped with makeshift mines. Homes and shops had been blown to rubble. Bullet holes pocked the few walls left standing.

The Taliban had invaded Now Zad with hundreds of fighters earlier that year. After desperate pleas from Afghan president Hamid Karzai, the British commanders who were responsible for Helmand under a NATO security agreement dispatched a platoon of Ghurkas to evict the insurgents. But the fearsome Nepalese warriors were outmanned by the Taliban. A tense standoff ensued as the insurgents roamed the city and the Ghurkas hunkered down inside the police station. Every few days, the Taliban would try to storm the compound, sometimes getting close enough to hurl grenades, but the Ghurkas, and subsequent contingents of British troops, managed to keep the enemy at bay with torrents of bullets and rockets. As the fighting escalated, most residents fled.

The Brits were bent on simple survival. Soldiers crouched in their guard towers, gazing at the city through rifle scopes. They named a once lush pomegranate grove just a few hundred yards away Sherwood Forest. A strip of walled compounds teeming with fighters from across the border—their shouts in Urdu revealed their provenance—became known as Pakistani Alley. If the soldiers could have left their Alamo, there would have been no Afghan policemen or soldiers to accompany them on patrol, at least none who were interested in anything more than self-enrichment. The portly police chief, who holed up in the same compound as the Brits, spent his days finding the last few residents to extort and the last few boys to molest.

U.S. Marine Brigadier General Larry Nicholson was appalled when he visited Now Zad on a February 2009 reconnaissance trip. The first thing he saw when he landed was a wall at the police station that was scrawled with graffiti: WELCOME TO HELL. American Marines had relieved the British the year before, and they had expanded the patrol zone by a few blocks, but they were still surrounded on three sides by insurgents hiding in trenches and abandoned houses. A debris-strewn no-man's-land lay in between, trod only by wild dogs. Injuries from IEDs—improvised explosive devices—were so common, and so dire, that the Marine company in Now Zad was the only one in the country to be assigned two trauma doctors and two armored vehicles with mobile operating theaters.

To Nicholson, a compact former infantryman whose ruddy complexion made his weathered face appear perpetually sunburned, the opposing forces staring at each other reminded him of what it must have been like at Verdun during the epic trench battle between the French and Germans in World War I. He met a Marine at Now Zad who told him, "Sir, we patrol until we hit an IED, and then we call in a medevac and go back" to the base. "And then we do it again the next day."

The first U.S. Marines had arrived in Now Zad in May 2008 on a mission to train Afghan security forces. The ninety-five-man reinforced platoon was led by Lieutenant Arthur Karell, a twenty-seven-year-old with degrees from Harvard and the University of Virginia who had postponed practicing law for the adventure of combat. When he landed at the NATO base in Kandahar, about a hundred miles to the southeast, he was given a satellite map of Now Zad marked with a small blue star that indicated where he was to build a police station to house newly trained Afghan policemen. But when he got to Now Zad, he discovered the blue star was four miles beyond the British perimeter. In between were Taliban bunkers and minefields. He crumpled up the map.

In his seven months in the city, the only civilians he saw were a few brave farmers from a nearby village who came looking for firewood. When he led his Marines on patrol, they were met with gunfire less than three hundred meters from the base. His platoon killed dozens of insurgents, but at a cost: One of his men was sent home in a casket, and 20 percent had to be evacuated because of injuries. At first, despite the danger, his Marines didn't complain. There were plenty of bad guys to kill. But even the most trigger-happy eventually started to wonder why they were in a town that had been abandoned. "There's nobody here," they said to Karell. "Why are *we* here?"

When Nicholson became the top Marine commander in Afghanistan in April 2009, he resolved to save Now Zad. IEDs had blown off the legs of more than two dozen Americans in and around the city. Fighting a war of attrition with fixed positions was not something Marines did, at least not in his book. "If we're not showing progress, if we're not showing movement towards stability, what the fuck are we doing?" he asked. The situation was emblematic to him of everything that was wrong with the war.

The officers working for him agreed, as did Helmand's governor, but his bosses at the NATO regional headquarters in Kandahar felt differently, as did the American and British diplomats at the reconstruction office in the provincial capital. They maintained that Now Zad was a ghost town that lacked the strategic significance to merit more troops and dollars. They believed the stalemate was a good enough outcome in an imperfect war: A small unit of Marines had succeeded in tying down hundreds of insurgents who couldn't launch attacks elsewhere. Nicholson was told not to worry about Now Zad.

But he would not let go. His job was to protect the people of Helmand, and that meant allowing the displaced to return home. He bristled when British and American officials told him that the former residents of Now Zad would not come back. That's how people in the West might behave, but Afghans, he believed, would act differently. The only real assets most Helmandis had were their homes and their land. Nicholson felt they would reclaim them if they could.

It seemed as though every day he received word of another American double amputee in Now Zad. Each folded, handwritten casualty notification his aide passed to him stopped his heart a beat longer. The losses of his brother Marines had to be worth something. Failing to act, he thought, would mean they had sacrificed lives and limbs in vain, and it would condemn more Marines to the same fate. He pondered what to do.

When Nicholson's political adviser, John Kael Weston, the diplomat he trusted most, arrived in Helmand that June and asked the general which outpost he should visit first, Nicholson did not mention the places where most of his troops were conducting counterinsurgency operations.

"Kael," he said, "you've got to go to Now Zad."

At first glance, the thirty-seven-year-old Weston seemed like a surfer who'd taken a wrong turn on the way to the beach, but his tousled hair and untucked shirts belied his place among the most erudite and experienced diplomats of his generation. Weston had spent more time in Iraq and Afghanistan than anyone else at the State Department. By the time he landed at Camp Leatherneck, the Marine headquarters in Helmand, he had already put in six consecutive years in the two war zones, with just a few short breaks to visit family and friends back home.

On the U.S. Embassy's organizational chart, Weston was listed as the State Department representative to the Second Marine Expeditionary Brigade. He was supposed to advise the Marines about Afghan government matters, palaver with local leaders, and keep his bosses in Kandahar and Kabul apprised of political developments in the Marine area of operations. Fellow diplomats who had similar jobs generally stuck to those requirements, but Weston saw his writ in more expansive terms. He was the brigade's political commissar. He constantly reminded the Marines that the military had been deployed in support of the Afghan government, not the other way around. And he was Nicholson's confidant. They had forged an enduring friendship while serving side by side for a year in the Iraqi hellhole of Fallujah. The general could open up to him, sharing doubts and gossip, in ways he could never do with the officers under his command. Their close relationship also meant Weston could do what none of the Marines could: When he thought Nicholson was making a mistake, he could walk into the general's office and say so.

Weston's helicopter landed in Now Zad at night. Moonlight illuminated the jagged cliffs as he descended. Over the next three days, he climbed a guard tower to see Sherwood Forest, where the dead pomegranate trees were rigged with explosives. He walked through the shuttered bazaar, praying that his next footfall would not be atop a pressure-plate IED buried in the dirt. Halfway through the patrol, he asked the corporal ahead of him, who was scanning the ground with a metal detector, how much training he had received to use the device. "Well, sir," the corporal replied nonchalantly, "not as much as you'd like to think."

Later on, Weston talked to a few Afghan men who had congregated at a mosque. Some told him the Marine presence was encouraging the Taliban to occupy the city, and others pleaded for the Americans to stay. The following day, he mourned with the Marines of Golf Company when they received word that Corporal Matthew Lembke, who had enlisted on his eighteenth birthday and served two tours in Iraq, then reupped to deploy with his buddies to Afghanistan, had died from an infection. Three weeks earlier, he had stepped on an IED while on a night patrol. The blast had blown off his legs and deposited the rest of him in the crater left by the bomb.

Weston had supported President Barack Obama's decision in early 2009 to deploy 21,000 more troops to Afghanistan. He too believed Afghanistan was the war that the nation had to fight after 9/11. The war that had to be won.

But after almost eight years of fighting, what did that mean? Weston shared Obama's view that the new troops—about half of whom were Marines under Nicholson's command—needed to be directed toward only the most critical areas, the most vital fights. Their job was to hammer the Taliban so that it no longer posed an existential threat to the Afghan government. In some cities and towns, that would require a protect-the-population strategy. In others, the Americans would have to strike hard and fast against insurgent redoubts, but leave the arduous work of security and governing to the Afghans. It was, after all, their country, and Weston knew well the dangers of trying to do too much for them.

As he prepared to depart the outpost, a young corporal approached him. "Sir, I just hope this all adds up," he said. "All of my friends are getting hurt over here." *That's why I'm here,* Weston thought. *My job, and the general's job, is to make sure that by the time those guys are out on foot patrol, it is going to add up to something.* Now Zad seemed like a blood feud to him. "It is truly an area where you've got a company of bad guys versus a company of good guys," he told his parents in an audio recording he sent them shortly after the trip. "The question for me, the general, and others at headquarters is going to be: What kind of further effort do you put towards a place like Now Zad?"

He would answer that question three months later. By then, Nawa, Garmser, and Khan Neshin—the districts that had been the Marines' initial focus—had grown relatively quiet. Nicholson wanted to address other problems in the province, and the arrival of a replacement battalion in northern Helmand provided an opportunity to make a big push in Now Zad. One night in early October, Nicholson made his pitch to Weston.

"I'm frustrated," he said. "I feel like a bulldog who wants two more links in my chain."

"You're on twitch muscles," Weston replied.

"I am. There are places I can't go right now and it's killing me," Nicholson said. "I'd like to finish Now Zad because I think there's a strategic payback and benefit of showing people what we're doing—we'll repopulate the second largest city in Helmand." (Only Nicholson thought Now Zad was once that big. Afghan records listed it as fourth.)

"The people have to want to come back," Weston said. "And right now, it doesn't sound like they want to."

Such raw discussions did not occur often among civilians and generals, but Weston and Nicholson trusted each other.

"If you clear it, they will come," Nicholson continued.

"I'm just being honest with you," Weston said. "I don't

believe in the time we've got that Now Zad is where we should focus our attention. Our report card ain't going to be about Now Zad."

"When Now Zad starts to be repopulated, it will be one of the biggest stories to come out of Afghanistan."

"If the world still cares about Afghanistan."

"The world will care about it," Nicholson said.

The next morning, Weston was in his office eating a bowl of instant oatmeal. He explained to me that his opposition to focusing on Now Zad was rooted not just in the risk of casualties in seizing an empty town. Committing more forces there, in his view, would mean that Nicholson would have fewer Marines to tackle places far more vital to Afghanistan's security.

Back in Washington, Obama was considering a request from the military to send 40,000 more troops to the war front. Nicholson and every Marine officer I met thought America needed more boots in Afghanistan. But not Weston. For him, military commanders needed to be more judicious in how they applied the forces already on the ground. He didn't believe Marines should be charging into remote hamlets in the eighth year of the war. He believed the war should be about triage—protecting the most important cities and towns so the Afghan government would have a fighting chance of holding on to power.

Two months earlier, he had been sitting next to Nicholson in a conference room during a planning session for an assault on Now Zad. Halfway through, Nicholson had been handed a folded note. A twenty-one-year-old Navy petty officer, Anthony Garcia, who had been serving as a medic for a Marine platoon, had been killed by a roadside bomb in a district almost as remote as Now Zad. The message said Garcia's comrades were still trying to remove his corpse from the smoldering wreckage.

That night, at fifteen minutes after midnight, Weston stood with Nicholson as Garcia's flag-draped body bag was hoisted across the tarmac, between a long row of ramrod-straight Marines, and placed inside a C-130 Hercules transport plane. The chaplain said a prayer, and Nicholson walked up the tail ramp, knelt before his fallen fighter, and paid his respects. The following day brought news that four Marines in the same area had burned to death in their Humvee after striking another bomb.

Weston knew war meant middle-of-the-night repatriation ceremonies, but he wanted each grieving parent who received a knock at the door from Marines in dress blues, bearing the worst possible news a father or mother ever could receive, to know their son had died fighting for key terrain.

In August 2007, exactly two years before Kael Weston gazed on Anthony Garcia's body bag, Senator Barack Obama had declared Afghanistan "the war that has to be won." He pledged to deploy more troops and increase reconstruction funds. "We will not repeat the mistake of the past, when we turned our back on Afghanistan," he had said. "As 9/11 showed us, the security of Afghanistan and America is shared."

For Obama, Afghanistan had been the good war, the war that began with two fallen towers, not the war that stemmed from faulty intelligence and exaggerated claims of weapons of mass destruction. Republicans and Democrats alike had embraced the Afghan operation—to exact revenge and prevent another attack, to sideline radical mullahs and allow girls to attend school. But the war in Iraq had distracted the Pentagon and the White House and had diverted troops, helicopters, and other essential resources from Afghanistan.

When he moved into the White House in January 2009, Obama sought to make good on his campaign promise. His administration's approach to salvaging the failing war, forged through sometimes contentious discussions among his national security team, amounted to calling a mulligan in the eighth year of the conflict: He doubled troop levels, dispatched thousands more civilian advisers, devoted vast sums to reconstruction, and demanded greater accountability from Karzai's government. The Pentagon and the State Department put their best people onto the challenge, many of whom had gleaned valuable counterinsurgency experience from their years in Iraq.

I traveled to Afghanistan soon after Obama's inauguration to observe the war he had inherited, and I returned more than a dozen times over the following two and a half years to track America's progress there. I flew with generals and hiked with grunts, feasted with warlords and walked fields with share-croppers, ducked my head during firefights and witnessed the human toll of roadside bombs. This book traces Obama's war, from early 2009 to the summer of 2011—from the surge to the drawdown. It is set in the southern provinces of Helmand and Kandahar, where most of the new troops were sent, and where the story of the United States in Afghanistan began in the late 1940s, when Americans launched an enormous development effort whose legacy is etched across the Helmand River Valley.

After observing the dysfunctional American attempt to secure and rebuild Iraq, I wondered whether we could get Afghanistan right. Had we learned from our failures? Would more troops, civilian advisers, and reconstruction funds resuscitate a flatlining war? Would a protect-the-population counterinsurgency strategy work in Afghanistan? Would the Pakistanis crack down on Taliban sanctuaries in their country, and would Karzai work in good faith with the United States?

Confronted with a stubborn insurgency in a primitive land, could officials in Washington adapt? Could we wage a good war?

PART ONE

Grand Dreams

1

An Enchanting Time

PAUL JONES ARRIVED in a Chevy pickup, billowing dust clouds in his wake as he crossed the desolate desert. The khaki-clad engineer had set out from his base soon after first light to observe a massive construction project aimed at transforming the long-neglected valley along Afghanistan's Helmand River into a modern society. Irrigation canals would feed new farms that would produce so much food that the country would export the surplus for profit. New towns, with Western-style schools, hospitals, and recreation centers, would rise from the sand. So too would factories, fed by electricity from a generator at a dam upriver. Jones had witnessed a similar metamorphosis near his house on the outskirts of Sacramento, and he was certain it could be duplicated on the moonscape of southern Afghanistan.

Jones was sixty-three but appeared as hale and trim as a man two decades younger, save for his graying hair, which he covered with a hat or helmet while outside. One of his sons, an Army aviator, had been killed in the war a few years earlier. His wife, who remained at the family home, could not fathom why he wanted to embrace a hardscrabble existence halfway around the world. He had been indecisive, despite his employer's urging, until he heard a preacher on an AM radio station out of Modesto: "Go into a far country—a strange land—inhabited by a different people. Let God within you point the way!" So he let himself be lured by the prospect of adventure and altruism. His country and his employer, the construction firm

Morrison-Knudsen, were doing something grand and noble. He wanted to be a part of it.

The year was 1951.

Before he departed the United States, his boss told him that the company's first residential project, encompassing 16,000 acres, "must be completed at once." The Afghan government had promised new settlers, who had begun traveling west and south to Helmand on meandering camel trains, that they would be able to farm irrigated fields within sixty days. But surveyors had not yet finished apportioning the plots, and construction crews had not even begun to dig the canals.

To oversee the work, Jones had to leave his comfortable base, which had whitewashed barracks, a weekly movie night, and food that, he reckoned, could compete with the best restaurants in San Francisco, whipped up by Afghans who had been trained by Americans in Kabul. One recent menu had featured steak, fried potatoes, fresh chard, and canned pineapple. There were even cans of Pabst Blue Ribbon beer to slug back at the end of the day. Almost everything at the base had been sent by sea from California or Oregon and then trucked for six hundred miles from Karachi.

Plans drafted by his fellow engineers specified that the first settlement be divided into four villages spaced exactly four miles apart. Each would have 120 identical single-story multi-family dwellings in long rows. Every family would receive an apartment—four to a building—and a half acre of land nearby on which to plant a personal garden. The families would also get at least 10 acres of farmland outside the village on which they were to raise crops for sale. Alfalfa, clover, cotton, grapes, fruit trees, and wheat were to cover a 2,000-acre experimental farm that would verify which crops were best for the new residents.

On that cloudless but chilly February morning, Jones toured Village No. 1 with Jan Mohammed, the director of building construction for the Helmand Valley agricultural commission. Jones recorded his recollection of the conversation and his guide's accent:

"What else will be on this project?" he asked Jan.

"We will have a central city. Here will be a big hotel—big

mosque—big business. . . . In each village we will have school through *eight* grade—*compoolsury* education for both boys and girls, as you say in *Amrika.*"

"And you will have high schools?"

"Oh, yes—high schools. Here *weel* be *ooneeversitee.*"

Jones wanted to know what crops the people would grow.

"Oh, many *theengs*—wheat, cotton, corn, sugar beets, alfalfa, clover, fruit. We will have sugar mill and *fabreek* factory."

What about electricity?

"We want that very soon," Jan said. "We *weel* have hospitals. We *weel* have sports area in each village."

"How long will it take to get going on these things, Jan?"

"Maybe ten to fifteen years."

"That will be marvelous."

As Jones watched Afghan laborers toiling under American supervision, he came to share Jan's enthusiasm. A modern Afghanistan would soon rise from centuries of conflict and neglect. He was certain he was witnessing "the beginning of a new civilization."

The Helmand River Valley has been the chalice of many dreams. The swift water lured nomads across the Desert of Death to replenish their urns. The fertile banks cradled Bronze Age civilization. The escarpments provided a majestic home for the emperors who lorded over a vast swath of Central Asia in the tenth century. One millennium later, the arid landscape that hugged the river inspired Afghanistan's king to transform his nation.

The development of the valley began during the Holocaust. The Nazis forced Jewish furriers to shut their businesses in Paris, Leipzig, and other European cities. Many of those able to flee moved to New York, where they had to find new sources of pelts. They soon turned to Afghanistan, whose hills abounded with karakul—Persian fat-tailed sheep. The soft, curly black fleece of their newborn lambs became lustrous coats and hats. By 1942, Afghanistan was exporting 2.5 million pelts a year to the United States. Because of currency-exchange controls that functioned as a tax, the sale of each pelt deposited a few dollars into the country's treasury.

At the end of World War II, Afghanistan had $100 million in gold and foreign-exchange reserves. As Europe began digging out of its rubble, the thirty-two-year-old king in Kabul, Mohammed Zahir Shah, decided to use the fur windfall to vault his primitive, landlocked nation into the modern era by harnessing the raging waters of the majestic Hindu Kush. He imagined the valley as a fertile oasis.

He was motivated, in part, by the prospect of resurrecting what Genghis Khan had destroyed. The Ghaznavid rulers who had conquered much of Central Asia ten centuries earlier had spent their winters along the Helmand River, not far from where Jones stood that morning in 1951. They had built imposing mansions and a towering arch, and irrigated their fields with an elaborate network of canals fed by the river. When the Mongols had descended on the area in the early thirteenth century, Genghis Khan had ordered not just the homes destroyed but the canals too. Then, to ensure that what had been lush farms would remain a desolate wasteland, he had salted the ground. If Zahir Shah could build a modern city next to those ruins in the southwestern hinterlands, it would strengthen his claim to the nation his father had seized seventeen years earlier, suggesting to his countrymen a connection between the Ghaznavid dynasty and the current occupants of the royal palace in Kabul.

The king also saw the project as a way to redraw the Durand Line, the 1,200-mile-long boundary demarcated by the British in 1893 between colonial India and unconquerable Afghanistan in an attempt to divide and control the ethnic Pashtun population along the frontier. Zahir Shah, who was a Pashtun, wanted to create a new country called Pashtunistan, to be carved out of what would become northern Pakistan and eventually absorbed into Afghanistan. Although it was an impossible quest—there was no way the new nation of Pakistan would cede territory—the idea of an ethnically homogeneous state shaped the king's thinking about development in the Pashtun heartland of southern Afghanistan. If he could deliver real benefits for his subjects on the Afghan side of the border, he figured, Pashtuns in Pakistan would notice and rise up to merge.

Zahir Shah had another goal, one far less quixotic than

reclaiming the glory of a lost civilization or seizing his neighbor's turf. Many in the hinterlands, particularly those from
other ethnic groups—Tajiks, Uzbeks, Hazaras—did not regard
the king as a legitimate ruler. Even many of his fellow Pashtuns
were suspicious of his government. Isolated in remote valleys
and towns far from the capital, Afghans exhibited the same
sort of rugged self-sufficiency that had characterized early
American settlers on the western plains. Their lives were contained in their villages. They married their cousins and spent
their lives tending fields and herding goats. They sought little
from the state, which had little to offer. In return, they wanted
to be left alone.

Reaching out to his subjects was nearly impossible. Paved
roads ended at the gates of Kabul. So too did the country's rail
tracks. There were few telegraph and telephone lines. (To call
Kandahar, the principal city in the south, which was three hundred miles away, the king had to use a radiophone.) His army
was tiny and largely cantoned in the capital; when the country
had to defend itself from invaders, the tribes formed militias,
which were disbanded when hostilities ceased. He hoped the
project would start to transform his rudimentary nation into a
coherent whole and extend his influence to the far corners of
his kingdom.

The king believed his nation had to embrace progress. If his
people were to rise out of poverty and illiteracy, taxes needed
to be collected, the population counted, roads built, health
clinics established, and schools erected. In the decade before
the war, he and his father had sought development assistance
from the Germans, who had constructed a radio tower, a power
plant, and a handful of small carpet factories and textile mills
in Kabul, all of which were run under a royal license. In 1945,
he decided to expand the modernization drive into agriculture,
seeking to create a breadbasket that could ease the pain of
frequent food shortages. German and Japanese engineers had
helped to repair two primitive canals off the Helmand River in
the 1930s, but they had eventually been evicted during World
War II under pressure from the British and Soviets. With the
hostilities over, the king envisioned a far grander development
effort. His Cornell-educated minister of public works had pro-

posed building a large canal to feed two new farming communities that would be carved out of the desert. The king thought
it a brilliant idea. Because the Afghans lacked the necessary
equipment and engineering expertise, they had to look overseas. The king turned to the world's newest superpower, the
United States. After all, it was the Americans who had enriched
his nation by purchasing so many karakul pelts.

In 1946, the royal government hired Morrison-Knudsen, the
giant engineering outfit that had built the Hoover Dam and the
San Francisco Bay Bridge. The king bequeathed the company
a Mughal palace outside Kandahar in which to set up shop.
Morrison-Knudsen's first task was to widen the road from the
Pakistani border to Kandahar. The supply route was essential
to the firm; it insisted that every piece of equipment, no matter
how small, be brought from the United States. The king didn't
mind because he had the money.

For some of the king's most influential ministers and advisers, who had been sent at great expense by the government to
attend universities in the United States, the project was about
more than just creating new farms. They wanted to bring to
Afghanistan the America that had dazzled them in their school-
days. New villages would be built, with modern schools and
health clinics. Nomads would be resettled, and families from
different tribes would live next to one another rather than in
separate villages. Girls would be educated, and women would
cast off the *chaderi* (what Afghans called the head-to-toe burqa).
Eye-for-an-eye Islamic justice would be replaced with written
laws and august courts. Professional government men from
Kabul would supplant the gray-bearded elders who wielded
power in the provinces. It was to be a grand social engineering
experiment, and the English-speaking, suit-wearing Afghans
who had the king's ear saw in Paul Jones and his fellow American engineers the ideal partners for the transformation of their
nation.

For Morrison-Knudsen, the $17 million project began in the
spirit of America's great postwar ambition. "In a country where
nails practically were unknown because houses are built of
mud, where wheels had not been seen until recent years because
camel trains moved through country where wheels could not

go, a forward-looking government has sought American engineering and construction know-how to bring it irrigation,
hydroelectric power, and modern roads to truck its potentially
great crops to market," the company boasted in an August 1949
employee newsletter. The firm described sending its men to
faraway Pacific islands to purchase military-surplus power
shovels, tractors, scrapers, and rolling machines that were then
shipped via the Panama Canal, the Atlantic Ocean, the Mediter-
ranean Sea, the Suez Canal, the Red Sea, and the Arabian Sea,
before commencing a thousand-mile rail-and-truck journey to
Morrison-Knudsen's base camp. By that fall, the company predicted, "the waters of the Helmand River . . . will be flowing in
the great Boghra Canal that the company has dug through the
desert wasteland."

But this lush agrarian vision soon ran aground. A Morrison-
Knudsen study found that the soil in the new farmland was
shallow, and below it lay an almost impermeable layer of sub-
soil. The Helmand Valley was like a giant planter box without drainage holes. When irrigated by Afghans, who tended
to flood their land, water pooled on the surface, and when it
evaporated, it left salts in the soil that stunted anything that
was cultivated.

The royal government began to develop reservations about
the project. Morrison-Knudsen's answer was to expand. Company executives advocated a far more ambitious development
program in the valley and the construction of a large dam and
reservoir in the upriver hills. The new price tag was $63.7 mil-
lion (about $600 million in 2012 dollars)—more than three
times the value of the original contract.

By then Morrison-Knudsen had already spent $20 million.
The "only tangible returns Afghanistan has are one short road,
one diversion dam, and one incomplete canal," the U.S. ambassador in Kabul, Louis G. Dreyfus, Jr., wrote in a cable to the
secretary of state. In response to the criticism, the company
admitted that "there should have been more . . . to show for
this large expenditure."

The Afghans couldn't afford a bigger project. Increasing competition from Russian and African karakul pelts had pushed
down prices, cutting into Kabul's tax and foreign-exchange rev-

enue. Pakistan, which controlled the principal transit routes linking landlocked Afghanistan to the Arabian Sea, exacted its revenge for the king's Pashtunistan fantasy by restricting and delaying the export of agricultural products, further squeezing the treasury. So the Afghans turned to the Americans once again—this time for a loan.

Impressed with a $100 million tranche the Export-Import Bank had provided the new state of Israel, the Afghans asked for $55 million. The request was rejected. The bank was skeptical that the wide-ranging program proposed by the Afghans and Morrison-Knudsen would succeed, citing the challenges of settling nomads, exporting goods through Pakistan, and marshaling an indigenous labor force large enough to perform the proposed work. The Afghans pared back their request, jettisoning small power stations, cotton gins, and spinning machinery for a textile mill. Dreyfus weighed in, warning Washington that the failure to provide the loan was "seriously undermining U.S. prestige. . . . Abandoned MK camps will stand as monuments of American inefficiency." Although the bank remained dubious, it eventually gave the Afghans $21 million.

With American money sloshing in, the engineers sought to get Afghan water flowing. Before beginning the work, Morrison-Knudsen planned to conduct soil and drainage studies of the entire valley—a standard prerequisite for such projects—to avoid ending up with waterlogged tracts. But when the Afghan government dismissed the need for such time-consuming analysis, the company did not object. It believed the venture was simply too big to fail.

Paul Jones soon grew alarmed. Jan Mohammed and his men failed to meet their construction deadlines. Afghanistan had only a few engineers, and most of them had already been hired by the Americans, often to serve as administrators. Morrison-Knudsen did not grasp that until it was too late, in part because the prideful Afghans were slow to admit they could not complete the work they had promised, which included digging the drainage ditches required to keep water from pooling on the farms. Many settlers wound up living in tents, building their own mud-walled homes, and watching their fields turn into marshes.

The Afghan government eventually asked Morrison-Knudsen to take charge of all of the engineering work. That, of course, required more funding, so the king's men had to return to the United States to ask for another loan. They got it, largely because of Cold War fears in Washington: If it did not pay, Moscow would, and that would allow the Soviets, who were already active in northern Afghanistan, to gain a critical foothold in the south.

Morrison-Knudsen caused its share of problems too. When the Export-Import Bank eliminated the incentive bonuses that had been promised by the Afghan government, the firm's work slowed. Later on, the company took several construction shortcuts and eliminated parts of the project that would come to be seen as vital, including groundwater surveys and road improvements.

In an attempt to increase oversight of the effort, the king created a new bureaucracy, the Helmand Valley Authority, and gave it responsibility for implementing the grand development scheme. The president of the authority was accorded a place in the king's cabinet, so that he could resolve disputes between various ministries that were hindering settlement activity. Washington also became more involved. Heeding Ambassador Dreyfus's warning that America's reputation was at stake in Helmand, President Harry Truman's administration dispatched a team of U.S. advisers in 1952 under his Point Four assistance program, which aimed to blunt Soviet influence in the developing world. One of the team's first tasks was to find a suitable town to house the Americans and Afghans working for the new Helmand Valley Authority.

While the team was tromping around the valley, Paul Jones's two-year contract with Morrison-Knudsen ended. He departed in January 1953, convinced that the drainage problems would soon be surmounted. Afghanistan, he believed, would become "the star of Asia."

The team eventually determined that a plot along the river not far from Qala Bost, the ancient Ghaznavid arch, was the best site, in part because it was situated near a grove of trees. An engineer, Frank Patterson, drafted a report with specifications for the "harmonious" new town—where to put the roads, schools, parks, market, and HVA center. He identified eighteen public buildings (among them a board of trade, a tourist office, and an archaeological museum) and ten commercial buildings (including a cinema and a clubhouse). He even described the width of various roads—residential streets were to be seven yards across, while main boulevards were to be twice as wide—and what sorts of trees should line them. Homes, he noted, should be designed without compound walls to "give a visual effect of openness."

The area had long been called Lashkar Gah—"army barracks" in Persian—because it was where the Ghaznavid kings had quartered their troops. Patterson wanted to name the new community Town of Helmand. The Afghans said Lashkar Gah was just fine.

Soon, however, the Afghans came up with a new name. They started to call the place Little America.

"It was an enchanting time," recalled Rebecca Ansary Pettys, who was among the first residents. She lived there for six years starting in 1958, when she was twelve years old. Her father, Amanuddin Ansary, was an Afghan who had received a doctorate from the University of Chicago and brought back a Finnish-American wife. He moved his family from Kabul at the request of the king, who wanted Ansary to put his American education to use in Helmand.

For the first few years, Pettys was schooled in a neighbor's home with the help of a correspondence program from Baltimore and the expertise of those in the town. Her father taught geology, one of the engineers gave physics lessons, the American wife of another Afghan official organized English classes. Pettys dressed as any American girl in the late 1950s would: knee-length frocks, saddle shoes, barrettes in her hair. When classes were over, she and her friends rode bicycles and gathered in one another's homes to listen to Elvis Presley and the Everly Brothers on 45 rpm records. They drank lemonade and ate ice cream. They frolicked in the community pool (where boys and girls could swim together), played by the river, and swatted balls on the tennis court. Once a week they would head to the nearby Morrison-Knudsen camp, where Paul Jones had lived, to watch movies. "Everything about our lives was American," she said.

One day, Rebecca drove with her father across the desert to see the construction of the canals. He explained how the project aimed to transform Helmand province and, by extension, Afghanistan. But all she saw was an arid and denuded landscape. Then she visited the Qala Bost arch on the outskirts of Lashkar Gah. She recalled her history lessons, and suddenly it all made sense to her. Her daddy was trying to return Helmand to its verdant past.

Ansary had been tapped for the job by his longtime friend Abdul Kayeum, who had been appointed vice president of the Helmand Valley Authority by the king. The two men had been among the first five Afghan students given royal scholarships to study in the United States. They lived together in the same Chicago boardinghouse, and Kayeum also married a woman he met in America. Both men wanted to plow what they had learned back into their native land and plant the seeds of a more prosperous future atop centuries of poverty.

The town developed in the way Frank Patterson had outlined, with perpendicular streets, almost-identical white stucco houses, and lush front lawns. Neighbors could wave at one another because, unlike in every other part of the country, tall walls did not ring each compound. The imposing HVA headquarters building sat along the river. Many of the American engineers who arrived after Paul Jones brought their wives and children from small towns in California, Texas, and Colorado. Most of them had worked on massive postwar irrigation projects in the American West for the U.S. Bureau of Reclamation. To them, Afghanistan was yet another adventure, but with hefty bonuses for serving in a hardship post.

Except that it was not really all that hard. The town store sold cold cans of Coke and packaged food that had been shipped from the United States along with American staples: books, blue jeans, toothpaste. Before the town hospital opened, Dr. Murphy's clinic treated all manner of exotic ailments with

American medicines. The clubhouse featured nightly card games and a Filipino barkeeper who mixed gin and tonics. There were weekly square dances and regular dinner parties where everyone got tipsy. On weekends, the adults lounged on front porches or under the gazebo at the pool. Servants did all of the cooking, cleaning, and gardening.

In its early years, the town was just two blocks wide and eight blocks long. The Americans, along with the Kayeums and the Ansarys, lived in a four-block-long row of stately homes. Afghan administrators and clerks lived in a stretch of more modest bungalows. The natives who worked as cooks, gardeners, and houseboys lived in a village outside Little America and were admitted into the town only during the day. But the Afghan government did not chafe at the segregation. The king's ministers and advisers saw the town as the Americans did: a modern community that village dwellers would soon aspire to create for themselves.

The historian Arnold Toynbee visited Lashkar Gah when Rebecca and her brother, Tamim, lived there, finding it "a piece of America inserted into the Afghan landscape." He observed that "American-mindedness is the characteristic mark of the whole band of Afghan technicians and administrators who are imposing Man's will on the Helmand River. . . . The new world they are conjuring up out of the desert at the Helmand River's expense is to be an America-in-Asia."

In 1959, Kayeum held up the example of Little America to help persuade the king's cousin and prime minister, Mohammed Daoud Khan, to allow all Afghan women to cast off their veils. Unlike in almost every other part of the country, Afghan women in Lashkar Gah never donned the all-covering chaderi, which forced the wearer to talk and see through a mesh window. In his town, Kayeum told the prime minister, Afghan women even wore bathing suits in the presence of men at the community pool. The prime minister, in turn, swayed the king. At that year's independence parade, the wives and daughters of the royal family and other high government officials appeared on the reviewing stand with their faces uncovered. Although several religious leaders opposed the gesture—some were arrested after preaching against the regime—the king and the prime minister held fast to their view that there was no basis in the Koran for the veiling of women.

In Little America, the decision encouraged Kayeum and Ansary to attempt even greater social change. When the Helmand Valley Authority set up a public school in the town, Rebecca's father figured she should attend with the boys. She arrived wearing a long black skirt, a white shirt, and a head scarf, and despite fears of a violent reaction from the inhabitants of nearby villages, her first days were free of incident. The next week, Abdul Kayeum's eldest daughter, Rona, joined Rebecca. Then two Afghan clerks decided to send their girls as well. The Lycée Lashkar Gah became Afghanistan's first coeducational school.

For many of the boys at the school, the experience was far more jarring. They were plucked from nearby villages by the government in an effort not just to educate them but to introduce them to a new way of life. Tamim Ansary remembered it this way:

> A jeep full of soldiers would screech into a village. A government rep would hop out and order the village headman to line up the young men. When they had assembled, he would ask them a few questions and make his choices on the spot: "You, you, and you—get your stuff. You're going to school." Then the jeep would roll on to the next town and the new students would be shipped to Lashkar Gah, where they were sprayed for lice and issued gray woolen outfits. So it was that most of my eighth-grade classmates were men in their twenties who dressed like Maoist infantry.

When word of the coed school reached the mullahs in Kandahar, a far more conservative city than Kabul, they resolved to put an end to the nascent women's liberation movement. At Christmastime that year, a mob rampaged through Kandahar, killing a few people and burning down a new girls' school, before government troops smothered the insurrection. Kayeum would learn later that the revolt had been part of a broader plot to attack Americans and progressive Afghans across the south. The residents of Lashkar Gah survived only because the reb-

els in Kandahar had started before the appointed time, allowing authorities to round up conspirators plotting attacks in
Helmand. Rebecca and the other children were petrified, and
their fear only grew a few days later, when they went to the
Morrison-Knudsen camp for movie night. The film was about
the anticolonial Mau Mau uprising in Kenya.

Although the plotters were imprisoned and some were
executed, the government responded by slowing its modernization drive. Officials in Kabul were concerned that the mullahs could easily organize another attack. But Kayeum did not
want to relent. If the government did not continue its efforts to
remove the veil and educate women, he argued, people would
conclude the clergy had won. When his fellow Afghans would
not listen, he warned Americans of the danger he saw in ceas-
ing reform efforts. In a 1962 meeting with the wife of the U.S.
Bureau of Reclamation chief in southern Afghanistan, he said
he had noticed an Afghan farmer observing a team of American technicians "with a very strange expression on his face,"
according to a U.S. Embassy memo written at the time. When
he asked the farmer what he was thinking, "the man told Kayeum that as he looked at the Americans, the thought came to
him that the land upon which they were standing was cursed
because the foot of the infidel had touched the land. . . . He then
predicted to Dr. Kayeum that within twenty years, the entire
Helmand Valley would be a wasteland because of the tinkering
by the infidels." But the embassy dismissed Kayeum's concerns
about such extremist thinking, writing in a cable that he "exaggerated the dangers to the American community in the south."

The anger at the social changes the government sought
could not be separated from growing frustration among the
new farmers about the quality of their land. To lure them
hundreds of miles from their ancestral homes, the government had told them they would receive cropland so fertile
that they would soon grow wealthy. But their fields yielded
less and less each year as salts accumulated in the soil. By
the mid-1960s, farmers in Nad Ali, one of the first tracts to
be developed by Morrison-Knudsen, reported that their har-
vests were a quarter of what they had been in the first year.
In other parts of Helmand, reductions ranged from a half to

two-thirds. Morrison-Knudsen's claim that a larger irrigation project would resolve the initial problems of waterlogging and salinity had proved false. The grand project to make the desert bloom was failing.

As the first signs of trouble appeared in the early 1950s, the Afghan government began complaining to U.S. diplomats in Kabul. As dissatisfaction increased, the embassy urged the State Department to commission an independent study of Morrison-Knudsen's work. The U.S. International Cooperation Agency, charged with implementing the Point Four program, hired the Tudor Engineering Company of San Francisco. In 1956, it issued a lengthy report that largely absolved Morrison-Knudsen and predicted that farm incomes would rise once the project was completed. It accused the Afghans of "unrealistic expectations" and noted that "the quality of workmanship is excellent." What the Afghans did not know at the time was that the Tudor Company was part of Morrison-Knudsen. Its office address was the same as that of Morrison-Knudsen's Afghanistan division: 74 New Montgomery Street in San Francisco.

The Tudor report failed to appease the Afghans. In 1959, the king's government terminated its contracts with Morrison-Knudsen. The firm was replaced by American technicians funded by the International Cooperation Administration, who advised an Afghan-run construction unit that inherited all of Morrison-Knudsen's equipment. The Bureau of Reclamation joined the effort soon thereafter, dispatching a team of hydrologists and soil engineers to Helmand. In 1961, the ICA was incorporated into the newly created U.S. Agency for International Development. Salvaging the irrigation project quickly became one of USAID's top priorities.

The new specialists discovered a fatal flaw in the design of the main canal. Had it been built higher, water would have flowed down the fields, and the excess would have run off into drainage canals. Because the main canal was too low and the fields were not flat, farmers tended to overwater in an attempt to irrigate all of their land, resulting in salt buildup that destroyed the soil. The solution proposed by the Bureau of Reclamation engineers was to move the farmers off their land, level the terrain with bulldozers, and then allow them to return. But the farmers feared they would receive less land or their plots would be shifted elsewhere. When the earthmovers arrived, the farmers met them with rifles. The American engineers were forced to back away.

There was one group of Americans who were welcomed warmly by the Afghans at the time: a motley lot of Peace Corps volunteers. Some were avoiding the Vietnam War draft. Many grew to love the cheap and plentiful hashish that could be procured in any Afghan bazaar. But all of them seemed interested in helping better the lives of the locals in a far less overbearing way than the Morrison-Knudsen engineers or the American-educated Afghans. And they offered to do so for a pittance. By the mid-1960s, there were more than a dozen Peace Corps volunteers stationed in Helmand. Most taught English in village schools, but they lived as the Afghans did—in mud-walled homes without electricity, eating goat stew and flatbread for dinner.

Jonathan Greenburg, who had signed up for the Peace Corps when graduate students could no longer automatically obtain draft deferments, was assigned in 1968 to an agriculture school established by the king on the grounds of a shuttered Morrison-Knudsen camp in the town of Garmser. It had once been a comfortable destination, with a pool, a tennis court, a clinic, and air-conditioned rooms. But the Afghans had been unable to maintain any of it. By the time Greenburg arrived, the pool had been drained, the tennis net was gone, the clinic was empty, and air ducts were no longer connected to anything that blew cool air. A few days later, the custodian introduced himself. "Mister, I speak English," he said. "I work for M-K. One, two, three. Jesus Christ. Fuck."

Over the following months, Greenburg walked through the fields Paul Jones had tried to irrigate. He concluded that an easier fix than bulldozing the land would be to encourage the Afghans to switch from growing only wheat to cultivating a mixture of crops, including vegetables that would be more tolerant of the poor soil and uneven irrigation. Onions and spinach were among his leading candidates. He set up a small demonstration farm with a few other Peace Corps workers, but the local farmers weren't interested; their diet consisted largely of bread and meat.

When Greenburg and other Peace Corps volunteers were feeling homesick or wanted to celebrate a holiday in the company of their countrymen, they hitched a ride to Little America. The USAID and Bureau of Reclamation engineers who moved into the Morrison-Knudsen homes were gracious hosts, but they were near the end of their careers and seemed drawn to Afghanistan only because of the additional salary and benefits they earned for being so far from home. Some of the spouses were afraid of the natives and even of the water; one woman took to putting iodine tablets in her bathtub. They overpaid their houseboys, cooks, and gardeners so extravagantly that the servants could afford their own servants. Their self-imposed confinement in the town led to boredom. One summer, the chatter was all about a wife who was carrying on an affair with her male Afghan housekeeper. "The women had nothing to do," remembered Peace Corps teacher Jane Willard. "It was very much a Peyton Place."

Their husbands were just as disconnected from the people they were supposed to be helping. Back in 1967, they had thought they would solve the problem of anemic farm production by introducing high-yield varieties of wheat. The seeds they handed out would ripen in half the time—allowing farmers to plant two crops a year—and each crop would generate twice the wheat. That was the theory. But the USAID advisers failed to account for the migratory patterns of the birds that flew over Helmand right before the harvest. That year, the agency wrote in a report, "the birds got fat and the farmers did not."

From 1960 to 1970, the Helmand Valley consumed almost three-quarters of all U.S. assistance to Afghanistan. In the early 1970s, the Americans decided to try once again to bulldoze the land. This time, they would begin with a 200-acre demonstration area. The plan was to move the farmers and their families to a desert escarpment while the land was flattened and new drainage ditches were dug. The Americans also wanted to make the area more orderly: Instead of each farmer working several small plots with meandering borders, the land would be divided into square parcels, even if it meant removing homes and trees. The Americans were convinced that once they completed the demonstration project, Afghans up and down the Helmand Valley would want the same improvements.

But once again, the Afghans were reluctant to leave their land. In March 1971, the USAID office in Kabul turned to Dick Scott for answers. The middle-aged Texan wasn't an engineer or scientist. He had studied anthropology and sociology, and he had worked on irrigation projects in Turkey. He traveled to Helmand and talked to the farmers. It quickly became clear that they were refusing to move not because they distrusted the Americans but because they didn't believe the Afghan government would allow them to reclaim their land. A few years before, when a small group of farmers had agreed to withdraw temporarily so their fields could be improved, the government had seized their property for a state-run agricultural project.

Scott urged his superiors at USAID to embark on a public information campaign to explain the new program to the farmers and reiterate that they would be able to return to their property. But the Afghan government insisted to USAID officials that the farmers knew enough about the project and would be willing to depart when the time came. USAID officials ignored Scott and ordered millions of dollars of earthmoving equipment to be shipped to Afghanistan. Once the machinery arrived, Afghan officials said they couldn't proceed with the project. But they kept the equipment.

U.S. funding for the salvage effort soon ran out. USAID officials thought about authorizing another multiyear program, but they concluded that the opposition among Afghans to leveling the land would doom further efforts. In July 1974, the project ended.

Then, a few months later, Secretary of State Henry Kissinger visited Kabul and met with Prime Minister Daoud, who told him that the Helmand Valley was an "unfinished symphony." Kissinger assured Daoud that the United States would live up to its responsibilities. Before long, the project resumed. This time, however, the job went to the U.S. Soil Conservation Service. Its specialists deemed impractical the Bureau of Reclamation's plan to bulldoze the land and instead advocated the construction of small ditches to drain excess water from the fields. The service convinced the Afghans that the drains should be dug by hand to employ as many peasants as possible.

On the first farms to receive new drains, yields increased to 75 percent of optimum production within a year. Excited Americans and Afghans hoped they finally had a solution to the problems that had hounded them for thirty years. But in 1978, before the program could be expanded across the valley, Afghanistan's Communist Party staged a coup. Washington ordered the engineers in the south to pack their bags. The following year, Soviet tanks rolled into Afghanistan. By then every American had left Little America.

It would not be the last time America would fail to achieve its goals in Afghanistan.

2

Stop the Slide

THE MARINE PILOT banked hard to the left and then the right through the sweltering night sky without navigational lights, pushing his Vietnam-era CH-53 Super Stallion transport helicopter to its limits as he descended toward a dirt field. Insurgents armed with automatic rifles and rocket-propelled grenades could have been lurking on the ground below. The passengers in the cargo bay, their brown camouflage uniforms speckled with hydraulic fluid from a leaky rotor shaft, experienced whiplash and then momentary free fall. The pilot wasn't taking any chances. His payload included the top Marine commander in Afghanistan, Larry Nicholson, who sat on one of the side-facing canvas seats in the back, eyes shut, unfazed by the roller-coaster descent.

The helicopter set down with a thud, and within seconds the passengers shuffled off the tail ramp toward the barely visible form of a Marine holding a red light stick. He escorted Nicholson's party into what appeared to be a bombed-out two-story brick building with no roof or windows. The only furniture, save for a few cots, were four-foot-long Javelin missile cases that had been converted into benches. Flashlights were verboten at night—white light could draw enemy fire—so everyone felt his way around. The resident Marines knew exactly how many steps to take before hitting a wall; the newcomers nearly toppled off a half-finished staircase with no banister.

It was late June 2009, and Nicholson had arrived at Patrol Base Jaker, a sandbar of allied control surrounded by a sea of insurgency. Before an advance party of U.S. Marines had shown up a few weeks earlier, just forty British and Danish soldiers had lived in the ramshackle encampment. They had been responsible for all of Nawa district, a swath of hand-worked farms and mud-brick houses along the western bank of the Helmand River where American engineers had dug irrigation canals six decades before. The soldiers were supposed to train a contingent of Afghan soldiers and policemen, but many of them were corrupt, incompetent, or simply lazy. As attacks increased, the Europeans spent less time patrolling and more time hunkered inside the base. Freed from interference, the Taliban set up checkpoints on the roads, taxed merchants in the bazaar, planted homemade bombs, and took potshots at Jaker from less than a mile away. Jaker's jittery occupants often responded with heavy machine guns and shoulder-fired missiles, which sometimes overshot their intended targets and struck nearby homes.

Most of the schools and stalls in the market had closed. The district governor spent much of his time away from the district, as did the area's few other government officials. Residents who had the means fled twenty miles north to Lashkar Gah, the provincial capital. Poor sharecroppers kept their heads down and worked their fields, hoping they would not get caught in the cross fire. Others stuck around to abet the insurgency—either because they supported the Taliban or because they were too fearful to refuse its requests for help. Nicholson deemed the situation intolerable.

He projected the image of a tough, gruff Marine who relished a good fight. But that façade hid a deft practitioner of modern warfare whose out-of-uniform interests included listening to the pop star Katy Perry and watching *Downton Abbey,* a British period drama on PBS's *Masterpiece Theater.* He drove an Audi and savored Italian red wine—his stint at the NATO defense college in Rome and at the alliance's headquarters in Brussels had turned him into a Europhile—but he kept that side well hidden from comrades who drove pickups and listened to country music. He had been born in Toronto, and he didn't want anyone to question the degree to which he loved apple pie.

Nicholson had been raised in Washington by his mother, who worked as a secretary at the British embassy. In 1968, when he was twelve years old, he would walk up the hill from his apartment on Massachusetts Avenue to the American University campus, where he joined protests against the Vietnam War. His extracurricular activities eventually prompted his mother to ship him off to boarding school and then to the Citadel, the military college in South Carolina. He joined the Marine Corps upon graduation.

On September 14, 2004, he had taken command of a regiment in Iraq, cocking his arm in a crisp salute as a color guard marched past. Before his predecessor had departed, he'd given Nicholson a bottle of 1999 Réserve Mouton Cadet and told him to open it on the last night of his tour. Because that was nine months away, Nicholson put the bottle of Bordeaux atop a tall wooden cabinet in his office, which was on a base outside Fallujah. That evening, as he sat behind his desk, he had trouble logging in to the military's computer network. He was the boss, so his call for help was answered not by a lowly grunt but by the major in charge of the communications team, a strapping Air Force Academy graduate who had offered to extend his deployment because a replacement had not yet arrived. Nicholson relinquished his seat and walked a few paces away, where he noticed an unplugged electrical cord on the floor. He bent down to find a socket.

At that moment, an insurgent rocket crashed through the window and detonated with an explosion so loud it sent Marines scurrying for cover a half mile away. The major died instantly. Nicholson remained alive, but barely. Because he had been squatting, the shrapnel spared his vital organs. As he was rushed into the base hospital, he repeated over and over, "Don't let them take my regiment away from me!" Doctors inserted a catheter into his bladder—prompting him to scream, "It's my shoulder that hurts, not my dick!"—and performed a tracheotomy before placing him on a medical evacuation flight to Germany. From there he was sent to the Naval Hospital in Bethesda, Maryland. He recovered after several painful months, and was given command of another regiment headed to Fallujah, where he would spend a year working out of the same office. The wine bottle had miraculously survived the explosion, landing upright on the floor with just a few scratches to the label. He put it on the top shelf of a rack at his home in Alexandria, Virginia, adorned with the Purple Heart he had been awarded after the attack.

For Nicholson, a different war lay ahead in Afghanistan. After years of focusing resources on capturing or killing Taliban members, the military wanted to try a new approach to stabilize the country. Nicholson had left Iraq just before General David Petraeus overhauled the U.S. battle plan in Baghdad and imposed a counterinsurgency strategy. COIN, as the military calls it, concentrates not on hunting down guerrillas but on protecting the civilian population from insurgents. The idea is to separate the good from the bad and focus on the good, depriving the insurgency of popular support. COIN theory draws upon what worked—and what didn't—in efforts to suppress guerrilla movements from Malaya to Algeria, but it requires resources and time. Protecting civilians means ensuring law and order, providing basic services such as education and health care, setting up government operations, training local security forces, and rebuilding infrastructure. COIN was the order of the day in Afghanistan, and it fell to Nicholson, who had more than 10,000 Marines under his command, to implement the new strategy in his patch.

After a brief tour of the patrol base—there was not much to see in the darkness—he huddled in an upstairs room with officers from the battalion responsible for the district. Despite the trappings of modern war in the downstairs command center—the laptops and telephones that linked them to an Air Force base outside Las Vegas where technicians sitting in trailers flew the unmanned, missile-equipped drones that circled over the Helmand Valley—Nicholson's meeting could have been a Civil War reenactment. A dozen officers looked at a map on a makeshift table illuminated by three flickering candles. They had reviewed their plans almost a dozen times, but the general wanted to talk it through once more. In two or three days, depending on the weather, a flock of helicopters would alight in Nawa in the wee hours of the morning and deposit hundreds of Marines. Another battalion would arrive in Garmser, the district to the south. It would be the Marine Corps's largest air assault since the Vietnam War. The goal wasn't so much to catch the Taliban by surprise—they knew the Americans were coming soon—as to hopscotch the belts of roadside bombs that ringed the districts. The Marines would start from the inside of each community and push outward to the fringes. Not only would this method be safer than working inward, but it amounted to smart counterinsurgency tactics. They would focus on protecting the people first.

But the matter of tactics was vexing the Marines that night. The new top commander in Afghanistan, General Stanley McChrystal, was preparing to issue a directive restricting the use of air strikes. McChrystal was a veteran Special Operations officer who had spent his career pursuing bad guys rather than protecting the people. In Iraq, he had directed covert teams that hunted insurgents and unleashed blistering firepower in residential areas. By the time he arrived in Kabul earlier that June, however, he was embracing COIN with the fervor of the recently converted. It was good politics: COIN was what top officials at the Pentagon and the White House thought would turn around the Afghan War. It also made good sense. The military had emphasized counterterrorism in the first five years of the war, spending the precious few resources Defense Secretary Donald Rumsfeld allocated to Afghanistan on raids to hunt Taliban leaders. Those operations had become a major irritant in the United States' relationship with President Karzai. He was particularly incensed by nighttime missions to kill or capture insurgents, which often involved U.S. troops storming into Afghan homes, and by the use of air-dropped bombs to flatten buildings used as Taliban hideouts. In many cases, insurgents would seek refuge in compounds inhabited by women and children—so as to use them as human shields or, if the house was bombed to bits, as pawns in their propaganda campaign to convince the Afghan people that coalition forces were indiscriminate murderers of the innocent. McChrystal wanted a rapprochement with Karzai, and he had come to believe the COIN axiom that killing one civilian creates ten new insurgents. Thus the new restrictions.

Nicholson had read a draft of the directive, and he thought

it was a little excessive. The new rules prevented air strikes on residential buildings unless troops were in imminent danger of being overrun or the house had been observed for more than twenty-four hours to ensure no civilians were inside. If the bad guys ran into a home, they would have a free pass, unless the Americans were willing to wait them out.

"If we have to treat every house like a mosque, it'll result in a whole lot more casualties," Nicholson growled. "We'll have to explain this to a lot of families."

Sometimes, Nicholson told the rapt officers in the candlelit room, using a precision-guided missile or bomb was safer for civilians than relying on ground-fired weapons. "Have you seen a nineteen-year-old lance corporal behind a .50-cal?" he said, referring to a powerful machine gun. "You're going to kill people three towns away."

He implored his Marines not to dwell on the rules; he would worry about them. But he urged them to be mindful of civilian casualties. After all, their mission was to protect the good people of Nawa, not to kill as many Taliban as they could. He told the battalion commander to hold a community meeting within the first forty-eight hours of the operation. "You're going to drink lots of tea. You'll eat lots of goat, and you'll need to be ready for some man-love," he said, noting the custom among Afghan men of holding hands in public. "None of you guys are homophobic, are you?" The Marines smirked.

Ninety minutes after he arrived, the metronomic *whoop-whoop* of an approaching helicopter interrupted the conversation. As he rose to catch the flight that would ferry him back to his headquarters, he warned the officers that COIN would not be simple—or quick. "The easy part will be finding and killing the Taliban. The hard part is everything else. They're a pragmatic people. After thirty years of war, they're not going to take sides right away. It'll take time. You can surge troops, but you can't surge trust."

When Nicholson asked Afghans how they felt about the United States, he almost always heard positive answers. Afghans tend to tell visitors what they want to hear, especially visitors surrounded by men with big guns. But the Helmandis also

looked back on the Little America project with genuine fondness. None of them seemed to understand that it had failed
to accomplish its original goal of modernizing Helmand. They
knew two essential facts: The canals that fed their subsistence
farms had been built by the Americans, and everything that
had happened after the Americans departed was bad.

The Communist revolution in 1978 and the subsequent
Soviet invasion had upended the province. The new government's land reform campaign, intended to liberate tenant
farmers from peonage, had targeted wealthy tribal leaders
who controlled much of the arable terrain in areas of Helmand
that had not been part of the Little America blueprint. Many
had been killed, and others had fled to Pakistan and beyond.
Although these khans were feudal lords, they had also settled
disputes, fended off bandits, and performed other basic acts
of local governance. Their absence created a power vacuum
that was filled not by the new Communist government, whose
secular agenda generated deep resentment in the conservative
south, but by the mullahs and upstart warlords leading the fight
against Soviet occupation. One of them was a middle-aged religious leader named Mullah Nasim Akhundzada.

Hailing from a family of modest means and social status,
the charismatic Mullah Nasim rallied a cadre of devoted warriors, quickly becoming one of the most prominent and powerful commanders in the mujahideen resistance. He savagely
attacked his rivals and soon claimed leadership of the Alizai
tribe by fighting others who aspired to the position. At one
point in the mid-1980s, intratribal warfare among the Alizais
in northern Helmand was so violent that residents welcomed
Soviet troops as peacemakers.

To fund his militia, Mullah Nasim turned to the opium-
producing poppy, which had been grown only sparsely in the
hills of Helmand as a palliative for the locals and as a small-time
cash crop in places where little else would bloom. In 1981, he
issued a religious decree stating that poppy cultivation was per-
missible if farmers needed to provide for their families. And
many of them did. Persistent drainage problems in the valley
made it difficult to grow fruit and vegetables; those who could
cultivate their land feared taking produce to market because of

the fighting. Poppy, however, flourished in waterlogged tracts, and the harvested opium paste could be stored by farmers for as long as two years.

Mullah Nasim then set out to dominate the burgeoning drug trade that he had encouraged. He purchased much of the crop by offering indebted farmers payment when they planted it. It was a shrewd deal: He bought low and then pocketed the difference when he sold the harvest at a profit; it also allowed him to extend his grip on the central and southern parts of the province. He soon shifted from condoning the cultivation of poppy to compelling it; his deputies threatened farmers with torture and execution if they refused to grow it on at least half their land. His family also profited from a network of processing labs they established in northern Helmand, fed by electricity generated at the American-built dam. Before long, Mullah Nasim was the richest, strongest man in the province. Only the northern district of Kajaki remained beyond his grasp because the khans there allied themselves with a rival mujahideen faction led by the warlord Gulbuddin Hekmatyar.

Having seized much of the province, Mullah Nasim offered to go legit in 1989. He told the U.S. Embassy in Islamabad that he would ban poppy cultivation in Helmand in exchange for $2 million in development aid. His specific motivation in abandoning poppy remains a mystery, but it may have been a short-term play to squeeze Hekmatyar. To prove to the Americans he was serious, Mullah Nasim issued an order prohibiting the crop, starving the heroin factories Hekmatyar ran along the border with the help of allies in Pakistan's intelligence service. The following year, as Mullah Nasim traveled to Pakistan to negotiate with the Americans, he was gunned down, allegedly by Hekmatyar's goons.

Mullah Nasim's brothers took his place, and by 1993, they had seized control of Lashkar Gah. One of them, Rasul, proclaimed himself governor. But his reign would be short-lived. The Taliban captured the province the following year, welcomed by residents who had grown weary of the Akhundzadas' brutality and of the infighting among rival mujahideen commanders. Rasul and the rest of the family refused to surrender to the Taliban and fled to Quetta, in Pakistan. After

Rasul died of cancer, his five-foot-tall son, Sher Mohammed, assumed leadership of the clan. He quickly forged an alliance with the Karzai family, which was also living in Quetta. Sher Mohammed cemented the relationship by marrying a sister of a prominent mujahideen commander from Kandahar whose other sister was married to Hamid Karzai's half brother Ahmed Wali Karzai. When U.S. forces toppled the Taliban in 2001 and installed Hamid Karzai as interim president of Afghanistan, one of his first moves was to appoint Sher Mohammed as the new governor of Helmand.

Helmand was the last province to slip from the Taliban's grasp when the Americans arrived. A militia chief who controlled the mountainous northernmost reaches of the province sheltered the movement's reclusive leader, Mullah Mohammed Omar, as he fled from U.S. and Afghan forces closing in on Kandahar. But once the Talibs left—either by crossing into Pakistan as Mullah Omar did or by melting back into the population—Sher Mohammed Akhundzada rolled into Lashkar Gah and welcomed other mujahideen warlords into the provincial government, dividing the spoils among key tribes. Abdul Rahman Jan of the Noorzai, who had helped the Akhundzada family smuggle opium, became the police chief, and Dad Mohammed Khan of the Alikozai, who presided over the province's largest opium bazaar, became the intelligence director. In 2002 and 2003, this trinity seemed to American officials to be the ideal leaders for the new Afghanistan: Despite their rough-and-tumble past and their involvement in the drug trade, they were virulently anti-Taliban and staunchly supported Karzai's fledgling government in Kabul. U.S. Special Operations forces—the only foreign military presence in Helmand at the time—turned to them for help in pursuing the Taliban. That relationship expanded their power. If you crossed them, you risked having them falsely report you to the Americans as a Talib, and that often meant zip cuffs, a black hood, and a trip to the military prison on Bagram Airfield.

All three strongmen—everyone called them SMA, ARJ, and Amir Dado—ran roughshod over the province. Instead of trying to reopen schools and provide other basic services, the squat new governor set out to reestablish his family's domi-

nance over the drug trade. His lieutenants encouraged struggling farmers, who had not received any meaningful assistance
from the United States or nongovernmental organizations, to
plant poppies—and they offered, as had been done during the
jihad years, to pay up front. By the spring of 2003, magenta
and fuchsia flowers sprouted across the fields of Little America, their petals concealing seed capsules that, when scored by
legions of migrant laborers, would disgorge a whitish sap that
could be refined into heroin. Every spring thereafter, more
poppy flowers waved in the fields. By 2006, Helmand was producing more opium than all the world's junkies could consume
in a year. The Akhundzadas and their cronies pocketed much
of the profit, but U.S. intelligence analysts believe a substantial
portion also was sent to top Afghan officials, including members of President Karzai's family. It was the price SMA had to
pay for his governorship.

Karzai made his first visit to Helmand in 2004. When he
returned to Kabul, he told Lieutenant General David Barno,
then the top U.S. commander in the country, that he was
impressed with the new wealth there. He gushed about all the
shiny sport-utility vehicles and gold watches he had seen. He
said nothing about drugs.

A patchwork of militias protected the warlords and their
interests by preying on the population. SMA's network of
gunmen focused on drug smuggling, while intelligence chief
Amir Dado's men earned a reputation for torture and vigi-
lante killings. But it was police commander ARJ's force that
most inflamed Helmand residents. His policemen shook down
travelers at checkpoints and helped themselves to what they
wanted in the bazaars. And they had their way with young
boys.

For those who are wealthy enough to employ a boy as
a servant or powerful enough to kidnap one, pederasty is a
common, socially acceptable practice among the Pashtuns of
southern Afghanistan. In the 1970s, ARJ was a leading member of a subculture among Noorzai tribesmen in Kandahar
that glorified *bacha bazi,* the Pashto term for sex with prepu-
bescent boys. Thirty years later, his policemen used their guns
and uniforms to help satisfy their urges. Mohammed Jan, a

weather-beaten farmer in central Helmand, told me that ARJ's men would snatch boys from the fields and haul them to their station. "They would use the boys for pleasure," Mohammed said. "If their fathers or their brothers asked about them, they would be beaten."

For those brave enough to complain, there was no avenue to redress grievances. The U.S. military did not establish a presence in Helmand until October 2004—and then it was only a small reconstruction office in Lashkar Gah staffed by a few dozen soldiers. The Afghan government also was of little help. People couldn't vote out governors or district chiefs. Under the country's new constitution, written by a Karzai-appointed committee, the president had the power to hire and fire every provincial governor and district governor. And the interior minister, who was appointed by the president, selected all of the local police commanders. If Helmandis wanted to get rid of SMA and ARJ, they had to wait until the next presidential election and hope Karzai wouldn't win a second term. That seemed unlikely. He had won the country's first post-Taliban presidential election, in 2004, in a landslide.

Starting in mid-2002, Taliban commanders who had fled to Pakistan began slipping back into southern Afghanistan and trying to reassemble networks of old comrades. Their initial forays into Kandahar province were unsuccessful; numerous U.S. forces were operating there, and residents were willing to report on Taliban activity. But when Taliban commanders reached Helmand, they were welcomed into villages as old friends. It wasn't that people there had fond memories of their brutal reign, rather that what had followed was so much worse. The Talibs preached in mosques, often invoking ARJ's name and reminding listeners that when they had been in power, their strict application of Islamic law had eliminated bribery and fighting among warlords. And they warned villagers that foreign troops would remain on Afghan soil forever if they did not act. It was a masterful propaganda campaign that fed into growing doubts about Western motives. Despite foreign leaders' grand promises to rebuild the country—transmitted by shortwave radio to even the most remote hamlets—the people of Helmand saw little evidence of international assistance.

Most U.S. forces had been pulled out to prepare for the invasion of Iraq. The few who remained barely seemed to notice the venality and violence of the local government.

The way SMA spread the wealth also helped the Taliban gain a foothold. He steered jobs and contracts to fellow members of his Alizai tribe. ARJ did the same for the Noorzai and Amir Dado for the Alikozai. The one big tribe shut out of the provincial hierarchy was the Ishaqzai. They had been slighted because they competed in the drug trade with the Alizai and the Alikozai, and because they were stereotyped as a band of thieves. Because they languished at the bottom of the tribal pecking order, they were ripe for exploitation. Taliban leaders appointed several Ishaqzai to key positions in the shadow administration they assembled in Helmand to show residents they could provide some services more effectively than Karzai's government. Taliban courts, which administered eye-for-an-eye justice, heard cases without delay or bribes. Young Ishaqzai men soon flocked to join the budding insurgency.

By early 2005, Helmand was no longer a quiescent backwater that U.S. officials in Kabul could ignore; it had become the world's leading producer of opium. The Taliban had seized the province's northern districts and were threatening to expand their reach southward to Lashkar Gah. The insurgents sent as many as five hundred fighters at a time to conduct withering attacks on ARJ's police force. U.S. troops could have been dispatched to beat back the insurgents, and U.S. diplomats could have striven to persuade Karzai to establish a more inclusive, less corrupt government in the province. But because President George W. Bush wanted to reduce American forces in Afghanistan and deploy them in Iraq, his administration asked NATO to take up the task of stabilizing southern Afghanistan. The Dutch agreed to move into Uruzgan province, the Canadians got Kandahar, and Helmand fell to the British. As drugs and militants were surging across the south, the Americans packed up and left.

British commanders planned to show the Americans, who were playing whack-a-mole with the Taliban in other parts of the country, how the pros executed counterinsurgency. In early

2006, before David Petraeus released his COIN manual and became the strategy's new leading evangelist, the Brits claimed unrivaled expertise in countering insurgencies. They had the legacy of quashing rebellions in Malaya and Northern Ireland, and their stabilization operation in the Iraqi city of Basra, which had begun when British soldiers removed their helmets and body armor to project an image of friendliness, had not yet been judged an abysmal failure because of a series of unseemly deals they had made with Iranian-backed militiamen.

Instead of chasing after the Taliban, Britain intended to concentrate its troops in and around Lashkar Gah to create what top generals called a "lozenge of security." Despite reports of increasing insurgent activity in northern Helmand, Brigadier General Ed Butler, the British task force commander, said his superiors assumed that troops would be able to move about freely and engage the people in the area around the provincial capital. British Defense Secretary John Reid suggested that soldiers would be peacekeepers, noting on a visit to Afghanistan before the deployment, "If we came for three years here to accomplish our mission and had not fired one shot at the end of it, we would be very happy indeed."

The British commitment came with a condition. To perform their COIN mission, British officials knew they needed an Afghan partner in Helmand, someone to be the front man for their government, reconstruction, and antidrug efforts. In most provinces, the obvious candidate was the governor, but that wasn't an option in Helmand. They regarded SMA as part of the problem, not the solution. In July 2005, Afghan counternarcotics agents working with the U.S. Drug Enforcement Administration raided SMA's house and found nine metric tons of opium. SMA claimed he had been storing material his men had seized, but to U.S. and British officials, it was proof positive of his involvement in drug smuggling. British diplomats in Kabul made clear to Karzai that SMA had to go, or else the troop deployment might not happen. That December, Karzai eased SMA out by appointing him to the Senate.

London thought it had scored an enormous victory. But SMA got his revenge. He persuaded Karzai to make his nephew the deputy governor. Then he dispatched many of his henchmen to join the insurgency, saying he no longer had a way to pay them. "I sent 3,000 of them off to the Taliban," he told a British journalist. The Taliban welcomed his men and funded them. It was a great investment: It would get its tentacles into SMA's drug trade, which would yield tens of millions of dollars every year to expand its guerrilla war.

SMA's decision coincided with a new Taliban offensive in southern Afghanistan led by Mullah Dadullah Akhund, a sadistic former mujahideen fighter who had mounted fearless attacks against the Soviets. Known as Dadullah the Cripple because he had lost a leg to a mine, he had joined the Taliban at its inception and quickly became a top military commander. His battlefield prowess and his reputation for beheading captured enemies drew the attention of Mullah Omar, who made him a trusted adviser and appointed him to help direct the group's advance east to Kabul in the mid-1990s, and then into northern provinces later that decade. But he eventually had a falling-out with Omar and senior leaders over orders he had given his men to slaughter thousands of ethnic Hazaras in Bamiyan province, home of the giant Buddha statues that his fighters also destroyed. He was brought back into command a few years later to help fend off the Northern Alliance, and he soon returned to his ruthless methods. He once ordered that five prisoners be tied to cars facing opposite directions; at his command, the cars drove apart and dismembered the prisoners. When the Taliban regime had crumbled under U.S. bombardment in late 2001, he had eluded capture and fled to Pakistan.

His bloodlust and his open support for al-Qaeda won him admirers among young Afghan and Pakistani men studying in the religious schools on Pakistan's side of the border that had become boot camps for the Taliban. His network, which soon grew to more than a hundred ground commanders and dozens of aspiring suicide bombers, functioned as a semiautonomous, al-Qaeda-affiliated arm of the overall Taliban insurgency. He saw himself as Afghanistan's equivalent of Abu Musab al-Zarqawi, the leader of al-Qaeda's Iraq operations. In the spring of 2006, Dadullah ordered his fighters into Helmand. With SMA's men out of the way, there was little resistance.

District after district fell to Dadullah's militants, who shuttered government schools and forced ARJ's policemen to cower in their stations. His commanders offered residents the same promises their predecessors had in the early 1990s: security, an end to corruption, and swift justice, often in the form of a lopped-off hand. But Dadullah's lieutenants were more interested in conquest than civil administration. To pay their fighters and fund their expansion, they commandeered residents' homes, taxed poppy farmers, and stole from merchants in the bazaars. Many Helmandis felt as if they had traded one set of devils for another.

When the British arrived in the summer of 2006, President Karzai did not want them to sit in their lozenge and work on development projects. He demanded they take back the districts Dadullah had seized. The new governor in Helmand, Mohammed Daoud, implored British commanders to be more aggressive. "We need you to protect us. You need to give us the freedom of movement. You must support me to be allowed to go around my own constituency. If I can't do that, why are you here?" Butler recalled Daoud telling him. "If the black flag of Mullah Omar flies over any of the district centers, you may as well go home."

Butler and his superiors acceded to Karzai and Daoud. They scrambled soldiers to the northern districts of Musa Qala, Now Zad, and Sangin. The contingents were tiny—often no more than a fifty-man platoon—because Butler had not been given the resources for a full-on combat mission. Of his 3,300-strong task force, only about 650 were fighting troops. The rest were support personnel, many of whom lived in a new headquarters constructed in the desert near Lashkar Gah. Butler had only six transport helicopters and far fewer vehicles than his men required, many of them lightly armored Land Rovers that offered scant protection from roadside bombs or rocket-propelled grenades. Proper flak vests, radios, and night-vision goggles were also in short supply, and the soldiers' plastic rifle grips, designed for chilly Britain, melted in Helmand's scorching heat.

The troops moved into abandoned government compounds. From there they were to secure the main town in each district and then push toward the fringes. But the Brits were set upon from the moment they arrived, sometimes by hundreds of insurgents wielding mortars, rockets, and grenades who sought to storm the compound walls. In scenes reminiscent of a medieval siege, the troops fought back from sandbagged guard posts, sometimes shooting directly down at Talibs no more than a few yards away. Sentries were pinned in their fortified positions for days at a time, eating rations while lying down and relieving themselves in plastic bottles they threw over the sides. The overwhelmed platoons had no spare personnel to send on patrol; they were consumed with survival, even after panicked commanders dispatched cooks, mechanics, and military policemen from the headquarters to frontline positions. The areas around their bases were too dangerous even for armored convoys, forcing the Brits to rely on their small contingent of helicopters for supplies of food, bottled water, and ammunition. Lots of ammunition. British troops expended four million bullets during their first year in Helmand.

Few Afghans in the province believed the British had come to help them. The same mullahs who had inveighed against ARJ turned their venom on the Brits. They claimed that the soldiers would deprive people of their livelihoods by chopping down poppy fields. They insisted that foreign forces had imperial designs on Afghanistan. But the most potent argument the Taliban made drew upon history. The Afghans and the Brits had fought two bloody wars in the nineteenth century, and the scars remain etched in the national psyche, particularly in the northern reaches of Helmand, where dozens of fighters had an improbable victory on the desert of Maiwand in 1880 before being trounced by the British later that year in Kandahar. Memories of Maiwand fueled hopes of another Afghan victory, while Kandahar sparked desire for revenge. To this day, "son of a Brit" is among the worst insults that can be slung in Helmand. On a trip to Musa Qala in 2010, I witnessed an Afghan army brigadier general, furious that a gate between abutting Afghan and NATO bases had been locked, upbraid two British government officials. "This is my country, not yours," the general fumed. "When your grandfathers were here, my grandfathers killed five thousand of them." U.S. and NATO officials had failed to grasp that enmity when they had urged the British to take over there.

Although London would eventually send thousands more troops to Helmand, it never seemed as if there was enough firepower to knock back the Taliban. Eventually the British agreed to a peace deal with insurgents in Musa Qala, which commanders and diplomats hailed as a great achievement, only to see it fall apart months later. In other areas the troops managed to break out of their platoon bases and establish small bubbles of security. Beyond was Taliban country. The Brits lived according to what they regarded as a gentleman's agreement: You have your side, I have mine. But the Talibs rarely kept their end of the bargain. If they had a chance to lob a mortar or plant a homemade mine on the British side of the line, they would.

The British called the perimeters FLETs—the forward line of enemy troops. The first time Larry Nicholson heard the term, he shot a look of disgust at his staff. "We don't do FLETs," he said. "We're Marines. There's no place we won't go."

Nicholson had found himself in Afghanistan because of Barack Obama. As an Illinois senator, Obama had thought that fixing the Afghan War would be relatively straightforward. The effort simply needed more resources. When he began campaigning for the presidency, he pledged to send two more combat brigades—about 10,000 troops—and increase nonmilitary aid by $1 billion. The 10,000 figure was what the top U.S. military commander in Afghanistan had been seeking, but the Bush White House had refused to act on it, in part because the Pentagon brass said that every available unit that was not training, resting, or otherwise committed was in Iraq. Although Bush eventually agreed to fulfill about half of the request in the summer of 2008, the military's needs expanded as the Taliban kept gaining strength and seizing more territory. By the fall of 2008, the new commander in Kabul, General David McKiernan, said he needed 30,000 more troops. But Bush punted. The new president would have to name the number.

As Obama prepared to move into the White House, he received three assessments on the war: one from Lieutenant General Doug Lute, who had been Bush's Iraq and Afghanistan war czar; a second from Admiral Mike Mullen, the chairman of the Joint Chiefs of Staff; and a third from General Petraeus, who had become chief of the U.S. Central Command, which oversees the region. With so many officials jockeying for influence in shaping his new administration's war policy, he decided to conduct another review, one that would sort through the three assessments and chart a path forward—not just in Afghanistan but also in Pakistan. Less than three weeks after Obama took office, the White House selected a former CIA officer, Bruce Riedel, who had been a foreign policy adviser to the campaign, to lead the effort.

Riedel assembled a team that included Petraeus and Lute as well as Michèle Flournoy, the undersecretary of defense for policy, and veteran diplomat Richard Holbrooke, who had just been named by Secretary of State Hillary Rodham Clinton to be the Obama administration's special representative for Afghanistan and Pakistan. The participants agreed that the overriding goal of U.S. policy needed to be the defeat of al-Qaeda. A key prerequisite was preventing members of the terrorist network from returning to Afghanistan from their safe havens in Pakistan. Most of the team believed the best way to accomplish that was to build a stable, reasonably functional Afghan state. That in turn required a counterinsurgency strategy and enough troops to protect communities and train Afghan security forces.

As those discussions were occurring, Mullen called up Lute and National Security Advisor James Jones and told them that the president needed to act on McKiernan's 30,000-troop request right away if he wanted additional forces on the ground by August to provide security for Afghanistan's presidential election. At the very least, the chairman said, the president had to make a decision about a first tranche of 17,000 personnel. Less than two weeks after Riedel accepted the job, and well before he was ready to present a strategy to the president, Obama met with his National Security Council to consider the matter. Riedel, who had been invited to the session, told Obama that if he did not approve the increase, the Afghan election might have to be postponed, which would amount to a huge blow to U.S. and NATO efforts to stabilize the country.

Three days later, Obama signed off on the 17,000. It was the marching orders for Nicholson and his 10,000-plus Marines to head to Helmand.

Everyone on Riedel's team believed the United States needed to have more troops in Afghanistan, but nobody could be sure just how many. The actual requirement depended on how much of the country merited counterinsurgency operations—parts of the north and west were deemed sufficiently stable—and how many Afghan security forces could be added to the mix. The team endorsed a further increase of 4,000 troops to focus on training the Afghan army, and they figured Obama would have to give McKiernan another 10,000 by the end of the year, which would more than fulfill his original 30,000 request. Several team members assumed that would be sufficient. After all, it was what McKiernan had asked for, and he was the commander on the ground. They did not travel to Afghanistan to discuss matters with the general.

At the Pentagon, however, Mullen and Defense Secretary Robert Gates were starting to wonder whether McKiernan really knew how many troops were needed. If McKiernan was serious about counterinsurgency, how could he not want more forces? Within the military, counterinsurgency had a clear meaning and a defined prescription: a troop density of twenty counterinsurgents for every thousand residents. If that formula were applied to parts of the south and east, where the Taliban was strongest, it would require at least tens of thousands of additional foreign troops.

In mid-March, as Riedel was finishing his assessment, Gates and Mullen met in a secure Pentagon room for a fortnightly video conference with their man in Kabul. McKiernan, a silver-haired former armor officer, began with a brief battlefield update. He was then asked about reconstruction and counternarcotics operations, both of which Gates and Mullen regarded as central to the COIN mission. In Mullen's opinion, McKiernan fumbled his answers. Gates and Mullen had been having doubts about McKiernan since the beginning of the year. They regarded him as too languid, too old school, and too removed from Washington. He lacked the charisma and political savvy that Petraeus had brought to the Iraq War.

McKiernan's answers that day were the tipping point for Mullen. Gates came to the same conclusion. But they opted not to do anything about it until the Riedel team had finished.

The review had been a rushed process that lacked wide consultation, field visits, or rigorous analysis. Holbrooke and Lute told their staffs that Reidel seemed to be drawing heavily on a book he had recently written about al-Qaeda. But that did not prompt concern among the president's West Wing advisers, nor did the endorsement of COIN as the prescription for Afghanistan's ailments. Riedel's forty-four-page report soon became the new administration's policy for Afghanistan and Pakistan. When Obama announced the strategy, flanked by Clinton and Gates before a row of flags in the Eisenhower Executive Office Building next to the White House, he stressed that his aims in Afghanistan and Pakistan were clear and focused: "To disrupt, dismantle and defeat al-Qaeda in Pakistan and Afghanistan, and to prevent their return to either country in the future." But the strategy for achieving that goal was expansive and expensive. Riedel's first recommendation called for a counterinsurgency strategy that would combine the efforts of the military and civilians working for the U.S. government.

Mullen traveled to Kabul in April to confront McKiernan. The chairman hoped the commander would opt to avoid a confrontation and retire, but he refused. Not only had he not disobeyed orders, he believed he was doing what Gates and Mullen wanted. *You're going to have to fire me,* he told Mullen. Two weeks later, Gates did. It was the first sacking of a wartime theater commander since President Truman had dismissed General Douglas MacArthur in 1951 for opposing his Korean War policy.

Mullen and Gates had settled on a replacement well before removing McKiernan. Stan McChrystal, who was working directly for Mullen as the director of the Joint Staff, was a general they trusted, and they felt confident he would ask for the resources necessary to win.

McChrystal landed in Afghanistan less than three weeks before the Marines' air assault in Helmand was set to begin. Most of the planning had been completed. Unless he wanted to delay the mission, he would have to hope the Marines listened to his admonitions, delivered almost daily in a videoconference with his subordinate commanders, about minimizing civilian casualties and maximizing resources to protect residents from insurgents.

Larry Nicholson needed no direction to fight differently. Despite his concern about McChrystal's planned restrictions on the use of air strikes, Nicholson had embraced COIN with zeal. Long before Petraeus had returned to Baghdad with his COIN bible in hand, Nicholson and his fellow Marine commanders in Iraq's volatile Anbar province had implemented key elements of COIN strategy. During his year in Fallujah, he had sought to reopen cement factories, recruit policemen, and win over tribal sheiks whose eventual decision to stand in opposition to al-Qaeda's Iraq affiliate proved to be the critical step in pacifying the province. He had even ventured to neighboring Jordan, traveling in an unmarked plane and wearing an ill-fitting suit stitched together in twenty-four hours by a Turkish tailor on his base, to persuade three key Fallujah elders to return to the city. When journalists credited Petraeus with bringing COIN to Iraq, Nicholson and other Marines bristled. "We were country before country was cool," he joked to those who served with him.

Nicholson's interpretation of COIN doctrine involved more than the fuzzy business of reconstruction, political deal making, and training local security forces. Enemy fighters needed to face a credible threat, one that would compel them to drop their weapons and reintegrate into society. If not, they'd have to be killed or captured. And the best way to make that happen was not through the incremental approach used by the British in other parts of Helmand or the U.S. Army's gradual saturation of Baghdad. His Marines would come in strong and fast—hundreds of them dropping behind Taliban lines under the cover of darkness. Two thousand others would arrive in armored trucks. By demonstrating overwhelming force right away, he hoped to frighten many insurgents enough that they would flee or simply become law-abiding citizens. If they wanted to go back to being farmers or laborers, he wasn't going to hunt them down. And if they ran into the desert, that meant his Marines would be free to work on reconstruction and development projects along the river valley.

Although this would not be an in-and-out mission like so many other U.S. efforts to flush the Taliban out of its redoubts in the early years of the war—the Marines planned to stay in communities along the river for years, not weeks or months—Nicholson ordered the air-dropped troops to avoid setting up bases in the first thirty days. He wanted them to remain on the move, walking from village to village to interact with people and keeping the Taliban guessing about their next destination. Food and water would be helicoptered in, as would more ammunition if they needed it. They would sleep under the stars. Once his captains got to know their villages, they could select the most advantageous sites on which to set up small bases. But they had to live near the people, not partitioned off in the desert.

As the day of the operation neared, Nicholson remained troubled by how few Afghan soldiers were available to participate in the operation. He wanted at least one Afghan for each of his Marines. What he had was one Afghan for every ten Americans. He complained to everyone who came for a visit—his military bosses, dignitaries from Kabul, even Jim Jones. But there were no Afghan forces to spare. Other units in the south already were stretched, and the Ministry of Defense in Kabul, dominated by ethnic Tajiks and Uzbeks from the north and west, did not want to pull soldiers from their parts of the country, even though those places were far less violent. With no other option, Nicholson's staff apportioned out their Afghans as a precious commodity, giving a few to each Marine company. When he heard at a mission rehearsal that one company would not receive any, he erupted. "That's not going to work," he huffed at a junior officer. "If locals see us by ourselves, it doesn't provide much. How are we going to engage them by ourselves?" The Afghan soldiers were divvied up again.

Five hours before the first helicopters lifted off to commence Operation River Liberty, Nicholson was in his plywood-walled office at the end of a barnlike building that had just been constructed by Navy Seabees. He should have been bushed—he had been catching only a few hours of sleep a night on a cot in the office—but he seemed excited and anxious. His foot tapped, and he crunched on a mint Life Saver. It was the biggest, riskiest mission of his career, and it had the potential to shape the new president's thinking about the war. Would his assault demonstrate that more troops and a new strategy could resuscitate a flatlining war? Or would it reveal a stronger, more resilient insurgency than Washington anticipated?

"We feel that we're at a decisive point and a decisive place," he said. "We're going to stop the slide and begin moving back in the other direction."

3

Marineistan

THE DAY AFTER HE ARRIVED in Kabul in June 2009, Stan McChrystal gathered officers on his staff to discuss the state of the war. They barraged him with "metrics" on PowerPoint slides—the frequency of Taliban attacks and the proportion of them the military deemed effective; the number of improvised explosive devices that had detonated and the few that troops had been lucky enough to discover before they blasted; the number and location of Afghan security forces across the country; and an evaluation of the Afghan government's effectiveness in each province. The data were grim, the conclusion obvious: The Americans and their NATO allies were losing.

The part of the country that concerned McChrystal most was the south, and the part of the south that concerned him most was not Helmand but the city of Kandahar and the eponymous province that encompasses it. Founded by Alexander the Great in 330 B.C. at the junction of trade routes between the Indus and Oxus valleys, Kandahar city has long been the sacred and symbolic homeland of the Pashtuns. It has more than two thousand mosques and a blue-domed shrine that houses a cloak said to have been worn by the Prophet Mohammed. In 1748, Pashtun king Ahmed Shah Durrani made it the capital of his empire, which included all of present-day Afghanistan and Pakistan and parts of Iran and India. In the 1940s and 1950s, Zahir Shah had ensured it was part of the Little America project. Morrison-Knudsen dammed the Arghandab River twenty miles northeast of Kandahar city, and the firm dug canals to irrigate farmland across the province. In 1957, the U.S. International Cooperation Administration, the predecessor of USAID, began constructing a modern airport with soaring, glass-walled arches that was supposed to serve as a pit stop for propeller planes flying from Tehran to Delhi. (The visionaries at the ICA, however, failed to foresee the jet age. By the time USAID inaugurated the airport in 1962, the Boeing 707s flying that route did not require refueling, and it sat largely unused until the Soviets turned it into an air base during their occupation. When U.S. troops arrived in 2001, USAID's boondoggle was the military's boon. It was the perfect place for a large military base.)

Kandahar eventually grew into the second largest city in the country, a dusty, traffic-choked mess whose flat landscape and perpetual haze afford none of the charm of other Afghan towns. But for the Taliban, it was the strategic prize. In the 1990s, just as every other band of conquerors had done for the last thousand years, they used it as a springboard from which they captured Kabul and much of the rest of the nation. If the Americans were going to retake Afghanistan, they needed to start with Kandahar.

That made perfect sense to McChrystal. What did not was how the U.S. military and NATO had arrayed their forces. By then, the British had 9,000 troops in Helmand because London kept adding more each year to confront expanding Taliban ranks. In its haste to reduce its commitments in Afghanistan, the Bush administration had handed off Kandahar to Canada, which had deployed only 2,830 soldiers. As with any military unit—the Americans were no exception—the tail was far longer than the tooth. Most Canadian soldiers were assigned to headquarters and support roles. Fewer than 600 went on patrol.

The 17,000 additional troops Obama had authorized in February were supposed to address the growing violence in the south, but most of those slots—10,672 of them—went to Larry Nicholson's Marine brigade, which had landed in Helmand two months earlier. Kandahar, which had a larger population, was slated to get a far smaller Army brigade—it would have only about 4,000 soldiers—and it would roll in far more slowly.

Those troops were not going to be ready to conduct combat missions for two more months.

"Can someone tell me why the Marines were sent to Helmand?" the incredulous McChrystal asked his officers.

Before McChrystal had departed Washington, Robert Gates had told him to take stock of the war effort within sixty days. The idea for the assessment had originated with Jim Jones, who grew alarmed when McChrystal told the Senate Armed Services Committee, during his confirmation hearing, that he did not know whether the 17,000 troops and 4,000 trainers Obama had approved would be enough. Jones believed the Pentagon was lobbying for more forces before the 21,000 had fully deployed—and after McChrystal's bosses had all but told the president they would not be asking for more that year. As a compromise, Jones suggested McChrystal refrain from additional comments about staffing and instead conduct an assessment of the war. Then, if he determined that he required more troops, he could make a formal request. For the White House, the assessment would buy short-term silence and ensure an orderly process to consider the matter. But the Pentagon was the real winner. For Admiral Mullen and other top commanders who were convinced that David McKiernan had underestimated the need for more U.S. troops, there was now an opening to campaign for more. All it required was for McChrystal to make a convincing case.

Although he was a relative unknown outside the military, the rangy, almost gaunt general was regarded with awe in the rings of the Pentagon. McChrystal had a habit of running ten miles a day. When he spent a year as a military fellow at the Council on Foreign Relations in New York, he would commute on foot, jogging twelve miles from his house in Brooklyn to the Upper East Side. He ate only one sit-down meal a day, although it was often a 5,000-calorie affair that involved a mess hall tray piled with burritos, pasta, and ice cream. While deployed, he put in nineteen-hour workdays that included two hours of exercise, leaving just five hours for sleep and no time for relaxation—and he exhorted those working for him to keep a similar schedule. Although some of his spartan behavior was for show—to ease his hunger, he snacked on Atomic Fireball cinnamon candy and energy bars when nobody was looking—there were no secret champagne-and-caviar indulgences. He slept in a room the size of a prison cell with a twin bed, a plywood armoire, and a tiny desk. His drink of choice when he was home was Bud Light Lime.

What had cemented McChrystal's reputation was his transformation of a supersecret team of Special Operations units into the military's most lethal and effective counterterrorism force. This hadn't been a matter merely of growing the ranks of the Joint Special Operations Command, building connections with the CIA, and pushing his men to make more daring assaults. He revolutionized the command's management structure, using his discretionary fund to buy, in the wake of the dot-com crash, newly available satellite capacity for data transmission so operatives anywhere in the world could have immediate access to evidence vacuumed up during raids. This allowed members of his far-flung team to collaborate on problems and spot linkages in terrorist networks. It was a stroke of genius, and it eventually helped the command track and kill the terror mastermind Abu Musab al-Zarqawi in Iraq.

All that work had occurred in the shadows. McChrystal had few connections to official Washington—to the members of Congress who would shape Afghan War policy and to the pundits who would opine about the war's success or failure. To bridge that gap, and to help conduct the assessment in the two-month time frame allotted, McChrystal poached talent in the Pentagon and beyond, including a top aide to Senate Armed Services Committee chairman Carl Levin and the deputy director of the State Department's stabilization and reconstruction office. He also convened an advisory group of outside experts from Washington's prominent national security think tanks to travel to Kabul for a month to help him draft the assessment and then sell the conclusion by writing op-eds, giving speeches, and talking it up at cocktail parties.

Among them was Andrew Exum of the Center for a New American Security, the most influential cradle of counterinsurgency strategists in the capital. He was the youngest of the outside advisers, but he had served in Iraq, and in 2004, he had led a platoon of elite Army Rangers in Afghanistan. He then left the military to study in Lebanon, where he learned Arabic, and afterward he got a doctorate in war studies from the University of London. With his lean, McChrystal-like build and his background in unconventional warfare, he formed a quick bond with the general. Exum knew enough about Afghanistan to understand that Kandahar was of critical importance, but he had no idea how tenuous the situation was until the group met with Sarah Chayes.

Chayes was a former National Public Radio reporter who ran an agricultural cooperative in Kandahar that made soaps from the oils of locally grown fruits and nuts that she sold in high-end shops in Boston and New York. Chayes had once been close to the Karzai family—one of Hamid's brothers had helped her get a start in Kandahar—but she had eventually had a falling-out with the president and his half brother Ahmed Wali over their connections to warlords and, she alleged, their involvement in corruption. Frustrated with the failure of commanders and diplomats to grasp how graft and malevolent governance were pushing Afghans toward the Taliban, she had accepted an offer to advise General McKiernan. She stuck around when McChrystal arrived, hoping to convince him and his staff that fighting corruption had to be a central element of their COIN campaign. She told them that Kandahar seemed to be slipping away. Ahmed Wali and his cronies were hoarding political power and foreign aid for themselves, and the have-nots were turning to the insurgency. She explained that the Taliban had taken control of the four districts that ring the city—Arghandab, Zhari, Dand, and Panjwai—shutting down schools, seeding roads with bombs, and forcing pro-government tribal leaders to flee. Exum grew alarmed. On a trip to the main NATO base in the south, he and others on the assessment team asked the top intelligence officer on the Canadian task force responsible for Kandahar for his take on the situation.

"I have no idea what's going on inside the city," the officer said, according to Exum's notes of the meeting. That was because the few Canadian troops in the city were focused on reconstruction activities, not providing security or gathering intelligence. Even development work was foundering. "We have promised a lot, and we have delivered very little," one senior Canadian commander told the group.

When he returned to Kabul, Exum asked U.S. Major General Michael Tucker, the soon-to-depart director of operations for all NATO forces, why more Canadians had not been sent into the city. Tucker said he did not want to dictate to the Canadians where to place their forces. "It is wrong," he said, "to tell a commander, from this level, to put troops in Kandahar city."

Exum happened to be sitting next to Tucker. When he did not want others to see what he was recording in the Moleskine notebook he took everywhere, he scribbled in Greek.

"This guy is a jackass," he wrote. "Kandahar—not Helmand—is the single point of failure in Afghanistan."

But it was not just a matter of will. The Canadians did not have the resources to do what was needed, either in the city or in the surrounding districts. It soon became clear to Exum that the number of Canadian troops in greater Kandahar was totally inadequate. Hence McChrystal's question about the Marines.

The decision to send the Marines to Helmand instead of Kandahar had been made by McKiernan, but he had been urged to do so by his subordinates in Kandahar, including a then-one-star U.S. Army general, John "Mick" Nicholson. (He is not related to Larry Nicholson, but the presence of two U.S. brigadier generals with the same surname in the same part of the country confused many Afghans.) When Mick Nicholson met with Exum and his teammates to explain his reasoning, his first point was about national pride. The Kandahar mission was Canada's largest overseas military deployment since the Korean War, and the Canadians had lost more troops as a percentage of their country's overall population at that point than the United States had. The prospect of handing off Arghandab district to the incoming U.S. Army brigade had already elicited strong emotions among Canadian officers. Military leaders in Ottawa were reluctant to ask for more help—some were convinced that security in Kandahar was improving, others didn't want to risk the embarrassment—and McKiernan didn't want to upset the Canadians by forcing them to cede additional territory. To Exum and others on the team, however, it seemed that

U.S. commanders thought that managing the NATO alliance was more important than winning the war.

The British had the opposite view about U.S. assistance in Helmand. Eager to minimize their high casualty rate, British commanders wanted to concentrate their forces around Lash-kar Gah and a few other key towns. They were happy to let U.S. troops assume responsibility for the remote parts of Hel-mand, so long as the transfer was portrayed as a transatlantic partnership, not an American takeover or a wholesale British withdrawal, along the lines of what had occurred in Basra.

Nicholson also insisted that the Marines could be used more effectively in Helmand for three other reasons: It was the epi-center of poppy production, the Taliban were conducting more attacks there, and Afghan officials had told commanders that foreign troops should stay out of Kandahar city, given its cul-tural and religious significance. But if the mission were to pro-tect the people, Exum thought, the new troops should be closer to the largest population center in the south, not where vio-lence was worst. The drug argument similarly made no sense to him, because Richard Holbrooke had just announced that to avoid antagonizing farmers the United States would no longer participate in the eradication of poppy fields; a CIA study also claimed that the Taliban got most of its money from illegal taxa-tion and contributions from Pakistan and Persian Gulf nations, not from drugs. And even if the Afghans were right about the psychological impact of foreign forces inside the city—some on the assessment team questioned that logic—the surround-ing districts seemed like the best home for the Marines. The Taliban's surge in Helmand was "a feint," Exum wrote in his notebook. "It draws our attention and resources away from Kandahar."

When he recommended that the Marines be sent to Hel-mand, Nicholson did not know it would be a force of more than 10,000. He had assumed that Marine commanders would dispatch the equivalent of an infantry brigade, which typically ranges from 3,500 to 5,000 personnel. That would have allowed the Army to send more troops to Kandahar. But the Marines insisted on bringing their own helicopters and logistics teams, and they wanted to set up their own large headquarters that duplicated some of the functions being performed on the giant NATO base at Kandahar's airport. To Nicholson, "it was a lot of overhead we didn't need."

By the time McChrystal arrived in Afghanistan, it was too late to redirect the Marines. They had built bases in Helmand, and they were days away from conducting their massive air assault along the river valley.

There was another reason the Marines had wound up in Helmand: They wanted it.

In discussions with senior Pentagon generals in charge of troop deployments in 2008, the Marine commandant, General James Conway, was willing to dispatch thousands of troops to Afghanistan as soon as the president approved a troop increase. His zeal for Afghanistan stood in contrast to that of his comrades in the upper echelons of the Army, who showed no such initiative. They had more than 120,000 soldiers in Iraq, and they were struggling to find enough rested and trained units to replace those coming home. Preparing for the possibility that they might have to deploy more forces to Afghanistan was not high on their priority list. Conway, however, could afford to turn his sights to Afghanistan because he was planning to pull his Marines out of Iraq. He believed the Marine presence in Anbar province had turned into a policing mission that was more suitable for the Army. He wanted his Marines to hunt bad guys, and by then there were more of them in Afghanistan.

But the gray-haired Conway, who maintained a linebacker's build and looked as though he could win a wrestling match with a nineteen-year-old lance corporal, drove a hard bargain. He required that any new forces be kept in a contiguous area where they could be supported by Marine helicopters and supply convoys. (Army officers thought the insistence on Marine helicopters was silly—Marine choppers are older, leakier, and generate more white knuckles than Army birds.) Conway's stipulation for discrete terrain and Marine-controlled airspace effectively excluded Kandahar. The geography of the province, and the Canadians' desire to hold on to key districts around Kandahar city, made it nearly impossible to carve out a Marines-only area there. Helmand was the next best option, even if it was less vital. It could be easily divided with the British.

Conway's requirement had its roots in World War II. Marines landing on the Pacific islands of Guadalcanal and Tarawa hadn't received the air support they had expected from Navy planes to hold off Japanese troops. Since then—in Vietnam and Iraq—Marine commanders have insisted on deploying with their own aviation and supply units. In the initial years of the Afghan War, the Pentagon broke with tradition and sent small Marine units into remote districts to help train and mentor Afghan soldiers. They were forced to rely on the Army for air support, particularly when they came under attack. But overstretched Army helicopter crews were sometimes slow to respond—to everyone, not just to the Marines—and the delays rekindled concern about abandonment within the Corps.

Conway made a second demand, this one even more remarkable: A three-star Marine general at the U.S. Central Command, not the supreme coalition commander in Kabul, would have to have overall operational control over the force going to Helmand. That meant McChrystal would lack the unilateral power to move the Marines to another part of Afghanistan or change their mission in anything other than minor, tactical ways.

The Pentagon brass was willing to meet all of Conway's conditions. They needed boots on the ground, and he was the only one offering to provide them.

After the Marines arrived in Helmand, the U.S. ambassador in Kabul, Karl Eikenberry, joked that the international security force in Afghanistan, then made up of forty-one nations, felt as if it had forty-two members because the Marines acted so independently from other U.S. forces. At the NATO headquarters in Kabul, officers noted that the Marines came with more caveats than some European armies. Before long, some American officials began referring to the Corps's area of operations as "Marineistan."

Conway's push for the Marines to take Helmand involved more than rejecting other parts of Afghanistan. He and his fellow Marine leaders beat the war drums for Helmand. They emphasized NATO statistics showing that it was the most violent province, conveniently neglecting to mention that the parts of Helmand in which they would deploy were home to little more than 1 percent of the country's population. And they brushed aside the CIA's analysis showing that poppy was not the principal source of Taliban funding, instead citing military intelligence figures suggesting that drug money played a primary role in bankrolling the insurgency. Marine officers soon started citing those figures as gospel. One colonel on Larry Nicholson's staff asserted to me that Helmand was as important to the Taliban as the Ruhr Valley had been to the Nazis.

Although Conway started to make his play for Helmand in 2008, well before the U.S. presidential election, it seemed a good bet—both Obama and Republican nominee John McCain had vowed to send more forces to Afghanistan. To avoid political blowback, Conway had limited his discussions to a handful of senior generals in the Pentagon, and Larry Nicholson wasn't among them. Nicholson thought he was going back to Iraq as the commander of Marine ground forces in Anbar. It was not until he traveled to Ramadi on a predeployment survey that he heard a rumor that he might be shipped off to Afghanistan instead. When he returned to Camp Lejeune in North Carolina, he asked his commanding officer about the possibility but was assured that he was headed to Iraq. A month later, on December 17, he got the news: Helmand, by spring.

He would get three infantry battalions and one equipped with light armored reconnaissance vehicles—each would have about 1,200 Marines—as well as an aviation group and a logistics element. The headquarters team was his to assemble, and he scrambled over the Christmas holiday. "The guys hanging around Lejeune on 17 December are not the kind of guys you want in your organization," he told friends. He called and e-mailed smart officers he knew across the country, quickly pulling together a contingent of battle-seasoned Iraq hands who were eager to apply their COIN lessons in a new desert. Nicholson treated the job offers as the real thing, but they were all tentative. Obama had not yet signed off on McKiernan's troop request.

In early February, still before Obama's decision, Nicholson traveled to Afghanistan to determine where to place his headquarters. The main British encampment in Helmand, which possessed an airstrip, seemed like the right place, but only a parking lot and a field were available to him. So he climbed up a guard tower and gazed at the open desert to the west. "Who owns that space?" he asked a British colonel. "Fucking you do, if you want it," the colonel replied. Nicholson described what he wanted to a team of Navy Seabee engineers. The next day, their bulldozers started flattening the land. Within two months, they would construct for him a vast base with a chow hall, toilets, sleeping quarters, and a command center with high-speed data connections. Much of it was in tents, but the Marines did not mind. It fit their expeditionary ethos. They called it Camp Leatherneck.

Nicholson's next challenge was figuring out where to send his Marines. None of his superiors, he said, told him, "We want you to go here, here, and here in Helmand." He knew he would have to send some of his forces to Garmser, a district along the river south of Nawa, so British forces could consolidate closer to Lashkar Gah. Beyond that, though, it was up to him.

He examined maps, pored through stacks of intelligence reports, and talked to officers who had been to Helmand. One place stood out to him: Marja, the farming community west of Lashkar Gah that had been carved out of the desert during the Little America venture. Over the previous few years, it had become the Taliban's own version of a forward operating base. It housed vast stockpiles of homemade explosives, large anti-aircraft guns, and dozens of insurgent commanders. Militants went about their business with impunity, not just building bombs but also growing poppy and storing opium collected elsewhere in preparation for shipment to Iran and Pakistan. The American-built canals that ringed the area served as defensive moats, which the Talibs reinforced with makeshift mines. It was a no-go zone for Afghan troops and British soldiers, and Marine pilots planned to take the unusual step of flying around it. Nicholson put it atop his to-do list.

"If Marja is the worst place you've got, let me go there first," he told McKiernan during the February trip. If the Marines went elsewhere, they would not be able to leave those places for a year or two—or longer. Not until they were ready to be handed off to Afghan security forces. Nicholson was scarred by his comrades' decision to leave communities along the Euphrates River in 2004 to mount an assault on Fallujah, allowing insurgents to exact retribution. "These people we were working with, these people whose trust we earned—they were dead men walking," he said. He vowed not to repeat that mistake.

"Larry, I'd love to let you go to Marja," McKiernan replied. "But I can't."

McKiernan said he could not risk having Marines engaged in full-scale combat immediately before—or even during—Afghanistan's presidential election that August. "It's going to be too political, it's going to be too big of a fight," he said. He worried that news reports of combat in Marja would "make it look as if Karzai is losing control of the country."

So Nicholson went back to his planners. With Marja off the table, they would go to Garmser and to Nawa, which sat along the river between Garmser and Lashkar Gah. Each would consume an infantry battalion. The third infantry battalion was committed to northwest Helmand province, in a collection of remote, sparsely populated areas that included Now Zad. Nicholson had inherited that mess. The U.S. team responsible for training Afghan security forces had asked the Marines to send a battalion there in 2008 to help the local police. But when Lieutenant Arthur Karell and his fellow Marines arrived, they found few police, and they soon got drawn into fights with insurgents traveling north from Marja. Although the northwest areas lacked strategic significance, Nicholson was not about to make a pullout one of his first acts, especially when he had few other places to go. He also wanted to demonstrate what that battalion, which had been among the Marine units that had failed to get enough air and logistical support from the Army, could accomplish when it fell under his umbrella.

That still left his light armored battalion without a mission, so he grabbed his operations officer and a big map and went to see Helmand's governor, Gulab Mangal. "Governor, I can't go everywhere," he said. "But if you were me, where would you go?"

Mangal asked for a few days to consider the question. When they met again, the governor had made red circles around the towns he felt were important. Like Mohammed Daoud before him, he believed every district was critical. But he drew attention to Khan Neshin, a poor and primitive district even by Afghan standards. "You should go all the way down there," he told Nicholson.

Deep into the Dasht-e-Margo—the Desert of Death—Khan Neshin was closer to Pakistan than to Lashkar Gah. Mangal said it had turned into a way station for Talibs traveling from Pakistani sanctuaries. Hitting them there, he argued, would protect communities to the north. That logic meshed with what Nicholson saw in his intelligence reports. But little was known about the area. The British had not spent any meaningful time in that part of Helmand, nor were any representatives from the Afghan government stationed in the area. "We have no freaking idea of what's down there," he told his staff.

American and British diplomats in Lashkar Gah thought the push to Khan Neshin was a bad idea. They had not allocated resources for reconstruction projects there, and the Afghan government lacked the capacity to provide basic services to people that far away. "It was a very poor decision—militarily, politically, resourcewise," one of them told me. But the Marines were insistent. They were going to bring peace to Khan Neshin, and they would use their own discretionary funds to pay for development projects.

Sending the light armored battalion to Khan Neshin meant that all of Nicholson's Marines would be committed. If he were to take on Marja after the election, he would need more troops.

Expecting stiff resistance, hundreds of troops from the First Battalion of the Fifth Marine Regiment swooped into Nawa an hour after midnight on July 2 in blacked-out helicopters, landing on fields they hoped had not been seeded with Taliban mines. They scurried off the aircraft, some heaving extra crates of ammunition, while others jogged ahead to begin searching the surrounding area for insurgents lying in wait.

The first hours of Operation River Liberty provoked anxiety in Nicholson's headquarters. How many Talibs would the men on the ground encounter? Would the principal threat be homemade bombs buried on roads and dirt paths or squads of insurgents shooting at them? Would a series of dust clouds moving into the area interfere with flights to evacuate the wounded? Nicholson's morning operations briefing had ended for the first time with a prayer by the chaplain: "Almighty God, we have trained and prepared ourselves. We ask for your protecting hand upon the troops involved . . . so that we would see order and peace brought to this land, and the forces of evil be dispersed and destroyed."

As the sun came up, one of the platoons in Nawa found a cache of bomb-making equipment in a mud-walled house, including metal pots that had been used to transform fertilizer into explosives. As they searched the compound, insurgents hiding in a tree line fired rifles and rocket-propelled grenades at the Marines, prompting an urgent call for attack aircraft. A pair of Cobra gunships soon buzzed overhead and pelted the insurgents with Hellfire missiles. Blood pressure levels eased in Nicholson's command center, where a live video feed of the battle, recorded by a Predator drone flying overhead, streamed on a flat-panel television. There were a few more similar incidents that day and the next. Then the Taliban melted away.

Attacks on Patrol Base Jaker, which had been an almost nightly occurrence, ceased. So did militant activity in other parts of the district. Marines would later stop vehicles full of young men driving out of the area, but the troops could apprehend them only if they carried weapons or drugs. In one car the Marines found a letter with instructions from a local Taliban leader to regroup in Marja, fifteen miles to the northwest.

There was no clear answer to why the Taliban had decided to fold in Nawa. The Marines believed overwhelming force was the critical factor. The combined strength of U.S. and Afghan troops in the district was about 1,500 for a population of about 75,000—exactly the one-to-fifty ratio suggested by most counterinsurgency theorists. That number allowed the Marines to practice the sort of COIN tactics McChrystal wanted. They set up two dozen small outposts, placing armed Americans within a short walk of every village. Each of the battalion's thirty-six squads conducted two foot patrols a day to meet residents and reassure them—often over cups of hot green tea—that they were safe, steeling them against threats made at night by a small band of insurgent holdouts. "We have enough Marines to shake everyone's hand," Lieutenant Colonel Bill McCollough, the battalion commander, said a few days into the operation.

But the campaign's success seemed to be the result of more than increased troop levels. The insurgents had overplayed their hand—residents chafed at the Taliban's taxation in the bazaar, closure of schools, and prohibition of music. Even more important, perhaps, were Nawa's unusually stable tribal dynamics. Most of the population was of the same tribe—the Barakzai—which meant the district was free of the infighting that the Taliban was able to exploit in other areas. Many Barakzai elders had turned a blind eye to insurgent commanders during the British years, when they felt NATO forces could not protect them, but once the Marines arrived, they cut those ties, although some of them still took a wait-and-see approach in dealing with the Americans.

McCollough, a blond Minnesotan who was so fresh faced that he looked younger than most of his just-out-of-boot-camp charges, didn't appear concerned that many insurgents had simply moved over to Marja. What if, I asked, they sought to return in a few weeks or months, once they had identified the Marines' weaknesses? "While they're regrouping, we'll be consolidating our gains," he boasted. "If those fish that went to Marja try to swim back into this pond, they'll find it tough to survive. Everything we do poisons the water for them."

The grand American counterinsurgency plan called for winning over the population by helping the Afghan government deliver basic services—to show that government could do more for the people than the Taliban could. That meant the Marines, the State Department, USAID, and the British-run provincial reconstruction office in Lashkar Gah would have to address a welter of challenges right away—and to try to make it seem as if all of the solutions were flowing from Karzai's administration. Nawa required a new district governor and civil servants. The police, run by a chief whom one Marine officer called "the Tony Soprano of Nawa," would have to be overhauled. Schools needed to be reopened. And new jobs had to be created. Otherwise the Taliban would once again be able to raise an army by offering disaffected young men ten dollars a day to plant bombs and snipe at military patrols. "Thirty days from now, the people will say: 'Okay. Great. You've cleared the Taliban out. Now what's in it for me?' " Nicholson said. "We have a very narrow window to bring about change."

But he was certain the transformation would occur. He had millions of dollars in commanders' emergency response funds to spend on reconstruction projects, the State Department and USAID had promised to send representatives to help rebuild schools and resurrect the economy, and the Afghans appeared ready to seize the moment. Later that summer, he received a report from McCollough about a group of young men the Marines had apprehended. The men had been digging holes along the road from the main irrigation canal to the bazaar. When men shoveled along roads in Afghanistan, it usually meant they were burying bombs, so McCollough had scrambled his quick-reaction force. But it turned out they were digging holes for electricity poles. Dozens of merchants had banded together to fund a homegrown hydropower project—a twelve-foot-high water wheel fashioned from metal shipping containers that would be placed in the canal and connected to a generator. The shopkeepers' investment, he reasoned, was a sure sign of progress: The people of Nawa felt so confident that conditions were going to improve, they were willing to put money on it.

A week into the operation, McChrystal flew into Jaker. It had become safe enough that he arrived at midday, his Black Hawk helicopter descending lazily onto a field behind the base. He toured the grounds as Nicholson had done ten days earlier and then sat down for a meeting with McCollough. But before the lieutenant colonel had spoken for a minute, the four-star general interrupted with questions: What do you need to know about how the community works? How much of the population can we really protect? Do people remember what the Americans did here in the 1960s?

McCollough said he had been approached by an old man a few days earlier who wanted to know if the Marine officer knew "Mr. and Mrs. Lerner," the American couple who had taught him English four decades before. McCollough had tried his best to explain that the United States is a large country and that he had not met the Lerners.

McChrystal told McCollough and his officers that he could not have been prouder of what they had done so far. But as he got up to leave, he admonished them to be patient. "The decisive terrain now is not geographical, it's in the minds of the people," he said. "We have to operate in a way that affects that."

After McChrystal departed, Nicholson sat down on a wooden bench. It was in the shade, but it offered little respite from the 125-degree heat. As he nursed a half-liter plastic bottle of water that was warm enough to steep tea bags in, he thought about the coming weeks and months. The push into Nawa had been flawless, and security had improved much faster than he had expected. Would USAID, the State Department, the Afghan government, and his Marines be able to muster the resources to meet local needs quickly enough?

"Our biggest challenge is catastrophic success," he crowed. "Are we ready for the success we're seeing?"

McChrystal's advisers continued to view the deployment of the Marines to Helmand as a distraction from more urgent problems in Kandahar, but soon after the general returned to Kabul, he realized the rapid changes in Nawa presented him with a fortuitous opportunity: It was the proof of concept he needed to convince the president and his war cabinet that the combination of more troops and a COIN strategy could turn Afghanistan around. He told his aides that Nawa had become his "number one Petri dish." It quickly became a popular destination for Pentagon officials and members of Congress traveling in the country, in part because McChrystal's staff encouraged them to visit, but also to verify the stories they were hearing.

In those initial months, Nawa didn't disappoint. The youthful McCollough explained COIN strategy to visitors with even greater zeal than McChrystal. The new district governor unfailingly played gracious host, often welcoming the delegations to his office—located on a corner of Patrol Base Jaker—for a lunch of greasy chicken and warm orange soda as he extolled McCollough and his Marines. The once shuttered bazaar bustled with merchants and shoppers. Each VIP tour included what Marines started to call the Nawa 500—a walking loop from Jaker through the market, by the school, and then back to the base. By late summer, McCollough felt confident enough in the security improvements that he strode the circuit without his helmet or body armor, and he encouraged his visitors to do the same.

In the summer of 2009, Afghanistan had 398 districts. McChrystal knew he did not need to replicate Nawa in each of them. Not all were as violent as Nawa had been before the Marines arrived—many parts of northern and western Afghanistan were relatively tranquil—and some districts were so strategically unimportant that they could be left to the Taliban. But McChrystal and his top deputy in charge of day-to-day operations, Lieutenant General David Rodriguez, a lean but towering former defensive end on the West Point football team, figured they had to achieve a Nawa-like transformation in dozens of other places—they had identified about eighty key districts—in order to weaken the insurgency enough that it would no longer pose a threat to the central government. That would require all of the forces under his command to embrace COIN as McCollough's Marines had. As McChrystal barnstormed the country in his first weeks on the job, he met many battalion and brigade commanders who insisted they were implementing COIN. He wasn't fooled; most of them were still far more focused on killing Talibs than protecting civilians. European allies who had responsibility for the northern and western parts of the country—the Italians in Herat, the Spanish in Badghis, and the Germans in Kunduz, Balkh, and seven other provinces—still viewed their mission as peacekeeping and reconstruction, despite growing Taliban activity in those areas. They spent more time on their base than off, and when they did leave, they rarely stepped out of their armored vehicles. The Germans even insisted on taking an ambulance along every time they departed their compounds. But many U.S. units were no better, concentrating their personnel in large, well-appointed camps, some of which had ice cream in the mess hall and recreation rooms with large-screen televisions, instead of dispersing them in small outposts as McCollough had done in Nawa. Life was tougher out there. There were no air conditioners or beds with mattresses. Days and nights were filled with patrolling and guard duty. Showers and food that didn't come from a ration bag were once-a-month luxuries. But living on the frontier was the only way to conduct COIN.

McChrystal soon realized his COIN challenge went deeper than how frontline units operated. His handpicked intelligence chief, Major General Michael Flynn, was an old friend from the Special Operations world, and both of them recognized the importance of intelligence that went beyond identifying the bad guys and their locations. To perform effective COIN, officers needed to know the tribal, social, and political relationships in their districts—who were the power brokers, and what were their connections? If you worked with one chieftain, what impact might that have on others in the area? But that sort of "white intel" was not a priority for analysts in Afghanistan. They were focused on bad-guy-centric "red intel."

All of the COIN problems seemed fixable to McChrystal if he could change the culture of U.S. and NATO forces within a few months. During his daily commander's meeting, which was piped to a half-dozen subordinate headquarters across the country, he underscored that troops had to operate differently, and he issued directives to restrict the use of air strikes, drive less aggressively, and escalate force proportionately. He wanted troops "off the FOBs"—forward operating bases—and out of their giant mine-resistant trucks with inch-thick bulletproof glass. They needed to be walking around and talking to Afghans, as McCollough's men were doing, even if it meant assuming more risk. Sure, riding in a mine-proof truck might protect soldiers from a roadside bomb, but the only way to prevent that bomb from being buried in the ground in the first place was for soldiers to build trust with the people. "I care less about U.S. and allied casualties than I do about protecting U.S. and allied interests," McChrystal told the assessment group. "But I would never ask a soldier to do something I would not do myself."

The general and his top aides also knew they needed more forces—that was another key lesson from Nawa—but he told his assessment team not to focus on a number. He wanted them to understand the perilous state of the war so they could explain the need to wage a real COIN campaign to politicians and journalists on the home front. That would prep the Washington battlefield for him. Then he would march in with his troop request.

In the end, the think-tank experts did not even write the assessment, as had originally been planned. McChrystal decided that would have miffed his superiors. The final document was drafted by him and a small coterie of aides, and it made the case for more boots on the ground, emphasizing that the approach of the moment—using coalition forces to try to hold the line until the Afghan army was big enough and competent enough to do the job—was untenable.

If NATO forces failed to reverse Taliban momentum within twelve months, he argued, defeating the insurgency might no longer be possible. Two pages later, he put his bosses on notice that a request for forces would follow: "Our campaign in Afghanistan has been historically under-resourced and remains so today. Almost every aspect of our collective effort and associated resourcing has lagged a growing insurgency—historically a recipe for failure in COIN. Success will require a discrete 'jump' to gain the initiative."

More troops alone, he stated, "will not win this war, but under-resourcing could lose it. . . . The status quo will lead to failure."

He was blunt in describing the posture of U.S. and NATO troops: "Preoccupied with protection of our own forces, we have operated in a manner that distances us—physically and psychologically—from the people we seek to protect. . . . The insurgents cannot defeat us militarily; but we can defeat ourselves."

Two weeks later, McChrystal sent in his request for more troops. There were three options—11,000, 40,000, or 85,000— and he laid out the risks and benefits of each. The low and high options were intended to be nonstarters. His advisers knew there was no way Obama would go for 85,000. The 11,000 option—most of those troops would be devoted to training the Afghan army—was described as almost ineffectual; he included it to emphasize the risks of having too light a force on the ground. What McChrystal wanted was the 40,000—four more brigades of combat troops with supporting aviation, logistics, engineering, and intelligence teams. That figure, he wrote, was based on his "professional military judgment," rendered after careful analysis. And that was on top of the 21,000 troops Obama had already authorized.

Four days after McChrystal sent his then-confidential assessment to Gates, I asked him how certain he was that more forces and a new approach would rescue the war.

"It's not too late," he said. "I'm confident of that."

4

The Wrong Man

GULAB MANGAL BOUNDED into the school auditorium clad in his finest tribal regalia—a dark wool waistcoat over a white shalwar kameez and a shiny gray silk turban, its excess fabric draped across his left shoulder. So many people had flocked to hear him that the crowd, all sitting cross-legged on the concrete floor, reached the tips of his black loafers. Others perched on the windowsills, blocking the desert breeze. The room felt hot enough to bake bread, which did not seem to trouble the weatherworn farmers and snowy-bearded grandfathers in attendance, most of whom had never experienced air-conditioning. But Mangal had not been hardened by a lifetime in the fields. Beads of sweat slid down his forehead, sprinkling those in the first row as he shook his head to make a point.

Helmand's governor had come to the school to hold his version of a pep rally. He knew it would take a few more months before the Marines and the Afghan government would be able to deliver what the residents of Nawa wanted—U.S.-funded development projects, salaries for teachers so schools could reopen, and a reformed police force—so he sought to buy time.

You need to stop those who are against the people of Nawa, against the government, against progress.

If you see Talibs in the area, talk to them and tell them to come to us. We can solve our problems with them together.

The Marines are good people. We should be happy they are here. Now it is everyone's job to help them improve security.

We cannot do what you want without your support.

When he finished, nobody clapped as vigorously as the Marine officers standing off to the side. The American COIN mission, of course, depended on connecting the Afghan people to their government, to convince them that their leaders could provide basic services—education, health care, justice based on laws—that the Taliban could not. Although the Karzai administration lacked the funds and staff to perform those functions right away, it could at least tell people it planned to help them in the near future. In much of the country, however, the government was at best a reluctant partner in the COIN effort. Most governors were Karzai cronies who had little interest—or skill—in public politics. Instead of trying to win over the population, they sat in their lavish homes and brokered personally enriching deals. To the Marines, Mangal's willingness to don a turban and travel to the backwaters of his province was vitally important. For five years, Helmand had had one of the worst governors in the country; now it had one of the best. After his first meeting with Mangal, Larry Nicholson came away thinking, *This guy is my most valuable weapon against the Taliban.*

The square-jawed Mangal, who sported a stubbly beard instead of the raggedy facial locks preferred by many Helmandis, could not have been more different from his predecessor, Sher Mohammed Akhundzada. Mangal was not a native son—he was born and raised in eastern Afghanistan—and he had served as governor in two other provinces before Karzai sent him to Lashkar Gah. He was a politically savvy technocrat who could interact with Western aid workers as effectively as he could with tribal elders. He was just the sort of local leader the Americans wanted and the Afghans needed.

There was more to his story, but he kept it well hidden from the people of Helmand. He had earned a literature degree at Kabul University in the 1970s, then a hotbed of socialist agitation. While a student, he had shortened his name from Gulab-

uddin to Gulab to burnish his secular credentials—the suffix
-*uddin* means "of the religion"—and he joined the Communist People's Democratic Party, which seized power in a 1978
coup. After graduation, he became a political commissar in the
Soviet-backed army. A few years later, he was rewarded with
a trip to Bulgaria for training, and he eventually was assigned
to the Ministry of Defense as an adviser. In 1985, he was sent
to prison after a purge ordered by the Communist president,
Mohammed Najibullah. Mangal insisted that he was jailed
because he had secretly joined the mujahideen, but it was not
clear whether that conversion occurred before he was detained
or after. He eventually returned to his hometown, where he lay
low during the subsequent civil war. After the Talibs were toppled, he was invited by the United Nations mission in Afghanistan to serve on a development board. The position involved
helping to organize the convention that approved the new constitution, and it led to his first governorship.

By the time he arrived in Helmand in March 2008, he had
reinvented himself. Although he preferred to wear a Western
suit and show off his thick, black hair, which he combed backward, he knew what his new constituents wanted. He dressed
in a turban and shalwar kameez when he was out and about.
He dutifully went to a mosque in Lashkar Gah every Friday,
organized large celebrations for the annual April holiday that
commemorates the mujahideen victory over the Communists,
and pledged to use government money to fund moderate religious schools so parents would not send their sons to Pakistani madrassas. One of his first acts was to assemble everyone
in Helmand who worked for the government. He approached
them with humility, telling them, "I work for you," but he
made clear he would not tolerate incompetence, absenteeism,
and graft. He persuaded the British government's aid agency
to fund the distribution of free wheat seed and fertilizer to
farmers to give them an alternative to poppy. And when he
heard that some of the country's best poetry had been written
in Helmand, he decided to hold a poetry festival in Lashkar
Gah, despite warnings from British officials that it could be a
magnet for Taliban violence. Five thousand people showed up,

and not a single attack occurred. Before long, Helmandis had stopped whispering about his Communist past and roots in the east. *This is what we've been waiting for. He's a good man. We trust him.*

Three months into his tenure, Mangal summoned British and American diplomats in Lashkar Gah for an urgent night-time meeting. "I've received very bad news," he began. He told them he had picked up reports that SMA and ARJ—Sher Mohammed Akhundzada and Abdul Rahman Jan—had struck a deal to work together to destabilize the province in an attempt to topple him and reclaim their jobs. The diplomats thought Mangal was being paranoid. A few days later, though, assassins killed the police chief responsible for Nad Ali and Marja, the two poppy-farming communities west of Lashkar Gah that had been constructed in the Little America period. U.S. and British officials believe ARJ ordered the murder of the chief to create a power vacuum that would allow him to reassert control over the police there. Within a month, the police had abandoned their checkpoints in the area, allowing Taliban fighters to stream in. Instead of sending more forces to wrest back the district, the British pulled out. They needed every available soldier to guard a massive convoy to transport a new hydropower generator to the dam in Kajaki that Morrison-Knudsen had built in the early 1950s. Installation of the turbine, which would provide electricity to Kandahar, was deemed a critical priority by the U.S. and British governments, even if it meant the loss of Marja and Nad Ali.

SMA had his opening to push for reinstatement. He told Karzai in August that Mangal was responsible for failing to secure Marja and Nad Ali, and he urged the president to fire the governor. The president agreed, but in the weeks that it took for his sclerotic bureaucracy to dismiss the governor, word leaked back to Helmand. When British prime minister Gordon Brown visited the region, Mangal told him of Karzai's plan. Brown grew alarmed. If Karzai removed Mangal, it would imperil the United Kingdom's stabilization mission in Helmand and prove embarrassing for Brown's government back home. When Brown met with Karzai the next day, he told the

Afghan leader that Mangal had the British government's confidence and that replacing him with SMA was not an acceptable alternative.

Karzai then telephoned Mangal. "You must give me three more months to prove myself," the governor told the president. Karzai backpedaled, telling him that the real subjects of his anger were British forces, who he believed were not doing enough to beat back the Taliban.

Despite his reversal, Karzai felt that removing SMA had been the wrong decision, and he resented the powerlessness that had resulted from his nation's dependence on foreign assistance. "The question is why do we have Taliban controlling these areas now when two years ago I had control of Helmand?" he told a senior State Department official during a meeting in the presidential palace. "When Sher Mohammed was governor there, we had girls in schools and only 160 foreign troops. The international community pushed me to remove him and now look where we are. My question for you is: Do you want a bad guy on your side or working for the Taliban?"

In Washington, a new president would soon be asking the same question about Karzai.

The Afghan president began talking as soon as his luncheon guests had taken their seats in the palace's wood-paneled dining room at a long table covered with platters of lamb and rice, baskets of flatbread, and glasses of pomegranate juice. He maintained that security was improving, poppy cultivation had been eliminated in many areas, and the economy was on the upswing. He looked across the table at the most important of his visitors and pledged to work closely with whomever won the American presidency.

"I'm at your disposal, Senator Obama," Karzai said.

The Democratic presidential candidate listened intently but revealed little about his views on Afghanistan over the two-hour lunch in July 2008. Only later that day, as a U.S. government jet flew him to Kuwait, did Obama confide in his two traveling companions, senators Jack Reed and Chuck Hagel, that he feared the situation was worse than Karzai had acknowledged.

By the time Obama moved into the White House, he harbored grave doubts about the man George W. Bush had lauded as a beacon of democracy and hope. Obama and his top advisers regarded Karzai as a mercurial tribal chieftain who condoned corruption, neglected governance, tolerated warlords, and alienated allies. To officials in the nascent administration, Karzai's behavior seemed rooted in his insincerity and incompetence, but even more so in seven years of American mismanagement.

Karzai was born in Kandahar, educated in India, and spent much of the 1980s living in exile in Pakistan. After the Soviets withdrew and their proxy president was toppled, Karzai returned to serve as a deputy foreign minister in a government that was supposed to be a coalition among various mujahideen factions. Instead of cooperating, though, the warlords fought among themselves, plunging the country into a civil war and flattening much of Kabul with tit-for-tat rocket attacks. Karzai sought to play peacemaker among some of the factions, but the then president, Burhanuddin Rabbani, accused him of plotting with a rival, Gulbuddin Hekmatyar, the warlord whose men had killed SMA's uncle. Karzai was arrested and taken to an interrogation center, where fortune smiled on him: A rocket struck the building, and he managed to escape. With the help of Hekmatyar's men, he fled back to Pakistan.

After the Taliban captured Kabul in 1996, he initially supported the hard-line Islamic movement. Many Talibs were fellow Pashtuns from Kandahar whom he had met in Pakistan during the 1980s, and he hoped they would finally be able to restore order to his anarchistic nation. He even considered, albeit briefly, becoming an ambassador for the new government. But once he grasped their brutality, he sought support from the United States and other nations to organize an anti-Taliban movement among his fellow ethnic Pashtuns, who make up about 40 percent of the country's population. The other principal ethnic groups—Tajiks, Uzbeks, and Hazaras—attempted to put aside past differences and band together as the Northern Alliance under the command of Ahmed Shah Massoud. Although Karzai's efforts foundered because he did not get the political and financial backing he wanted, he did establish a reputation—in Tehran, Moscow, and Washington—as a moderate Pashtun interested in the reconciliation of his country.

Then came September 11, 2001. About three weeks after the attacks on New York and Washington, I was invited to a small dinner at the spacious Islamabad home of U.S. Ambassador Wendy Chamberlin. As I sipped a drink in her living room, in walked a nearly bald but bearded man dressed in a gray Nehru-collared shalwar kameez. He came alone, sat on a chair across from me, and introduced himself as Hamid Karzai. I had no idea who he was, but I listened as he spoke of the savagery of the Taliban regime—the beheadings, the beatings of widows who had been reduced to begging on Kabul streets, the obliteration of the giant Buddha statues in Bamiyan. Everyone expected the United States to strike back at the Taliban sometime soon in retaliation for hosting Osama bin Laden and his al-Qaeda network. But nobody knew what would happen. Would the Talibs fight to the last man, as their ambassador to Pakistan had vowed? And who would replace them if they were toppled? Massoud had been murdered by al-Qaeda operatives on September 9, and no other opposition leader had the same clout. Chamberlin entered the room and invited Karzai to the veranda for a private conversation. As he walked out, he turned around for a moment. I expected one last observation about the Taliban, but he had America on his mind. "We Afghans are counting on the United States," he said. "We can't do this without you." I wanted to ask him what he wanted beyond the Tomahawk missiles and massive "daisy cutter" bombs that would soon pelt the Talibs ensconced in his country. But after his talk to the ambassador, he slipped into the night.

A few days later, he returned to Afghanistan, traveling by motorcycle to the mountains north of Kandahar, where he hoped to organize his fellow Populzai tribesmen to fight the Taliban. Word of his return soon leaked out, spread by Afghans and Americans eager to claim that an indigenous Pashtun resistance movement had begun. By then I had moved on to Quetta, the lawless desert city where Karzai had lived while in exile. Every three or four days, a few journalist friends and I would set off for the family's house, our beat-up taxi weaving past three-wheeled rickshaws and donkey carts, to inquire about his progress. We would always be invited into a room with plush red carpets and pillows along the walls, where his half brothers Shah Wali and Ahmed Wali served us candied almonds, raisins, green tea, and claims that Hamid's ranks of those opposed to the Taliban were growing by the day. When we heard reports from military sources that Karzai had been evacuated to Pakistan after Taliban fighters attacked him, his brothers steadfastly insisted that he was in Afghanistan. (The reports turned out to be accurate.) He even said so himself in a BBC radio interview. The following week, we obtained his satellite phone number and gave him a call. He told us he was in the mountains of Afghanistan's Uruzgan province. By then he probably was telling the truth. He did go back, but with protection from Special Forces soldiers and CIA paramilitary operatives, one of whom would save his life during an errant U.S. air strike. Although the Taliban had vowed to make a last stand in Kandahar, it melted away by early December. Karzai's tribal alliance helped pressure the Talibs, but it was not determinative. Other Afghan exiles with guns and money, including longtime rivals of the Karzai family, sought to flush the Taliban from Kandahar. And there was a blistering bombing campaign by the United States. But Karzai and his brothers had managed to shape the perceptions of Afghans, and the world, with their comments—and fabrications—to the press. He had become the liberator of southern Afghanistan.

When Afghan leaders assembled in Bonn that winter to form an interim administration, the person who had the most support for the presidency—among not only Afghans but the international community—was Karzai. He impressed Western nations with his spirit of conciliation. He reached out to powerful warlords, pledging to include their representatives in his government, not to hold them accountable for the violence of the rough-and-tumble years after the Soviets left. But it was a strategy born of desperation: Although he and many of his fellow Afghans hated the strongmen, he lacked a militia of his own to stand up to them. To Washington, however, he looked like Afghanistan's Nelson Mandela, an avuncular statesman who could unite the country's disparate, oft-warring factions.

When Karzai did seek to project his authority, he often faced opposition from the Bush administration—not because it always wanted him to be a peacemaker but because it didn't want to commit the resources, particularly troops, to support him in the first few years of his presidency. In early 2002, Karzai and U.N. special envoy Lakhdar Brahimi asked the United States to authorize the deployment of NATO forces beyond Kabul to other major Afghan cities. Although Secretary of State Colin Powell supported the move, Defense Secretary Rumsfeld opposed it because he did not want to allocate additional U.S. troops to the country. In the end, Bush sided with Rumsfeld. That same year, Karzai asked the U.S. military to remove Ismail Khan, a warlord turned governor who had enriched himself through smuggling and other illicit activities. Karzai argued that doing so was essential to establish the authority of the central government. But the request was rejected in Washington on the grounds that U.S. troops were not to engage in "green-on-green" actions—siding with one Afghan faction over another, even if one side was the president on whom the United States depended.

The most significant U.S. act that weakened Karzai early on, according to his allies and diplomats, was the decision to funnel almost all of the U.S. government's reconstruction assistance to for-profit development contractors, nongovernmental organizations, and the United Nations—not through the Afghan government, which U.S. officials didn't think was up to the task of administering the aid. The result was that Karzai's government was starved of resources to pay its workers or provide services. In February 2003, as the U.S. military was preparing to invade Iraq, Karzai took the unusual step of testifying before a Senate committee. He was asked if he had any advice for the United States. "Whatever you do in Iraq should not reduce your attention on Afghanistan," he said. By then, however, many U.S. military assets had already been diverted to Kuwait, the launchpad for the Iraq War. Afghanistan, clearly, was not the priority.

As Taliban attacks mounted, overwhelmed American soldiers increasingly resorted to calling in air strikes, which resulted in more civilian casualties. When Karzai's complaints in private to American officials failed to diminish the use of aerial bombardments, he started to denounce the U.S. military in his speeches, prompting consternation in Washington. "The Karzai that gives Washington such a headache today is, in large part, a product of how we dealt with him," Robert Finn, the U.S. ambassador to Afghanistan during the first two years of Karzai's presidency, told me soon after Obama took office. "We didn't give him the resources he needed—be it money or troops."

In November 2003, as the U.S. engagement in Iraq was becoming more violent, the Bush administration dispatched Zalmay Khalilzad, its foremost expert on Afghanistan, as its ambassador to Kabul. An animated former professor who speaks Dari and Pashto, the country's two principal languages, Khalilzad was far more than an envoy. He was effectively the country's chief executive—with Karzai the figurehead chairman—for the nineteen months of his ambassadorship. By his own account, Khalilzad ate dinner six nights a week at the presidential palace, where he met with Karzai and his advisers into the evening. Karzai made no significant decision in that time without Khalilzad's involvement and sometimes his cajoling and prodding. In 2004, a paroxysm of factional fighting involving the warlord Ismail Khan convinced Khalilzad that Khan needed to go. But by then Karzai had changed his mind about strongmen like Khan. With so few foreign troops in his country, he was reluctant to antagonize the warlords. So Khalilzad flew to Herat for discussions with Khan, a visit he coordinated with the top U.S. commander, Lieutenant General David Barno, who arranged for U.S. fighters to fly over the warlord's compound in a show of force. Khalilzad then announced that Khan would be moving to Kabul to become a cabinet minister. A few days later, Karzai issued an edict to that effect. "Karzai was being his usual indecisive self, so Zal drove the steel rod up his spine," said Thomas Lynch, who was Khalilzad's military assistant.

In June 2005, Khalilzad was made the U.S. ambassador to Baghdad. He was replaced in Kabul by Ronald Neumann, a soft-spoken, pipe-smoking veteran diplomat assigned by Secretary of State Condoleezza Rice to normalize the relationship between Washington and Kabul. That meant no dinners at the palace every night or involvement in the minutiae of government. Karzai began to slide off the rails. He refused to remove incompetent subordinates, and he fired officials whom the U.S. Embassy regarded as effective. He named as his anticorruption chief an Afghan American who had been imprisoned in Nevada on drug charges for nearly four years. At times, however, Karzai was prescient. He publicly faulted the Pakistani government for not stemming the cross-border infiltration of Taliban fighters. But when he first articulated that complaint, he was told by the United States to cease and desist because President Bush did not want to upset Pakistan's leader at the time, General Pervez Musharraf.

By late 2006, as concern grew in the White House over Karzai's leadership, Bush initiated biweekly videoconferences with Karzai, who sometimes held his infant son, Mirwais, on his lap during the conversations. "It was a lot of 'How are you doing? How is your son?'" according to a senior U.S. government official who attended some of the sessions. But the familiarity came at a cost. In late 2007, Bush's National Security Council authorized aerial spraying of defoliants on poppy fields because of concern that drug profits were financing the Taliban. Bush was passionate about the strategy, declaring at one meeting "I'm a spray man myself." The plan was to force the Karzai government to accede to spraying and then use that acquiescence to overcome opposition from the U.S. military and the British government, both of which were worried that eradication would push farmers to side with the Taliban. But when Karzai objected during a videoconference, saying the sight of spray planes would "look like chemical warfare" to the Afghan people, Bush backed down without a fight. "He had come to the point where he related so closely to Karzai that he yielded to his instincts," the official said. "When it becomes personal and it becomes more like partnership edging toward friendship, the personal dynamics are such that it's harder to put the heat on."

Obama's national security team learned of the frequency and tenor of Bush's videoconferences during the presidential transition. "The president of the United States had become the case officer for Afghanistan," said a senior Obama foreign policy adviser.

For Karzai, a dinner in February 2008 with Joseph Biden, then the chairman of the Senate Foreign Relations Committee, and two other committee members—Chuck Hagel and John Kerry—was a portent of what a Democratic administration would bring.

"Mr. President, how are you attempting to control the corruption in your government?" Hagel asked Karzai.

"Who is corrupt?" Karzai responded. "Show me. Give me the names."

Hagel noted that Karzai's half brother Ahmed Wali, the chairman of the provincial council in Kandahar, had been accused of links to narcotics trafficking. But Hagel couldn't cite specifics, and Karzai refused to budge. When the conversation moved to poppy cultivation, Karzai insisted that his government was making good progress.

"Mr. President, you're not doing very well," Biden responded. "Your poppy production is at record levels."

Biden disputed other Karzai claims of achievement. The back-and-forth circled again to corruption, and when Karzai still refused to acknowledge any problem, Biden stood up and threw his napkin on the table. "This dinner is over," he said, and he walked out.

Ten days before Obama's inauguration, Biden returned to Kabul to see Karzai. When the Afghan leader told the incoming vice president that he looked forward to building with Obama the same sort of chummy relationship he had with Bush, Biden replied, "Well, it's going to be different. You'll probably talk to him or see him a couple of times a year. You're not going to be talking to him every week."

There were some secrets presidential envoy Richard Holbrooke locked away in his vast mental vault, divulging them only to colleagues at senior reaches of the American government with top-level security clearances. There were other matters he deemed fit for sotto voce conversation in the Georgetown salons and Upper West Side town houses he frequented upon

his return from Kabul and Islamabad, even if the bureaucrats below him classified those topics as confidential. He was
old school in that way—he spoke openly with businessmen,
retired diplomats, think-tank analysts, and journalists whose
work he respected or he deemed influential. It was not just a
way to get his views circulating among the chattering class; it
proved to be an invaluable way to test ideas and perhaps even
pick up a few new ones. He believed many of the most useful
insights came not from presidents, generals, and ambassadors
but from those outside government, be they in refugee camps
or at swanky dinner parties.

In the early months of the Obama administration, Holbrooke
regarded the question of what to do about Karzai to be suitable for cocktail parties. There was little disagreement among
Obama's national security team that Afghanistan needed better leadership. The assessments of the war conducted during
Obama's transition accurately concluded that the incompetence and venality of the Afghan government were the principal reasons people were siding with the Taliban. Admittedly,
Karzai presided over a shell of a bureaucracy that lacked the
staff, structure, and resources to perform even basic functions,
such as paying teachers' salaries or allocating gasoline to police
trucks. But Obama's advisers nonetheless believed Karzai
should have been doing more. He could have taken a firmer
stance against graft. He could have traveled outside Kabul
more frequently. And he could have appointed more techno-
crats to his cabinet instead of warlords and cronies. To the new
team in Washington, the effort to fire Mangal was an example
of the problem with Karzai. "He's incompetent," Holbrooke
told me. Over at the White House, Doug Lute concluded to his
staff that Karzai had "plateaued as a leader." At the Pentagon,
senior generals saw him as more of a problem than a partner in their counterinsurgency efforts. But most on Obama's
team grudgingly concluded that there was no viable replacement. The principal alternatives to Karzai were not Pashtuns,
and it seemed difficult, if not impossible, to fathom how a
non-Pashtun president would be able to quell an insurgency
among Pashtuns, who already were skeptical of their government. Those advisers acknowledged that a flawed Karzai was

better than no Karzai. They also remained hopeful that they could modify his behavior by realigning his relationship with the new administration. There would be no more of the bonhomie of the Bush years; they would talk tough and restrict access until he reformed, which they assumed he would do soon enough because he depended on the United States for the security of his capital and the sustenance of his government.

Holbrooke, who had served as a foreign policy adviser to three previous presidents, was far more skeptical. Unlike others at the pinnacle of the Democratic foreign policy establishment, he had made several trips to Afghanistan as a private citizen during the Bush years, and his observations had led him to conclude that Karzai could not be redeemed. He knew that Washington lacked the power to tell him to go and Obama's team had no desire for the CIA to foment a coup as it had with Ngo Dinh Diem in South Vietnam. But Karzai was up for reelection in a few months, and Holbrooke thought that would be the ideal moment to clean out the presidential palace.

The Obama administration's official position on the election was that it did not have a position. When speaking before the cameras, various officials, including Holbrooke, said the U.S. government wanted to see a free and fair process; as for the outcome, that was up to the Afghans. When he wasn't speaking on the record, Holbrooke articulated a different desire: He wanted as many challengers as possible, and he even tried to persuade some Karzai rivals to run. By increasing the overall anti-incumbent vote, he hoped to force a runoff. If that occurred, he figured opposition supporters would band together to oust the president. It sounded far-fetched, but Holbrooke liked to shoot the moon.

"Isn't Ghani impressive?" Holbrooke said to me at a Washington reception. He was referring to former finance minister Ashraf Ghani, who was in the race, and Holbrooke really wasn't asking a question; he was touting the man he thought should be the next president of Afghanistan. Ghani had the sort of credentials that impress American diplomats. He had earned a doctorate from Columbia University, worked at the World Bank, and pushed for changes to Afghanistan's new constitution aimed at reducing graft. As a Pashtun, he satisfied the ethnic requirement, but he would not have been pulled aside for additional screening at an American airport based on his appearance: He was clean-shaven, he wore Western suits, and he spoke flawless English. He hired the political strategist James Carville to help advise his campaign, which set up a Web site and sent out regular e-mail messages, helping him win over a handful of urban, computer-literate elites who probably would have voted for him anyway.

A towering man with an irrepressible personality, Holbrooke had bucked State Department convention and irritated more than a few Foreign Service officers by assembling his own team of "Af-Pak" experts drawn largely from academia and nongovernmental organizations. These experts thought his obsession with Ghani was crazy. One of them told Holbrooke that Carville "was smoking something" if he thought Ghani had a chance of winning. Ghani had no real constituency in the provinces, and he was a miserable campaigner. His soft, nasal voice was better suited to speaking on panels about postconflict state building than directing the actual construction. Holbrooke should have known better—he had been around long enough to know that those who wow on the Washington social circuit rarely have sufficient street credibility among their people. But he was convinced that Ghani could prevail or at least make a strong enough showing to be a player.

When Holbrooke went to Kabul, he arranged to be photographed meeting with Ghani and other opposition candidates, including Abdullah Abdullah, the former Northern Alliance foreign minister. Holbrooke also instructed the new U.S. ambassador in Kabul, Karl Eikenberry, to attend rallies held by Ghani, Abdullah, and other Karzai rivals. Holbrooke was not worried about the repercussions of his actions. He was certain Karzai was going to lose.

The meetings with rival candidates and the visits to their rallies incensed Karzai, who regarded those gestures as an affront from a nation that had long been a loyal ally. "If he had any doubts what Holbrooke and Eikenberry thought of him, it was made very clear during the campaign," said Umar Daudzai, Karzai's chief of staff at the time. "The American message was 'We want you out.'"

.   .   .

The presidential election that August turned out to be a fiasco. Hundreds of polling sites did not open. The Taliban mounted dozens of attacks. In places where balloting occurred, international observers reported rampant efforts to bribe and coerce voters. Much of the fraud was perpetrated by Karzai's cronies, who stuffed boxes with thousands of identically marked ballots for the incumbent.

Despite the Pentagon's claim to Obama earlier in the year that the 17,000 additional troops were essential to conducting the election, those forces played only a minor role in the overall security effort. In fact, the new troops helped to facilitate the vote-rigging by protecting polling sites in Helmand and Kandahar where Karzai supporters engaged in some of their most egregious ballot tampering.

To avoid antagonizing Karzai, Eikenberry had urged Holbrooke not to visit Afghanistan during the election. But Holbrooke didn't want to miss it. Although it was clear by election day that Ghani had no chance of winning, Holbrooke's advisers thought Karzai had a good chance of being defeated by Abdullah Abdullah.

The morning after the election, as vote counts and reports of malfeasance were trickling into Kabul, Holbrooke hosted a meeting at the U.S. Embassy with his counterparts from other NATO nations. Parroting uncorroborated reports from one of his staffers—just a few percent of the ballots had been counted by then—Holbrooke said it appeared that Abdullah might have won. At the very least, he said, the election appeared to be headed for a runoff because many ballots for Karzai would probably be excluded because of fraud. After the meeting, a Turkish diplomat who had been listening by telephone called one of Karzai's top aides and told him what Holbrooke had said.

When Holbrooke met Karzai for lunch a few hours later, the Afghan leader was fuming. As soon as Holbrooke broached the possibility of a runoff, Karzai exploded. He accused Holbrooke of meddling in the election. Although Holbrooke denied that he had demanded a runoff, the damage was done. Karzai told his aides that he did not trust Holbrooke and did not want to see him again. His aides conveyed the message to officials at the U.S. Embassy.

White House and National Security Council officials blamed Holbrooke for making a bad situation far worse. They ordered him not to appear on Sunday talk shows. When it became clear that Karzai would not cross the 50 percent threshold needed to prevent a runoff—there were too many fraudulent ballots—the White House sought to broker a compromise between Karzai and Abdullah to avoid holding another election, which would have been too logistically challenging and burdensome for the military. But instead of relying on Holbrooke to forge the deal, the White House dispatched John Kerry, the chairman of the Senate Foreign Relations Committee, who patiently paced through the gardens of the presidential palace with the Afghan leader, sharing the story of alleged voting irregularities in Ohio during the 2004 presidential election. As Kerry mediated a window-dressing arrangement for Karzai to accede to a runoff in exchange for Abdullah agreeing to withdraw—meaning there would be no second round and Karzai would get another five years in office—Holbrooke sat in Washington and stewed. He knew the United States needed an effective partner at the head of the Afghan government. But it wouldn't have one anytime soon.

5

The Road to Ruins

ON CHRISTMAS EVE 2001, while many of Dick Scott's countrymen made toasts to America's victory in Afghanistan, he fretted in his tiny cabin nestled in the foothills of the Rocky Mountains. He had lived in Afghanistan for seven years in the 1970s, working as a social scientist for USAID. In the late 1990s, he had been among the very few Americans who had traveled into Taliban-controlled Afghanistan, where his efforts to repair the Little America irrigation system had so impressed the mullahs that they had allowed him to drive around the south without a chaperone. Although he had retired from USAID a decade earlier, the seventy-year-old Scott understood farmers along the Helmand River Valley better than anyone else in the United States, and he believed the fall of the Taliban provided a remarkable opportunity to wean Afghans from growing poppy—if bureaucrats in Washington acted quickly.

That evening, he sat in front of his computer and typed out a six-page, single-spaced letter to his former employer. The answer, he wrote, was cotton. Farmers had been growing cotton in Helmand since the mid-1960s, when the British had built a gin in Lashkar Gah. Many of them preferred it to poppy. It was, after all, a legal crop. Cotton also yielded far more revenue per acre than wheat or vegetables. But before farmers would switch back to cotton, they wanted the Afghan government to agree to provide the same incentives it had in the 1970s: ample credit, free fertilizer and seeds, and a guaranteed purchase price. When Mullah Nasim Akhundzada had sought to expand poppy cultivation in the early 1980s, he simply had copied the government's cotton business model, which had been abandoned a few years earlier with the Soviet invasion. It was too good a deal for the farmers to refuse.

If farmers didn't sow their fields with cottonseed that spring, however, the need for cash would drive them to grow poppy the following autumn. Scott urged USAID to refurbish the government-owned gin in Lashkar Gah and another about twenty miles to the north, in the town of Gereshk, which the British had built in the late 1970s because so much cotton was being produced in Helmand. He also recommended that the agency bring in better seeds, start an agricultural credit program, and clean out irrigation canals throughout the valley.

Scott's Christmas Eve letter wound its way through the USAID bureaucracy. A month after he sent it, he got a call from an international development firm that had been awarded a USAID contract to promote cotton and other crops as alternatives to poppy in Helmand. Did he want to work on what he had proposed? Scott had been convinced of the agricultural potential of southern Afghanistan since his first trip there in the early 1970s, and his passion to fulfill the dream of Little America seemed to grow with each passing year, even though he lived half a world away. Retirement had turned him into an obsessive—what he wanted, more than anything else, was to see cotton bloom on the fields of Helmand. He said he was willing to depart Colorado that night.

When he got to Afghanistan, he discovered that the gin in Gereshk had been bombed by the Americans because a small group of Taliban fighters had been using it as a base. Scott had no choice but to focus his efforts on the gin in Lashkar Gah. He allotted the state-run gin's operators enough money to honor IOU chits it had given to farmers the previous year, and he had replacement parts for the gin's machinery sent by air from the company outside Atlanta that had supplied the original equipment. But he soon realized that much more work needed to be done. A larger volume of seed had to be distributed to farmers, and the central government had to lift restrictions on the gin's purchasing power. None of that seemed complicated to Scott;

it just required some diligent work. But he hadn't counted on everyone erecting obstacles in his way.

The initial U.S. assistance to restart the cotton industry led several enterprising Afghan businessmen to set up small gins of their own in other parts of Helmand. To Scott, it was a sign of cotton's popularity, and if farmers resumed growing the crop to the extent they had in the 1970s, the private gins would pick up business the state-run facility couldn't handle. But the director of the gin deemed the private operators unneeded competition and complained to the minister of mines and industry, who happened to be a relative. The minister contacted Helmand governor Sher Mohammed Akhundzada, who ordered the police to seize all of the private gins.

Afghan officials were concerned about competition because the Lashkar Gah gin was one of only a few sources of revenue for the new government in Kabul. Scott hoped that USAID's promotion of cotton would mollify the Afghan government—increasing the overall harvest, he reasoned, would create a rising tide that would lift both the government gin and the private ones. But once USAID officials grasped the Afghan government's role in cotton—the state ownership of the Lashkar Gah gin, the price supports, and the fertilizer handouts—they wanted nothing to do with the crop. "Until the gin is privatized," an embassy official told Scott, "you can be sure there will be no American help for cotton."

USAID's opposition was rooted in the agency's antipathy toward subsidies. For cotton to be an attractive crop for Afghan farmers, the government gin had to agree to buy cotton from farmers at rates that could sometimes be above world prices. To USAID's agriculture experts, that was bad economic policy. They also argued that neighboring Pakistan and Uzbekistan produced cotton far more efficiently than Afghanistan. Scott found those arguments ludicrous and hypocritical. There was ample domestic demand for Afghan cotton, and it was U.S. government subsidies to American cotton growers that had depressed world prices, which was why price supports were needed in Afghanistan in the first place. "It's fine for us but not for them?" he groused.

That winter, farmers desperate for credit turned to opium brokers, who offered them bags of seed and wads of cash. The following spring, vermilion flowers dotted the landscape. The next year brought even more. Within a few years, poppy blanketed most of Little America's farmland.

By then Scott had returned home to Colorado. He was the expert, and he had been willing to stay, but USAID thought it knew better. He kept writing letters to friends in the development world about the need to help Afghans with cotton. But he stopped sending them to USAID. Instead of being part of the solution, his former employer had become part of the problem.

Soon after the U.S. military overthrew the Taliban government in 2001, senior Bush administration officials began to argue about the best way to rebuild a country whose rates of malnutrition, illiteracy, and infant mortality were among the highest in the world. Some development specialists at USAID advocated a longer-term focus on agriculture, which they deemed the key to economic sustainability, and on "capacity building"— training Afghans to do things themselves. But officials at the White House and the Pentagon wanted projects with a quick impact—schools, roads, and health clinics that could be completed in a year or two and would generate goodwill among the Afghan people. In early 2002, the White House ordered USAID to build or refurbish a school and clinic in each of the country's nearly four hundred districts. A school and clinic in every district made for a snappy sound bite, but there was no allocation of funds to hire teachers and physicians to staff the structures. When the construction started, the problems got worse. USAID required the contractor to build American-style schools that would be sturdy enough to withstand strong earthquakes. That required taking cranes to remote villages, many of which lacked roads. As costs ballooned, USAID revised its design requirement. The new specifications swung too far the other way, resulting in roofs that sometimes were so flimsy they couldn't bear the weight of wintertime snows. As reports of caved-in schoolhouses trickled back to Kabul, some international advisers to the Education Ministry saw a blessing: Each collapsed building was one less school that the Afghan government would have to staff.

Another prized project was a highway from Kabul to Kandahar. President Bush demanded that it be completed in less than a year. USAID met the goal, but to do so, it allowed contractors to deposit such a thin layer of asphalt that in some spots it washed away when the snow melted the following spring.

It was not until mid-2003, almost eighteen months after the Taliban government fell, that USAID started its first national agriculture program. It received less than 5 percent of the annual reconstruction budget. "Investments in agriculture take time. They don't produce results overnight—and that's what the administration wanted," said Mark Ward, a former senior USAID official who participated in high-level discussions with White House officials.

By 2004, reports that poppy cultivation was reaching record levels, particularly in Helmand, began to alarm administration officials. When the White House agreed to spend $775 million the following year on counternarcotics programs, USAID saw an opportunity. It pitched a program called Alternative Livelihoods that was based, in part, on the belief that poppy cultivation would drop if young men were offered short-term employment around planting and harvest time that paid better than working in the fields. It got the money.

Because budget cuts over the previous two decades had forced the agency to jettison staff who could run development and reconstruction programs, it turned to contractors. Chemonics, a for-profit development firm based in Washington, D.C., received the Alternative Livelihoods contract for southern Afghanistan in late 2005. One of its first projects was to build a road. Andrew Natsios, the USAID administrator at the time, had recently seen cobblestone roads in Bolivia's Chapare rain forest that had been funded by a U.S. Alternative Livelihoods program to discourage coca planting. He figured that hiring people to build such roads, which were inexpensive but required extensive manual labor, could be a new tool in the fight against poppies in southern Afghanistan. Chemonics readily agreed and flew in eleven Bolivian engineers.

The Bolivians trained forty-six Afghans in the art of placing fist-size river stones on the ground. Then they set about constructing a road from Lashkar Gah to the crumbling Ghaznavid arch at the edge of the city. Once a sixth of a mile was complete, Chemonics held a celebration that featured a speech by U.S. Ambassador Ron Neumann touting the promise of stone roads in combating drugs.

Chemonics had plans to build many cobblestone roads across southern Afghanistan, but Afghan leaders objected. They had been willing to humor the Americans with the path to the archaeological ruins, but what they really wanted were gravel and asphalt roads. They claimed the cobblestones hurt their camels' hooves. So Chemonics shifted to other cash-for-work projects, such as cleaning irrigation canals, that were more palatable to local officials. Although it allowed USAID to claim that it had generated hundreds of thousands of days of labor, the overall impact was like that of a sugar rush: It didn't last. Poppy farmers always managed to find enough help—largely because unemployment was so acute—and cultivation in southern Afghanistan reached all-time highs. And when U.S. funding for short-term labor dried up, many locals went to fight for the Taliban.

The Chemonics contract, which USAID increased to $166 million in 2007, included money for the construction of a business park, a women's center, an Internet café, and a recreational facility. But what Afghan farmers needed was agricultural credit and expert advice to improve their yields. USAID didn't offer those services. The few farm-related activities that the agency funded through the Alternative Livelihoods effort were so ham-handed that they sometimes generated results counter to what the agency sought. USAID naively assumed that doling out free wheat seed and fertilizer would be enough to get farmers to stop growing poppy when in fact the drug crop was far more lucrative. Many farmers who accepted U.S.-sponsored handouts simply sold the wheat seeds in Pakistan or ground them to make flour, and they used the fertilizer to nourish their poppy fields. Several former Chemonics specialists told me that the company, which by then had received more than $430 million worth of Afghanistan reconstruction business from USAID, had not complained to USAID project managers because of concern it might jeopardize future contracts with the agency. USAID officials were unable to see the problems for themselves because they seldom left their fortified compound in Kabul.

Soon after the cobblestone-road fiasco, Yosuf Mir, a stout and garrulous Afghan man who dreamed of owning his own business, traveled to Kandahar from his home in northern Virginia to look for ways to help his native country and make a few dollars. He was struck by the poverty and the prevalence of poppy flowers. He asked farmers why they were cultivating a crop that was illegal and un-Islamic, rather than cotton. "They told me, 'What else can I do? We don't have the seeds. We don't have the fertilizer. We don't have anyone to sell to. There's nobody to give us credit except for the drug dealers.'"

The solution seemed obvious to Mir. The Afghan government was seeking to sell the state-run textile factory in Kandahar. He would buy it.

He and his brother pledged $1 million of family land in Afghanistan in exchange for a twenty-year lease. When the factory reopened, he estimated that it would lead 35,000 farmers to resume cotton growing. Once the bales were ginned in Lashkar Gah, he planned for his facility to spin into action and employ as many as 12,000 people. "We would," he said, "create a real alternative livelihood for the Afghan people."

Mir needed help to realize his dream. He didn't have the funds to repair the factory and supply it with a reliable source of electricity. The family land was his only real asset. He worked as an interpreter at a courthouse in Virginia and drove a taxi to make ends meet.

When Mir approached Chemonics, the leaders of the Alternative Livelihoods program said they would help rehabilitate the factory. They in turn asked USAID for authority to do the work. USAID rejected the request within weeks. There were new leaders at the USAID headquarters in Kabul who were even more opposed to promoting cotton than their predecessors who had dealt with Dick Scott. It did not matter that cotton was the most viable competitor to poppy or that Afghans wanted to grow it. As before, the need for subsidies and the government's ownership of the gin were deal breakers for the new team at USAID.

The man who made the decision to reject assistance for the cotton factory was Loren Stoddard, USAID's director for Afghan agriculture and alternative development programs. Before joining USAID, he had worked as a produce salesman in Utah. And before arriving in Kabul in 2006, he had spent four years with the agency in Guatemala, where he had earned plaudits from his superiors for helping to facilitate business deals between local farmers and Walmart. He wanted to do more of the same in Afghanistan. The key to resuscitating the economy, in his view, was for farmers to specialize not in cotton but in what the country grew best—other than poppy—and what buyers in other nations wanted to import: pomegranates, almonds, pistachios, raisins, and fruit, including apricots, that could be dried or turned into juice. He was fond of noting that Afghanistan had been one of the world's largest exporters of dried fruits and nuts before the Soviet invasion. The first step in making that happen, he maintained, was to line up purchasers, not focus on farmers. "Rich farmers sell first and then grow," he told me. "Poor farmers grow first and then hope somebody will buy it."

Stoddard's vision wowed his superiors at USAID and the embassy, but it was harder to persuade farmers in much of Helmand to switch to fruits and nuts. Although a few northern towns had pomegranate groves, orchard plants had never been cultivated on the Little America farmland. Farmers there knew how to grow wheat, cotton, a few vegetables—and poppy; they would need to be taught how to raise and prune fruit and nut trees. An even more significant factor was time: It takes three to five years for most orchard trees to start producing. How would the farmers make ends meet in the meantime? And how would they export their goods in the midst of an insurgency? Cotton had the virtue of maturing in one season, and there was a ready market for it. But Stoddard was adamant. "Cotton is not a viable crop for Afghanistan," he declared. "AID will not fund it."

Convinced that Stoddard was wrong, Mir refused to give up. He sought to bend the ear of any government official in

Washington who would meet with him. Finally he typed out a three-page letter to President Bush:

> Mr. President, we are just asking for a little help to rebuild these plants and to put thousands of rural people to work. This will help improve local security and reduce the growing of drug crops and drug trafficking in this region. We need your help to get U.S. Government agencies and experts to support these redevelopment and security-improvement efforts.

Two months later, he received a response from the State Department's Afghanistan office:

> Unfortunately, the Bumpers Amendment prohibits USAID's Alternative Development Program from offering your company assistance with these crops. The amendment, passed by Congress in May 1986, prohibits foreign assistance in the agriculture sector where such assistance would be in connection with the growth or production in a foreign country for export of a commodity that would compete in world markets with a similar commodity grown or produced in the United States. This includes cotton, tobacco, and alcohol.

To Mir, the message was mind-boggling: Protecting King Cotton was more important than defeating the Taliban. Several U.S. officials familiar with the matter told me that USAID could have asked the White House to issue an exemption, given the national security importance of stabilizing Afghanistan, but senior officials at the agency refused to promote a crop in which Afghanistan did not have a comparative advantage in world markets. "Their thinking is all about free trade—that Afghanistan is better suited to produce pomegranates and raisins than bales of cotton," said one USAID official who disagreed with the agency's stance. "But what about the goal of keeping people from shooting at our troops?"

By late 2008, Mir had to furlough the last two hundred employees of the textile factory, several of whom had worked there since the Soviet occupation. Most of them, Mir said, went off to fight for the Taliban.

In late 2006, Chemonics had won another USAID contract, initially worth $102 million, to work on agriculture pro-
grams. The experts the firm recruited figured they would have
a chance to implement the sorts of assistance projects that
Afghanistan badly needed. They proposed setting up a commercial poultry operation that would employ women in fifty
villages and produce as many as 45 million eggs a year, reducing the country's reliance on imports from Pakistan and Iran.
And they urged extending a project that had been set up under
an earlier USAID contract to establish and restore grape vineyards. "It would have produced real change in the lives of hundreds of thousands of Afghans," said Gary Kuhn, the executive
director of Roots of Peace, a nonprofit organization that would
have done the vineyard work for Chemonics.

But Stoddard believed the contract should concentrate on
promoting "buyer-led development." That meant sales and mar-
keting activities, not field-level work to help farmers increase
production. The grapevine project was killed. So was the egg
venture. To implement his vision, Stoddard ordered Chemonics to use the contract money to hold a series of agriculture
fairs that would give Afghan farmers a chance to display their
wares to foreign purchasers, to organize promotional shipments of pomegranates to supermarkets in the Persian Gulf
region, and to establish "agribusiness brokerage centers" to
facilitate business deals. He also wanted the Afghans to start
growing new crops that he thought they could export. Among
them was saffron, which fetches more per pound than opium
paste. He authorized several projects to cultivate the reddish
spice, which USAID's public relations team touted in breath-
less press releases. But when the first crop was ready, traders
were unable to export it. Because Afghan farmers relieved
themselves in their fields and rarely washed their hands, their
saffron contained a thousand times more fecal matter than saffron grown in neighboring Iran, the country's principal competitor in world markets.

Stoddard's crowning achievement was going to be a sprawling commercial farm with miles of strawberry fields and thousands of cashmere goats. The effort began with an entreaty

from Bush to the billionaire chairman of the Dole Food Company at a 2006 Republican Party fund-raiser. Go to Afghanistan, Bush urged David H. Murdock, "to see what you can do to help." After a tour of the country the following April, Murdock told U.S. officials he wanted to build a 25,000-acre plantation modeled after Dole's vast holdings in the Philippines. But a few months later, he changed his mind. He had concluded that the transportation and security challenges were insurmountable.

That did not dissuade Stoddard. Mindful of the president's interest in the project—and convinced that the real reason Murdock had dropped out was because he had not received a thank-you call from Bush—Stoddard decided to go it alone. He allocated $40 million in reconstruction money to the venture and directed Chemonics to hire workers and purchase equipment. He was convinced the farm would "help Afghans realize there was a bright future ahead of them" by demonstrating modern agricultural techniques and generating an appetite for Afghan-grown products around the world.

Murdock had wanted the farm built on a vacant parcel because he feared tenant disputes. After Dole withdrew, USAID decided to stick with the empty-land strategy, despite the concerns of some at Chemonics that the site that the agency had chosen might not be suitable for commercial agriculture. It was not until a year later, after several million dollars had been spent, that USAID officials realized why Afghans had not cultivated the land themselves: The groundwater and soil were too salty to grow crops. "It was a total waste of resources," said Frauke de Weijer, a development specialist who worked with USAID contractors building the farm.

Even if there had been enough water to run the farm, several agriculture specialists familiar with the venture said it would have been out of place in a country where most people cultivate small plots of land by hand. "It was one man's pipe dream," a specialist who worked on the project for Chemonics told me. "It made no sense."

Stoddard, who subsequently received a prestigious assignment with USAID in Peru, had free rein to design and implement agriculture projects as he wished in Afghanistan because "nobody—nobody at the White House, nobody at USAID headquarters, nobody at State—really understood agriculture," said former USAID official Mark Ward.

USAID had employed dozens of agronomists and agriculture economists during the Vietnam War, but by the time the Afghan War started, there was only a handful of people with specialized training in agriculture development on staff. Most of its scientific and technical experts had been sent packing in the 1980s and 1990s as budgets were cut and the workforce shrank. "This is what happens when you eviscerate a federal agency," Ward said. "There's a consequence. You may not see it right away. In this case, we're seeing it a generation later, when we need AID to help us win a war—and it can't."

Richard Holbrooke didn't know much about farming—he wasn't even a backyard gardener—but he had read enough assessment reports and talked to enough outside experts to conclude that U.S. agriculture and counternarcotics policy in Afghanistan under the Bush administration was "an unmitigated failure." The problem, in his view, was not just the Alternative Livelihoods debacle but the U.S. government's support for eradicating the poppy crop. Bill Wood, the ambassador who had preceded Karl Eikenberry in Kabul, had come to Afghanistan from Colombia, where he had overseen U.S. funding for the aerial spraying of defoliants to wipe out drug plants. He had spent two years pushing President Karzai and other Afghan officials to agree to a similar approach but had succeeded only in earning the moniker "Chemical Bill." Karzai adamantly opposed the use of spray planes, arguing that they would remind Afghans of the Soviet occupation. While both sides bickered, Washington funneled money to an Afghan counternarcotics police unit that bulldozed and burned the fields of unlucky poppy farmers.

To Holbrooke, eradication by spraying, torching, or tilling was all the same—it was a huge mistake. Bush-era officials and many military officers insisted that the Taliban was heavily involved in the drug trade and that crop destruction was necessary to deprive the insurgents of funding. But Holbrooke maintained otherwise. He cited the CIA study that claimed the Taliban got more money from Pakistan and Persian Gulf nations than from drugs. Holbrooke argued that destroying fields only hurt poor farmers. Many of them had received cash up front that they had already spent. Without a poppy crop to sell, they became indebted to drug brokers. That made them perfect recruits for the Taliban, who offered day wages that allowed them to repay their loans. Eradication fueled corruption—a well-placed bribe could often protect your field—and it led to growing anger among southern Afghans toward Karzai's administration. The drug barons also thrived: Reducing the supply of opium drove prices up, which fattened their wallets.

The Bush strategy on counternarcotics and Alternative Livelihoods, which consumed almost $3 billion from 2005 to 2008, "was the single most wasteful, most ineffective program that I had ever seen," Holbrooke seethed to me in the spring of 2009. "It wasn't just a waste of money. . . . This was actually a benefit to the enemy. We were recruiting Taliban with our tax dollars."

He believed assisting Afghans with farming needed to be at the top of the U.S. reconstruction agenda. After all, more than 80 percent of working-age males in the country were small-scale farmers. Helping them grow more food would give them a financial incentive to side with their government against the Taliban. The experts he consulted recommended an integrated solution: credit and training for farmers, new roads so they could get their goods to market, cold-storage facilities so produce wouldn't spoil, and processing factories to dry grapes into raisins and crush pomegranates into juice. He knew that many farmers would balk at the prospect of waiting as long as five years for fruit saplings to mature, so he hoped to encourage them with cash handouts and opportunities for short-term employment. "They need the kind of soup-to-nuts agricultural support that Roosevelt gave the farmers during the Great Depression—roads, markets, irrigation, seeds, fertilizer, educational materials," he said. "Afghans are smart farmers. . . . They just need the right kind of help from us."

To implement his grand vision, he wrested control of Afghan agriculture policy from USAID and told agency leaders that he would be signing off on all new projects. He sent

Alternative Livelihoods programs and buyer-led development initiatives to the compost heap. But he wanted to do more than just shift the focus to farmers. He also demanded that USAID do business differently. He instructed the agency to issue smaller contracts, work with more Afghan-run development organizations, and provide more funds to Karzai's government. Under the Bush administration, USAID had focused money and attention on American-run programs instead of helping Afghans assume responsibility for their own affairs. In late 2008, when the newly appointed agriculture minister, Mohammad Asif Rahimi, moved into his Kabul office, he was shocked by what he found—or, rather, what he didn't. There was no phone, no Internet connection, no secretary. "It looked like the Taliban left a week ago," he said. Holbrooke promised Rahimi that everything would change.

For Holbrooke, it all came down to money. He believed the United States needed to spend big if it wanted quick results. He advocated for a huge increase in funding: Bush sought $1.25 billion for Afghan reconstruction in the last year he was in office; in part because of Holbrooke's prodding, Obama added more than $800 million soon after taking office and then requested $4.3 billion for the 2010 fiscal year from Congress, which gave him nearly $4.1 billion. The push to dole out cash was infectious. At a May 2009 strategy session on Afghanistan policy—the attendees included Holbrooke, Petraeus, McChrystal, and Lute—Eikenberry implored USAID and State Department managers to increase the size of their initiatives. "We have an opportunity to think unconstrained," he said. "If you used to ask for $22 million and now you're asking for $24 million, that's not thinking boldly."

Holbrooke got his first chance to turn up the volume that spring when USAID presented its new agriculture plan for Helmand and Kandahar. Modeled after a program in the north that gave farmers discounted wheat seed and fertilizer, USAID planned to offer farmers in the south subsidized seeds to grow vegetables and melons, which would fetch them more than wheat and corn and, U.S. officials hoped, help lead some of them to forsake poppy. The initiative, which was supposed to address the shortcomings of the earlier Alternative Livelihoods efforts, also called for organizing farmers into cooperatives and equipping them with tractors, water pumps, and hand tools. In addition, USAID would fund the construction of hundreds of miles of new gravel roads in both provinces so farmers could take their goods to market.

Like all USAID programs in Afghanistan, this one was known by its acronym: AVIPA, which stood for Afghanistan Vouchers for Increased Production in Agriculture. To Holbrooke, it seemed like a fundamental break from the past and an important first step in achieving his goals. He hoped the program would expand after a year to include the construction of storage and processing facilities.

USAID proposed spending $150 million on AVIPA. It was a staggering amount of money to disburse over just one year in two insecure provinces.

When Holbrooke heard the figure, he said, "Double it."

Money would no longer be a problem. The strategy for spending it—and fighting the war—would not be resolved as easily.

6

The Surge

KAEL WESTON ESCHEWED the trappings of Foreign Service imperiousness. He wore jeans instead of pressed khakis. His default posture was to listen, not lecture. He told Marines that if he could be anywhere else, he would be hiking in the American West, where he had been raised. He refused to sit around the base all day, writing cables and convening meetings, as many other diplomats did. He walked side by side with the grunts on patrols. He told the lowliest lance corporals that they were the most important Marines in the fight. He endeared himself to the officers because he instinctively knew when to push back and when to accept the Marine way of war—and he never, ever called the generals by their first names. Larry Nicholson was the exception, because they were friends, not just colleagues, and because they'd have taken a bullet for each other. When other officers asked Nicholson why he brought his political adviser on every trip and into every meeting, he told them Weston was "the sharpest civilian I know."

Weston had joined the State Department in 2001 after failing out of a doctoral program at the London School of Economics. Soon after the September 11, 2001, attacks, he was assigned to the U.S. Mission to the United Nations, where he helped lead the American campaign to impose financial sanctions on senior al-Qaeda and Taliban leaders. Eager to make his mark, he went to Baghdad in 2003 and witnessed firsthand the dysfunction in the Green Zone. He soon left the comforts of the Emerald City for Anbar province, then the most dangerous part of the country. He extended his tour by two years to work with the Marines in Fallujah—before, during, and after the bloody operation to retake it from insurgents. From his perch in a small outpost within the city, there was no escaping the human toll—the body bags filled with pulverized young Americans, the charred and mangled Humvees, the Iraqi funerals that occurred almost every day. He had arrived in Iraq thinking the war had been a grave mistake, and each passing day only confirmed that sentiment. But he believed he had an obligation to help his countrymen in uniform repair the mess their political leaders had created.

His boss at the time, embassy political counselor Robert Ford, wrote in an evaluation that Weston "had the toughest, most dangerous assignment of any State Department officer worldwide." Ford, who would later be named ambassador to Damascus and refuse to be intimidated by Syrian dictator Bashar al-Assad's thugs, said that Weston was braver than any other State Department official he had ever met.

When he was in the Green Zone, Weston had organized a social group for the handful of his fellow Democrats amid the crowd of Republican political appointees who worked for the U.S. occupation administration. He called it Donkeys in the Desert. Once he moved to Anbar, though, he rarely talked politics. Marine officers were overwhelmingly Republican, and they didn't have much interest in the field of Democratic contenders for the 2008 election. But Weston was obsessed. He read whatever he could find in *The New York Times* and *The Washington Post*. One senator piqued his interest more than any other candidate, and on January 27, 2007, he penned him a letter:

Dear Senator Obama,

A Marine friend of mine was reading your book at a chow hall here, at Camp Fallujah, tonight. You write about your visit to Anbar in 2006 and the briefing you received on the Marine base.

I had been scheduled to participate in that meeting, as the Department of State representative assigned to the province alongside 1st and 2nd Marine Expeditionary Forces. (I have been in Iraq for three and a half years, most of that time in the Fallujah/Ramadi neighborhood.) On that day, however, I remained downtown in order to address some difficult Fallujah city council issues—five local leaders, friends, have been assassinated in the last year. Later, the generals told me that your departure had been delayed due to weather. Unlucky you, unlucky me.

I say this because of all the presidential contenders, past/present/future, who have passed through Anbar—and it seems like most have at some point (Senators Kerry, McCain, Biden, Clinton, Hagel, Feingold, Brownback, Thune)—you are the one I wanted to meet most, even more than Sen. Hagel. For all others, I have had that opportunity. And I was honored, to be sure, but you stand apart in an altogether different category in my mind.

Those of us still serving in these dangerous Iraqi deserts need your voice and message in the Iraq debate back home. More than that, we want a new politics that speaks again to the great traditions of not just one party but of one country, ours. You capture that theme, genuinely, like no one else. Throughout my time in this tough assignment (best and worst job I will ever have), I have looked to Washington for the kind of leadership traits that I see among our Marine captains, colonels and corporals in the mean streets of Anbar. It has been dispiriting. Another Greatest Generation—whose apolitical patriotic steel is being forged here among tens of thousands of Americans—deserves better. Maybe the situation is at last beginning to change with deliberation taking place in your Senate meeting rooms. Please, for us, continue it and forcefully.

I am leaving Iraq before long and have decided to go basically straight from Fallujah to Springfield [Illinois] in order to hear your formal announcement in person. I just want to be there. Anonymous. In the crowd. Part of the energy. I will then soon head to Afghanistan's Khost Province, along the Pakistan border—the real 9/11 geography—for a follow-on assignment.

Please keep up the necessary fights in D.C. You have

supporters in this combat zone, where we are every senator's constituent. Sometimes it is hard to imagine anything close to "hope" in an environment like Anbar and
Iraq given the blood red fog of this war, but you and your
message represent that. I also keep telling Fallujans that
at the bottom of Pandora's box (which we have opened, I
fear), something remains: hope.

   With you in the presidential picture, I am more hopeful
about endings in Iraq and beginnings at home, in our country we miss so much and remain honored to represent.
Sincerely,
(John) Kael Weston

Weston was drawn to Obama by his early opposition to the
Iraq War. In October 2002, five months before the invasion, at
a time when most Americans—including many of his fellow
Democrats—had come to believe the Bush administration's
repeated claims that Saddam Hussein possessed chemical and
biological weapons, Obama called it "a dumb war, a rash war,
a war based not on reason but on passion, not on principle
but on politics." None of the other Democratic contenders, in
Weston's view, had gotten Iraq right from the get-go.

He departed Fallujah the morning his closest Iraqi contact
in the city was assassinated. When he got to Springfield, word
quickly spread among Obama's aides that someone had traveled from Iraq to hear the announcement. After Obama spoke,
a staffer escorted Weston to a small antechamber in the basement of the statehouse. In walked Obama, and an introduction
was made. He asked Weston if he had really come all the way
from Fallujah. They spent several minutes talking about Iraq.

Obama listened intently, Weston recalled, "not like D.C.
types who always look over shoulders for someone more
important." Weston said the United States needed to start to
hand off responsibility to Iraqi forces, but he thought Obama's
plan to drop to 40,000 troops by early 2008 was unrealistic
and unwise. When it was time to leave, Obama asked Weston
to stay in touch. He didn't take Obama up on the offer, only
because he didn't want to bother him.

Soon after that meeting, Weston moved to Khost province

for a yearlong assignment. He earned the trust of the locals but irked his superiors when he used part of his development fund to repair madrassas, reasoning that supporting those schools in Afghanistan would keep young men from traveling to far more fundamentalist institutions in Pakistan. When he finished there, he returned to Iraq. But after Obama took office, Iraq felt less important to Weston. He supported the president's decision in early 2009 to send 21,000 more troops to Afghanistan, and when he heard that his friend Nicholson was among them, he called in favors to leave Baghdad early and get himself assigned to the Marine brigade. As he set out for Helmand that June, he regarded the U.S. mission in southern Afghanistan as the last opportunity to save a failing war and realize the dream of Little America.

Weston didn't think it was possible to achieve an outcome that his fellow Americans would see as a victory. Afghanistan was too complicated, too messy, for that. But he believed the new troops could prevent the country from slipping back into the grasp of the Taliban. American warriors and diplomats could buy the Afghan government time to build its army and police force, to field civil servants in the provinces, to show the people it could provide a little something to meet their needs. The result wouldn't be perfect—it probably would look pretty ugly—but it would fulfill America's obligations. Even though there were few, if any, al-Qaeda terrorists lurking about Afghanistan—most of them were across the border in Pakistan—he believed the United States had made an implicit promise to the Afghans when it had launched the war in late 2001: If they stood against the Taliban, they would have a shot at a better, freer life.

After five years in Iraq trying to make the best of George W. Bush's grievous error and a year in Khost trying to win the right war with too few resources, the stars had finally aligned. His candidate—the underdog he had supported when nobody thought he had a chance—was the commander in chief. And his buddy Larry—the toughest, smartest Marine officer he knew—was going to lead the charge. But as Weston arrived at Camp Leatherneck, his excitement was tinged with apprehension. He wanted to do right by both his heroes, but they had different instincts. The president sought the sort of limited war in which Weston believed: Not every village had to be pacified, not every valley seized. The Americans needed to focus on retaking and safeguarding critical cities and towns so the Taliban no longer posed an existential threat to the government in Kabul. The Marines saw the mission in far more expansive terms: They wanted to charge up every hill and kill every bad guy. Their volume dial had two settings: zero and maximum.

Weston loved the Marines as much as he did Obama. He admired their history, their willingness to assume extreme risks, their no-frills ethos. And he believed he could reconcile their kill-'em-all approach with the president's desire for surgical combat.

He landed at Leatherneck three weeks before the Marine brigade's push into Nawa, Garmser, and Khan Neshin. As he listened to Nicholson's deputies describe the operation, Weston was sold on the strategic importance of Nawa and Garmser. They were large farming communities along the Helmand River that had been part of the Little America development program. The operation would also allow the British, who had tried and failed to pacify the districts, to make a face-saving claim that they were handing off to the Marines instead of withdrawing. But Weston didn't see the value in sending an entire light armored battalion down to Khan Neshin. He held his fire, though, because he had just arrived and he wasn't about to pick a fight with Nicholson without getting some sand in his boots.

Then he went to Now Zad. Once he saw the abandoned, demolished city and talked to the Marines who lived there—for whom seemingly every patrol yielded another casualty—he decided to speak his mind. When he returned to Leatherneck, he drafted a cable to the embassy that outlined his objections. He focused not on the tactics of an anti-Taliban operation—that was Nicholson's domain—but on what would come later. Moving the population back would require significant resources, he argued, and it was not clear that the Afghan government was willing to support the effort. Now Zad, he wrote, "does not presently measure up to other areas in terms of inherent strategic importance."

That October, as I listened to Weston and Nicholson argue into the night over the merits of sending more Marines to Now Zad, I wondered whether there was a middle ground between Obama's view of the war and the military's. Nicholson wanted to use the resources at his disposal and the precious months he had left on the ground to transform his patch of desert and allow Governor Mangal to raise the Afghan flag in every one of Helmand's districts. Weston feared the Afghan government and army wouldn't keep pace with the Marines. Could the Afghans hold on to the areas the Americans cleared of insurgents? Or would the Marines' sacrifices be for naught? Now Zad didn't feel worth it. He feared more American blood would be spilled needlessly.

"Does Now Zad matter to the Afghans, or does it just matter to us?" Weston asked Nicholson.

"I've got the governor calling me twice a week," Nicholson responded. "It matters to him. It fucking matters to him."

"He wants to raise the flag everywhere," Weston said.

"Why shouldn't he?" Nicholson retorted. "He wants to govern his province."

"We need to look at where the people are," Weston said. "There's nobody in Now Zad. As we enter the ninth year of the war, is that really where we need to be?"

The next afternoon, a similar debate played out in the windowless White House Situation Room. It was the fourth session President Obama had convened with his war cabinet to weigh McChrystal's request for more forces. The discussions, which often stretched to two hours, amounted to a reexamination of the administration's overall strategy in Afghanistan—a redo of the rushed review conducted earlier in the year. Back then, it had cost nothing for Obama to sign up for counterinsurgency. Now that he had received his first real bill—McChrystal wanted as many as 85,000 more troops on top of the 21,000 that the president had approved in February—it was time to question core assumptions: *Would COIN work in Afghanistan? Was Hamid Karzai's government really a partner? Wasn't Pakistan the bigger problem? Why not just focus on al-Qaeda terrorists seeking to attack the United States? Why not concentrate*

U.S. resources on building an Afghan army that could lead the fight against the Taliban?

Obama, who had been awakened early that morning to hear that he had won the Nobel Peace Prize, sat at the head of the mahogany table, the presidential seal adorning the wall behind him. To his right were Biden, then Gates, and then Mullen in his blue service dress uniform, with four gold bands on the sleeve denoting the highest rank in the U.S. Navy. Beyond them were the president's chief of staff, Rahm Emanuel, and Tom Donilon, the deputy national security advisor. To the president's left sat Jim Jones, Hillary Clinton, and Susan Rice, the ambassador to the United Nations. Next to her was Dennis Blair, the director of national intelligence, and then CIA director Leon Panetta. Holbrooke and Petraeus filled the last two seats on the left. McChrystal, Eikenberry, and Anne Patterson, the ambassador to Pakistan, joined the meeting from half a world away, appearing on large video screens facing the president. Doug Lute and a few other NSC staffers sat along the side walls, as did the president's top political adviser, David Axelrod, but most of those chairs were empty—no straphangers were allowed, given the sensitivity of what was to be discussed. Small monitors around the room indicated that the meeting was "Top Secret/SCI"—sensitive compartmented information—the highest level of classification.

Obama encouraged impassioned discourse among the participants during the strategy review, but not even those sitting around the table knew where he stood on the matter. White House aides believed he was genuinely conflicted—every option seemed to be long on peril and short on promise. He also wanted the aura of impartiality: If he chose to reject the troop increase, he did not want any of the attendees to think, or suggest in public, that he had approached the issue with anything other than an open mind.

Although the president had not explicitly polled everyone around the table, the first three meetings revealed a deep division among the war cabinet. Those in uniform—Mullen and Petraeus—strongly supported McChrystal's COIN strategy and his call for more forces. They believed COIN had turned Iraq around, despite strong evidence that the two most

important factors in improving security—the ebb of sectarian violence and the decision by Sunni tribal chiefs to stand
against al-Qaeda—had been in play before the surge troops
had arrived in Baghdad to implement Petraeus's COIN strategy. In Afghanistan, COIN did not involve separating warring
parties in a civil war but something far more challenging: trying to persuade Pashtuns to cast their lot with Karzai's government instead of the insurgency. The problem was that Karzai's
administration was often more rapacious and corrupt than the
Taliban. How could COIN work when the locals were turning
to the insurgents to protect them from their supposed protec-
tors? COIN also required patience; it can take years before a
besieged population feels safe enough to demonstrate allegiance to their nation. But the commanders played down those
risks and costs. After the Baghdad surge, America's military
leaders embraced COIN with the fervor of the converted. It
became their defining ideology, just as free-market economics
and Jeffersonian democracy were to the neoconservatives who
had led the United States into Baghdad.

The civilians in the war cabinet were not sold on the
McChrystal plan. Biden, Emanuel, and Axelrod were among
the most skeptical. The vice president doubted that Karzai and
the Pakistani government would be truly supportive of a more
expansive COIN campaign. Instead, he argued, the military
should focus more of its existing resources in the country on
pursuing Taliban leaders and any al-Qaeda operatives sneak-
ing back into Afghanistan from Pakistan. In private conversations with the president, Axelrod and Emanuel questioned the
cost—in dollars, American lives, and support among Obama's
base of Democratic Party voters—of sending tens of thousands
more troops to spend several years on foreign soil. Eikenberry
seemed unconvinced by McChrystal's request. The NSC team
of Jones, Donilon, and Lute was also doubtful, but they allowed
the vice president to articulate their fears. Panetta and Blair
hung back, but they too regarded al-Qaeda, not the Taliban, as
the real threat, and they knew from CIA reports how venal
and predatory the Afghan government really was. Holbrooke
had the same reservations, but he also wondered if more force
might compel the Taliban to negotiate a peace deal. He, how-

ever, suppressed his tendency to quickly take sides because the secretary of state, his boss and protector, had not yet staked out a position. Nor had the secretary of defense. Clinton and Gates were the two shrewdest political players in the room, and they knew it made no sense to show their cards early.

The session was McChrystal's first opportunity to talk about his troop options with the president and the civilian members of the war cabinet. The meeting began with one of Blair's deputies speaking about the Pakistani government's support of the Taliban. Then McChrystal launched into a thirty-minute presentation using PowerPoint slides that had been printed and distributed to the participants. His comments, and the ensuing discussion, revealed the civilians' limited understanding of the military.

McChrystal showed Obama slides illustrating on a map of Afghanistan how he would deploy personnel under the three force options. The troops were depicted with blue bubbles. The COIN converts—McChrystal, Petraeus, and Mullen—believed that as security improved in each zone, the troops would be able to focus on contiguous areas, expanding the diameter of each dot as an inkblot spreads on a sheet of paper. The low-end choice—11,000 troops to focus on training Afghan security forces—yielded just a handful of small blue dots. Nobody paid much attention to that slide because McChrystal had described it as ineffectual. He had included it to emphasize the risk, in his view, of sending too few additional troops. In the scenario of having 85,000 troops at his disposal, a substantial portion of the country's population centers was covered in blue. That option was dead on arrival, and McChrystal knew it. It was offered to make the option of providing him with 40,000 troops—the number he believed he needed—seem more reasonable. That was the slide on which everyone focused.

The bubbles were clustered in three areas: Helmand, Kandahar, and the regions around Kabul. The national ring road from Kabul to Kandahar, which had been built by the United States in the 1960s, also would be protected, as would a few Pashtun-dominated pockets in the north and west where insurgent activity had increased. McChrystal emphasized that the troops would be used to secure key population centers, particularly the areas around the city of Kandahar, which, he reminded the participants, was a symbolic and strategic prize for the Taliban. If Kandahar fell, the insurgents would have a critical foothold to seize Kabul and the rest of the nation.

As he examined the bubbles, Obama homed in on the disconnect between his relatively narrow goal—the defeat of al-Qaeda—and McChrystal's desire to conduct a large COIN mission aimed at beating back the Taliban and strengthening the Afghan government so terrorists would not be able to reestablish bases in the country. CIA and military intelligence reports that had been shared with the president and the war cabinet indicated that the few al-Qaeda operatives in Afghanistan—some estimates put the number at fewer than a hundred—were largely in the country's mountainous east. The 40,000-troop slide had smaller blue bubbles in the east than in the south. McChrystal had assessed the east to be of less importance than the south, and he planned to move additional forces there only after improving security in the south.

"Stan, we've said that our focus is the defeat of al-Qaeda, but it seems to me that al-Qaeda is in the east," Obama said to McChrystal. The general paused for several seconds—long enough to make some attendees think he was at a loss for words—before he launched into a defense of his overall COIN strategy. The only way to prevent al-Qaeda from returning to Afghanistan, he argued, was to protect the people. If the United States focused its energies on chasing terrorists in remote valleys, as it had for the previous seven years, the Taliban would continue to seize more territory. If insurgents toppled Karzai's government, it would open the door for al-Qaeda's return.

From his seat along the wall, Doug Lute wondered why so many troops were being sent to Helmand. The province was home to less than 4 percent of the country's population, but it was slated to receive thousands more troops on top of the nearly 11,000 Marines that Nicholson already had on bases there. Lute hoped the president or one of his civilian advisers around the table would raise the question, but nobody did. In more than two hours of discussion, the war cabinet never asked McChrystal why so many Marines were needed in Helmand, even though their concentration in the province had a direct bearing on the troop request. The civilians didn't know enough about Afghanistan to focus on that issue. They were also concerned about micromanaging the war, of looking like President Lyndon Johnson picking bombing targets in North Vietnam. But Lute believed they were missing a point that could have recast the discussion. Instead of arguing about COIN—whether Karzai would improve and whether the Pakistanis would crack down on the sanctuaries—they should have focused more on how the forces would be used. That would have revealed how the military had squandered the first wave of troops Obama had authorized.

After the meeting, Lute and his staff assembled a list of follow-up questions for McChrystal that were to be addressed at the next session of the war cabinet. Lute asked McChrystal to provide more explanation of the location of the bubbles. At the next meeting, McChrystal talked briefly about the need to "demonstrate momentum" in Helmand, to show the Afghan people—and the Talban—that the Marines could finish what they started. To Lute the answer felt unsatisfactory, but once again, nobody around the table pressed McChrystal.

Off in Helmand, Weston felt the same way. He was too far removed to receive readouts from Eikenberry about what was discussed in the Situation Room, so he e-mailed friends who worked at the State Department for tidbits—the pickings were thin—and he read every news account he could find with his maddeningly slow Internet connection at Camp Leatherneck. He knew two essential facts: McChrystal wanted 40,000 more troops, and if he got them, as many as 10,000 of them would be heading to Helmand. Weston was convinced that Helmand did not need any more boots on the ground. The only fight the Marines needed to wage was in Marja, because it was such a large and destabilizing Taliban sanctuary, but that could be accomplished by reallocating troops from misadventures in places such as Khan Neshin and Now Zad. He believed that other parts of the province should be secured by Afghan troops on their own timeline. "With more forces, you can do more," he told me the morning after his argument with Nicholson over Now Zad, "but do we really need to be doing those things?"

Weston did not believe that his fellow Americans should

pack up and leave en masse. He didn't want to re-create the power vacuum that had occurred after the Soviet withdrawal, especially given Afghanistan's meddlesome neighbors and the popular fear of a Taliban resurgence. What the Afghans needed was a long-term commitment from the United States. But Weston, who religiously watched the Sunday morning talk shows—the American Forces Network carried them in the afternoon—and talked politics with every visitor from Washington, knew that an open-ended surge was not politically viable. Growing numbers of Americans had concluded that the war was no longer worth fighting, and he predicted that it would be hard to reverse that perception as the conflict entered its ninth year, even if the Marines could liberate Now Zad and Marja. On the wall next to his desk, he taped a chart from a newspaper showing how long other American wars had lasted. By the following spring, Afghanistan would eclipse the Revolutionary War as the nation's longest.

To Weston, the answer was neither the go-big approach favored by the generals nor the narrow counterterrorism model advocated by some in the war cabinet that might have contained threats emanating from the country but condemned its residents to the hell of a prolonged insurgency or another civil war. He wanted to go long. The president needed to determine how many troops he was willing to commit to Afghanistan for ten years or more, and then he needed to pledge that level of support to the Afghan people. That meant no surge, and it probably meant fewer troops than were deployed at that moment. But Weston was convinced that a smaller but enduring force would appeal to the Afghans, who chafed at the presence of so many foreign soldiers on their soil; compel Karzai's government to stop using the coalition as a crutch; and force the Americans to focus on essential missions instead of blood feuds in places such as Now Zad.

Weston was too ambitious to sit in his plywood office and wait for his hero in the White House to make up his mind. He decided to write a cable to the embassy that would be powerful enough to get sent on to Washington. Instead of filling it with his own views, he solicited input from seventy-five Helmandis, including Governor Mangal, Afghan army officers, and even some day laborers.

"Of course, 40,000 more U.S. troops will solve terrorism in Afghanistan!" Mangal joked to Weston. The governor, who had become America's closest ally in Helmand, declined to support any increase for his province beyond what Nicholson needed to clear Marja. Helmand residents, he said, needed to see more of their own soldiers on the streets.

At the Afghan army base next to Camp Leatherneck, Weston spent two hours talking to three dozen officers and enlisted personnel. "The whole world knows that the U.S. is a superpower," said a grizzled soldier who had been fighting for thirty-six years. "But most people want you to send assets to Afghanistan that bring peace, not more assets that bring war. More war equipment is what the enemy wants here." His comments elicited the most applause from his fellow soldiers. Weston scribbled them in his military-issue notebook and then typed them into the confidential cable.

The collective sentiment of Helmand residents, he wrote, "boils down to a theme of (a) don't leave, (b) keep partnering, but also (c) don't think sending in new U.S. military forces is the best option.

"Most apparent in these conversations—whether in a room filled with animated ANA [Afghan National Army] officers and soldiers or conversing with elders in front of mud compounds and rundown bazaar shops—was an implied question: Just how long will the coalition stay in Afghanistan? The size of our ongoing troop commitment seemed to matter less in their minds than U.S.-led coalition stamina, the extent to which our side of the partnership will endure."

A week after Weston sent his cable to the embassy, Eikenberry transmitted a cable of his own to Clinton. It was classified at the highest level for diplomatic messages, and it was further stamped "NODIS"—no distribution beyond intended parties. The first page made it clear why. "I am concerned," he wrote, "that we underestimate the risks of this expansion of our mission." Sending additional forces, he argued, "will delay the day when Afghans will take over, and make it difficult, if not impossible, to bring our people home on a reasonable timetable." He went on to list six reasons why a surge would not succeed:

1. President Karzai is not an adequate strategic partner. The proposed counterinsurgency strategy assumes an Afghan political leadership that is both able to take responsibility and to exert sovereignty in the furtherance of our goal—a secure, peaceful, minimally self-sufficient Afghanistan hardened against transnational terrorist groups. Yet Karzai continues to shun responsibility for any sovereign burden, whether defense, governance, or development. . . .

2. We overestimate the ability of Afghan security forces to take over. . . .

3. We underestimate how long it will take to restore or establish civilian government. The proposed strategy assumes that once the clearing and holding process has been accomplished in a given area, the rebuilding and transferring to Afghans can proceed apace, followed by a relatively rapid U.S withdrawal. In reality, the process of restoring Afghan government is likely to be slow and uneven, no matter how many U.S. and other foreign civilian experts are involved. Many areas need not just security but health care, education, justice, infrastructure, and almost every other basic government function. Many have never had these services at all. Establishing them requires trained and honest Afghan officials to replace our own personnel. That cadre of Afghan civilians does not now exist and would take years to build. . . .

4. The proposed strategy does not remedy an inadequate [NATO] civilian structure. . . .

5. The proposed strategy may not be cost-effective. Sending additional combat brigades will require tens of billions of dollars annually for years to come. . . .

6. More troops won't end the insurgency as long as Pakistan sanctuaries remain. . . .

Madam Secretary, I would ask that you pass this assessment to the White House, if you deem it appropriate, in advance of the Principals' Committee.
Respectfully,
EIKENBERRY

The cable delighted Biden and his top security adviser, Tony Blinken, who had been pressing the ambassador for his unvarnished view of the proposed surge. During the meeting in which McChrystal had presented his troop options, Eikenberry had voiced mild skepticism, telling the war cabinet that it "shouldn't expect significant breakthroughs" for at least a year. Blinken and Lute wanted to hear more of that point of view. McChrystal, after all, had submitted a lengthy assessment, but nobody had asked Eikenberry for one, even though he had sent a stream of cables and other messages to the State Department that summer questioning Karzai's competence and partnership. ("We're playing football," he wrote in one, but "I'm not sure what sport they're playing.") A few days after the meeting, Lute sent Eikenberry a note urging him to submit his thoughts in writing.

During the discussions that fall, Biden assumed the role of skeptic in chief. Unmoved by the claims of McChrystal, Petraeus, and Mullen, he kept questioning the rationale for additional forces: *How do we know counterinsurgency strategy works in Afghanistan? Why don't we first try to develop a proof of concept?* There was no secret good-cop, bad-cop agreement between Obama and Biden. The vice president had long been dubious about sending more forces to Afghanistan, and Obama simply let him articulate his assertions and questions. If anything, Biden's barrage forced the commanders to justify their claims, to proffer more data, to examine alternate points of view. The Eikenberry cable provided another opportunity for Biden to make his case. Four days after it arrived in Washington, Biden sent a memo to Obama spelling out his concerns about the military's principal justification for more troops:

I do not see how anyone who took part in our discussions could emerge without profound questions about

the viability of counterinsurgency. Our military will do
its part: They will clear anything we ask them to clear.
They will hold anything we ask them to hold. But no one
can tell you with conviction when, and even if, we can
produce the flip sides of COIN that are required to build
and transfer responsibility to the Afghans: an effective and sustainable civilian surge, a credible partner in
Kabul, basic governance and services, and competent
Afghan security forces. We simply can't control these
variables, yet they're essential to the success of COIN.

Biden and Blinken did not want to cut and run. They were
willing to send about 20,000 additional troops so long as they
were focused on training the Afghan army and conducting
missions to kill or capture Taliban leaders. Their proposal was
dismissed as unworkable by Mullen, Petraeus, and McChrystal,
all of whom argued, without clear evidence, that it would be
impossible to conduct successful counterterrorism operations
without a COIN mission to gather intelligence. But one top
commander thought Biden and Blinken were moving in the
right direction: General James Cartwright, the vice chairman
of the Joint Chiefs of Staff. He was a former Marine fighter
pilot who did not share his Pentagon comrades' love of COIN.
Like many of the civilians in the Situation Room, he thought it
too costly and too unlikely to succeed. Cartwright had his staff
analyze the Biden plan. He eventually concluded it made the
most sense. His staff determined it would require the addition
of 25,000 more troops, not 40,000.

Weston's State Department cable never made it to Biden,
Blinken, or Lute, but it did get into Holbrooke's hands. The
nuanced argument about endurance appealed to the veteran
diplomat. He had been trying, with little success, to build support among the war cabinet for opening talks with the Taliban.
He believed a settlement was the only way the conflict would
end, especially considering the corruption of the Karzai government, the incompetence of the Afghan security forces, and
the safe havens in Pakistan. But none of the other principals,
save Clinton, supported that approach. Mullen, Petraeus, and
McChrystal thought it was too soon to talk. They wanted to

surge first and then accept the surrender of top Taliban officials; the commanders did not really want to negotiate, but
they were willing to offer emoluments to insurgent foot soldiers if they put down their weapons. Intelligence and NSC
officials worried that if the Obama administration made deals
with Taliban leaders who had not renounced al-Qaeda, it would
appear that the United States was negotiating with terrorists.
The president's political advisers had yet another reason to
balk: Holbrooke's aggressive campaigning on behalf of Clinton
during the 2008 presidential primaries had left scars.

Like Weston, Holbrooke believed a long-term commitment
was vital—if the United States showed that it wasn't leaving
Afghanistan, Taliban leaders would eventually come to the
negotiating table. Surging would complicate that calculus
because the only troop increase the country could afford, in
his view, was a relatively short one, and that would send the
opposite message about U.S. staying power, even if it resulted
in more Talibs being killed or captured. But he kept his reservations to his small and loyal staff. Clinton had not yet staked
out a position on the troop request, and he could not afford
to alienate the one person in the war cabinet who liked him.
Instead, he instructed his staff to write reports for the White
House that picked apart the military's key assumptions. One
noted that McChrystal's plan to grow the Afghan army and
police to a combined strength of 400,000 would require every
literate man between eighteen and thirty to join the security
forces.

Holbrooke could have been a vital ally to Biden, Lute,
and Eikenberry in their efforts to block a surge, but none of
them could abide him. Biden thought Holbrooke was an ego-
tist; Eikenberry grew tired of Holbrooke constantly trying to
bigfoot him; and Lute felt that Holbrooke—who sometimes
called four times in an hour—treated him as an errand boy.
An anti-Holbrooke attitude soon infused the NSC. When his
staff sent over its analyses, they sometimes languished unread
in in-boxes.

As the afternoon sun slipped behind the Lincoln Memorial on
the Sunday after Thanksgiving, Obama summoned his war

cabinet to the Oval Office. Biden, Gates, Mullen, Cartwright, Petraeus, Jones, and Emanuel took seats in the room. The president had made up his mind. He would be signing orders, he said, to deploy 30,000 more troops to Afghanistan. It was a compromise between McChrystal's 40,000 and Biden's 20,000, and between Cartwright's 25,000 and a 35,000 option proposed by Gates. The president also said he would give Gates the authority to send 3,000 more if needed under exceptional circumstances.

The surge came with conditions set forth in a six-page terms sheet. The most significant requirement was that U.S. forces start coming home in July 2011. He took the deadline from the military's documents stating that American troops could clear areas of insurgents and then transfer responsibility for them to Afghan security forces in eighteen to twenty-four months. July 2011 was two years from the start of the first clearing operations under his watch, the Marine push into Nawa, Garmser, and Khan Neshin. He said he planned to mention the deadline when he spoke to the nation from West Point in two days to announce the new strategy. Setting a date would force the Afghans to work faster in building their government and security forces, he said, and it would ensure that the Pentagon would give him the in-and-out surge he wanted, not a slow series of deployments followed by even slower reductions.

He also informed his commanders that he was not going to increase the Afghan security forces to 400,000; the NSC would set growth targets each year. And he made clear that the strategy was neither the sort of comprehensive counterinsurgency sought by McChrystal, Mullen, and Petraeus, nor the narrow counterterrorism mission sought by Biden and Cartwright. Rather, it was a hybrid—counterinsurgency in some areas and counterterrorism in others. "This is not full-blown counterinsurgency or open-ended nation building," he noted.

It took a day for the news to filter down to Camp Leatherneck. Nicholson smiled when he read the message. He would get all 2,500 Marines he wanted for Marja—the first of them would arrive in a week—and probably a few thousand more to push into northern parts of Helmand that the British wanted to vacate. The July 2011 deadline troubled him—*would the*

Afghans question our resolve?—but he did not dwell on it. He'd be home by then. Obama had made the right decision, the general thought, and he credited the president with displaying courage in the face of opposition within his party. Nicholson knew that his Marines had helped shape the outcome—their progress in Nawa and beyond had proved that counterinsurgency could work in Afghanistan. Now the stakes were even higher. Obama was betting there could be more Nawas, and the first test would be Marja. Once again, it would be up to Nicholson to show that it could be done.

On December 1, Obama announced the surge and the deadline in a prime-time address from West Point. Forty-eight hours later, hundreds of Nicholson's Marines swooped into Now Zad.

Weston felt hammered. His president, the man he had traveled from Fallujah to meet, had failed him. Questions banged around inside his head: *Where was the moral courage Obama displayed back in 2002? How could he think this would succeed? Why didn't he listen to his civilian advisers?* The surge and the deadline were the worst possible combination. It meant expansion but no enduring commitment. No longer would Weston be able to make the case to the Marines that they should be strategic and sparing with their operations, and no longer would he be able to tell the Afghans that the Americans were going to stay until the Afghan government was strong enough to secure the country. Nicholson would have the forces to go wherever he wanted. But how long would they be in Afghanistan? He recalled Georges Clemenceau's admonition, adapted by General Jack D. Ripper in *Dr. Strangelove:* War is too important to leave to the generals.

PART TWO

Shattered Plans

7

Bleeding Ulcer

AS I WADED THROUGH waist-high water in Marja, I cursed the engineers of Little America. The north–south canals that Morrison-Knudsen had constructed, traversing the desert polder as straight-arrow as the avenues of Manhattan, were more than irrigation marvels. They were perfect defensive moats, wide and deep enough to keep out MRAPs—the hulking, mine-resistant, ambush-protected trucks, equipped with machine guns and grenade launchers, that had replaced Humvees as Marine combat vehicles. Small concrete bridges spanned the canals, but they had been rigged with homemade bombs. The Marines refused to drive over the bridges until the explosives disposal experts had completed their sweeps and painstakingly removed each mine. That meant the first wave of American troops to enter Marja in February 2010, and the journalists who accompanied them, had to make their way on foot. And that involved crawling across muddy poppy fields and jumping over drainage ditches.

Each Marine hauled about a hundred pounds of gear: rifles, ammunition, food, water, radios. Some brought along shoulder-fired rockets. Others carried medical kits and stretchers. Because upright troops presented larger targets for the insurgent snipers who seemed to be in every cluster of mud-walled homes, the Marines kept low to the ground—crouching, kneeling, and worming on their bellies through soggy tracts as rounds cracked overhead. On the first day, it took us nine hours to travel one mile.

For the Marines I accompanied, Charlie Company of the First Battalion of the Sixth Marine Regiment, the day's mission was simple enough: Head west for a little more than a mile to link up with Alpha Company in preparation for a mission to secure a cluster of government buildings. Scrutinizing satellite photographs of Marja before the assault, Marine commanders assumed the municipal government center was the large, rectangular building catercornered from the main police station. Seizing that part of town became a key objective.

Larry Nicholson had wanted to charge in with his Marines, but Kael Weston had talked him out of it. The grunts didn't need a general in their midst as they forged ahead. After spending a day on a desert staging base, Nicholson and Weston returned to Camp Leatherneck, where they tracked progress by watching video feeds from surveillance drones.

At 6:30 a.m., Charlie Company set off on foot, accompanied by a contingent of Afghan soldiers fresh out of boot camp. We hadn't been walking fifteen minutes when the first shots rang out. Everyone dropped to the ground. We looked for the shooter. But there were no more shots, just the crowing of a rooster.

There would be no straight path to the destination. The adobe-walled compounds along the way—and for hundreds of feet to the north and south of the route—would have to be cleared. The Marines wanted the Afghan soldiers who were accompanying them to knock on doors whenever possible. As Nicholson had in Nawa, he reminded the Marja Marines in pep talks before the operation that the people were the prize. *Don't alienate them. Don't barge into homes unnecessarily.*

A few minutes later, another shot echoed across the poppy field. Word quickly made it down the line: A Marine ahead had fired on a menacing dog while searching a housing compound. Before anyone could find the owner to make amends, a burst of gunfire strafed us from the west. The Marines and the Afghan soldiers returned fire with M4 carbines and belt-fed machine guns. Eighteen minutes later, what sounded like a lawn mower engine could be heard overhead. A small, unarmed drone launched from a nearby base circled above. A radio report from headquarters revealed what the Marines couldn't immediately see from the field: Three insurgents, one of whom was carrying a walkie-talkie, had been killed.

As a squad from the company's Third Platoon moved gingerly forward, unsure if there were more insurgents undetected by the drone, the 1/6 Battalion commander, Lieutenant Colonel Cal Worth, received a report over his radio: Bravo Company had just hoisted the Afghan flag at a bazaar to the northwest. Before the operation, he had told his men that the Stars and Stripes was not to be raised in Marja. "No end-zone dances," he said. "This is their country."

By then it was safe to approach the owner of the dog, a middle-aged farmer named Jawad Wardak, who was standing in front of his spacious mud-walled house with five young men who he said were his sons and nephews. Stacks of dried poppy stalks strewed his driveway, and his fields were filled with poppy shoots.

"I'm very sorry about your dog," Worth said through an interpreter. "Hopefully we haven't done any damage to your home."

Wardak shrugged. "It's no problem," he said.

"We're bringing the government of Afghanistan back here," Worth said.

Wardak scowled but said nothing.

One of the Afghan soldiers assigned to the Third Platoon asked Wardak's nephew for food.

"We'll give you a meal," Worth told the hungry soldier. "This is not why we're here. We don't want to impose ourselves. We're guests here."

But the nephew came out with three large pieces of flatbread anyway. The soldier grabbed them and hustled off to his comrades.

Beyond Wardak's house was a Little America irrigation canal. Fording it required wading through thigh-high water, but there was no other option. A team of route-clearance Marines, with devices that detect and detonate roadside bombs, had already found a dozen explosives on the road that paralleled our path through the fields. To the south, Charlie Company's Second Platoon had discovered a ten-foot-high wall embedded with seventy bombs.

As soon as we crossed the canal, Worth confided to me that his Marines did not plan to check every house. "We're engaged in a counterinsurgency," he said. "We're not going to be kicking down every door."

As he uttered the word "door," a piercing crackle of gunfire came from a housing compound to the northwest of Wardak's house. Everyone dived to the ground.

The Marines responded with their rifles, first with a few shots, then with a fusillade. The hostile gunfire continued. Then the Marines unleashed mortars and shoulder-launched rockets. After ten minutes the firing ceased. When Marines and Afghan soldiers entered the house, they found four dead insurgents.

The rest of the day brought more of the same. At 4:30 p.m., we straggled into a walled-off courtyard to link up with Alpha Company.

The following week was equally grim. For all the Pentagon's talk of surgical modern combat—of satellite-guided bombs and networked computers on the battlefield—Marja was war the old-fashioned way. We ate field rations and defecated in plastic bags. We bedded down under the stars in abandoned compounds. In the mornings and evenings, we clustered around small fires fueled by stalks of dried poppy. Nobody had laptops or DVD players—anything that required electricity had been stored in footlockers at a staging base in the desert. Because the Marines had to stuff their packs with food and ammunition, sleeping bags and tents were left behind. And so was machismo when the mercury dipped to freezing at night. Those lucky to get a few hours of sleep in between shifts of guard duty huddled close together under thin plastic camouflage poncho liners, sometimes spooning one another.

On the fifth evening, the 1/6 Marines finally had a moment to relax. As the sun set over the rubbled market where they had made camp, four of them sat around an overturned blue bucket and played cards. A few opened dog-eared paperbacks. Some heated their rations-in-a-bag, savoring their first warm dinner in days. Many removed their helmets and armored vests. Then—before the game was over, the chapters finished, the meals cooked—the war roared back at them. The staccato crack of an incoming round echoed across the market. In an instant, the Marines grabbed their vests and rifles. The .50-caliber gunner on the roof thumped back return fire, as did several Marines with clattering, belt-fed machine guns. High-explosive mortar rounds, intended to suppress the insurgent fire, whooshed overhead.

And then I saw the stretcher. That first incoming round had struck a nineteen-year-old lance corporal in the face, just below his Kevlar helmet. He had been on the roof of a house to our south, scanning the orange-hued evening landscape for signs of Taliban, when he was hit by a single shot from an enemy sniper. Four of his comrades carried him back. His body was covered with a thin metallic blanket to prevent shock, and his head was wrapped in gauze that quickly turned red. A medevac helicopter was summoned, but by the time a team of elite Air Force rescue personnel swooped in, their MH-60 Pave Hawk skimming the ground to avoid insurgent fire, the Marine had stopped breathing. Pieces of his brain spilled onto the stretcher. The gauze, pulled off so that a comrade could perform CPR, fluttered from the sides like streamers. His four buddies, their twisted faces betraying both anger and grief, handed him off to the Air Force crew. Then they returned to their positions. There was no time to mourn, not if they were going to get the sniper.

Fifteen minutes later, an A-10 Warthog jet, equipped with a 30-mm cannon that can fire 3,900 explosive, armor-piercing rounds per minute, squealed overhead and obliterated the sniper's compound. By then, however, the shooter had fled.

He would return the next day. As would a few dozen other insurgent holdouts, who would take their shots and reseed the roads with bombs. They would kill a few more Americans. Still, the Marines had expected another Fallujah, with hundreds of hard-core militants ready to fight to the death. What they got instead was Baghdad—the bad guys melted back into the population, or fled. The Taliban may have been crazy, but they weren't crazy enough to take on 3,000 heavily armed Marines. A week into the operation, Marja had grown so quiet that there were days without a single attack.

When the Marines reached the area identified on Worth's map as the "government center," they discovered that what they had made out to be the flat roof of the municipal building on the satellite images was only a concrete foundation. The supposed police station was a bombed-out schoolhouse.

Stan McChrystal had wanted the Marja mission to be a model for the campaigns that would follow. It would show Americans and Afghans fighting side by side. It would demonstrate the ability of more troops to rapidly improve security. It would allow the State Department to showcase the benefits of its promised surge of personnel and reconstruction projects. And it would give Hamid Karzai an opportunity to prove wrong the State Department's pessimism about the Afghan government's ability and willingness to help its citizens.

Three months before the operation began, a team of American and British civilian advisers encouraged Governor Mangal to select a district chief and assemble a contingent of municipal employees who could start working as soon as the Marines secured the government center. The advisers were to deploy with the Afghans, and they would bring office supplies, computers, and other trappings of civil administration. "We have government in a box, ready to roll," McChrystal boasted.

Once the Afghan presidential election had concluded, McChrystal had been so eager to tackle Marja that he had urged Nicholson to start the operation while Obama was debating whether to approve the surge. McChrystal thought it would help make his case in Washington that more forces could have a dramatic impact, and it would allow him to use most of the surge units to address an even more pressing challenge in Kandahar. He figured the Marines could free up the troops to assault Marja by thinning out in Nawa, Garmser, and Khan Neshin. But Nicholson refused to release his Marines from their other posts for the new mission. He believed that reducing the Marine presence in those areas would encourage the Taliban to return. If you want me to do Marja, he told McChrystal, I need more forces.

Nicholson's tactic worked. Not only did he get two additional battalions for Marja, but Helmand wound up with one-third of all the surge troops. By April 2010, there would be about 20,000 Marines in the province—in addition to 10,000 British troops—and the Marine Corps would get to establish its own NATO regional headquarters at Camp Leatherneck.

McChrystal was torn. He wished he did not have to devote so many of his surge forces to Helmand—he obviously thought it was less critical than Kandahar—but he also believed what he had told Obama and his war cabinet during the surge debate: The Marines needed to finish the job that had been started there. McChrystal couldn't ignore Marja, and he couldn't risk allowing Nawa or Garmser to slide back into the hands of the Taliban. To him, expanding in Helmand would demonstrate momentum to the Afghan people. "We had to show we could fulfill our commitments," he said.

The Marines, as they had in early 2009, wanted to send far more personnel than McChrystal and his senior staff thought necessary. But there was little McChrystal could do about it. Jim Conway, the Marine commandant, insisted on establishing a Marine-run regional headquarters headed by a two-star general once Nicholson finished his yearlong assignment. The new headquarters, which many senior U.S. and NATO officers deemed unnecessary, required a lot of rear-echelon staff, sucking up valuable surge positions that could have been devoted to additional infantry units in Kandahar. In exchange, however, he was willing, yet again, to send his troops to Afghanistan much faster than the Army was.

Although the two Marine battalions earmarked for Marja arrived less than fifteen days after Obama's December 1 decision to surge, they needed time to acclimate and prepare for the operation. The extra weeks gave McChrystal an opportunity to persuade Karzai to seize the moment and become a wartime president. For the previous eight years, Karzai had exercised almost no role in military operations except to criticize them if civilians were killed. McChrystal planned to fly Karzai to Lashkar Gah so he could meet tribal leaders and tell them that a full-on Marine invasion of Marja was good for everyone. But Karzai did not believe that. He insisted on bringing former governor Sher Mohammed Akhundzada on McChrystal's plane, and when they arrived at the *shura,* the president told SMA to sit in front of Mangal. The current governor had been hoping for a clear-cut statement of political support and an endorsement of the Marja operation. Karzai provided neither. Instead he lavished praise on SMA, mentioning him two dozen times in his remarks and suggesting repeatedly that he was the solution to problems in the province.

McChrystal remained undeterred. He needed Marja to be the marquee battle of his surge, even if the more critical fight had to occur in Kandahar. He wanted to show progress to the Afghans, to his fellow Americans, and to Obama. The Marines did their part to pump up the mission. They choreographed an elaborate plan to insert hundreds of troops by helicopter to commence the attack on what they called D-Day, and they summoned every major television network, wire service, and newspaper with a presence in Afghanistan to cover what they promised would be a "major event."

Two weeks before the invasion, McChrystal met with more than a hundred top Afghan and U.S. officers to talk through the initial stages of the operation. After everyone else had finished discussing their elements of the battle, he stood to address the room:

> For a number of years, we struggled to get enough
> resources to do this mission. We now have enough. For
> many years, we talked about being real partners and
> fighting this war together. Now we are real partners. For
> many years, we struggled to get people to pay attention
> to Afghanistan. Now everyone is paying attention. The
> people of Marja will watch this operation carefully. Peo-
> ple from every corner of Afghanistan, from Nuristan to
> Badghis, will watch this operation carefully. There will
> be people in [the Taliban's high command in] Quetta
> who watch what happens carefully. And in every capital
> of the world, they will watch what happens carefully.
> What they will see is a complete change from what they
> have seen in the past.

The attack on Marja hardly reflected the "complete change" McChrystal had promised. Once the assault commenced, I soon observed that shaking down residents for bread was the most innocuous of the Afghan National Army's sins. U.S. commanders and Afghan Defense Ministry officials in Kabul claimed that Afghan officers were helping to plan day-to-day operations and leading the fight. It was a lie. The ANA battalion attached to the 1/6 Marines had just finished its basic training, and its men, most of whom were illiterate, lacked the skills to organize even the simplest missions. They could not read maps or understand that one platoon needed to hang back and provide cover for their buddies searching homes. They had been trained to use their U.S.-issued M-16 rifles, but when it came time to fire, none of them bothered to take aim using his weapon's sights. They simply shot in the general direction of the insurgents—exasperated Marines called it "spray and pray"—and they usually unleashed a torrent of bullets that depleted their ammunition clips. In the first few days, the only people the ANA soldiers shot were themselves—in the foot, the hand, the leg. One problem may have been what they were smoking. When the Marines and the Afghans bedded down in homes for the night, the Afghans grabbed the rooms, leaving the Americans to sleep in freezing courtyards. Once inside, the Afghans smoked so much hashish and marijuana that intoxicating clouds wafted into the night air.

Their officers were no better. When one ANA soldier walked off in the wrong direction while on a patrol, a Marine informed the soldier's commander. He shrugged. "If he dies, he dies," he told the Marine, who shot him a disgusted look and then went running after the soldier. Another morning, I woke to the screams of a Marine gunnery sergeant. "You fucking worthless lazy sacks of shit!" he yelled. "If you don't get that water right now, I will march you in circles for six hours like I do with my Marines who disobey orders!" Petrified that he might be shouting at me and my fellow journalists—we were in the next room—I crawled out of my sleeping bag. The Afghans were supposed to get up at 4 a.m. to collect bottles of precious drinking water dropped from a helicopter, but they chose sleep over work.

Later that morning, I tracked down Captain Iqbal, the commander of the ANA company at our outpost. While his Marine counterpart had plotted the day's operations, Iqbal had eaten breakfast and bathed with water from a hand-pumped well. He wasn't planning to head out with his men, as the Marine captain would. Being an officer in the ANA had its privileges, and staying safe on the base was chief among them. Puffing on a cigarette, he complained that his men didn't have enough supplies—though they got the same amount of food and water the Americans did—and he bristled at McChrystal's order to minimize civilian casualties, which had been translated and transmitted through the ANA ranks. "If that wasn't the case," he claimed, "the ANA could take Marja."

Leadership was clearly a problem, but why weren't the ANA grunts fighting harder? Their poor showing couldn't just be chalked up to a lack of training and equipment—after all, an untrained corps of slippers-wearing Afghans, most of whom were armed with no more than AK-47 rifles, had defeated the Soviets in the 1980s. Most of the foot soldiers in Iqbal's company were ethnic Tajiks, Uzbeks, and Hazaras from northern Afghanistan, the very people whom the Pashtun Talibs had persecuted in the 1990s. Surely, I thought, they wanted to defeat the Taliban. But when I asked several of them why they had joined the ANA, I heard a totally different reason. "Of course we hate the Taliban, but we joined the ANA only because we couldn't find other work," said Amir Shah, a twenty-one-year-old Uzbek from Balkh province. He was the sole source of income for his family, and he couldn't afford to get killed. "It's better for us to let the Americans chase the Taliban."

At least the ANA limited their greed to bread. Members of a national paramilitary police battalion brought in to operate checkpoints and guard the main bazaar helped themselves to the contents of shuttered stores: food, soft drinks, cigarettes, blocks of opium. They were so rapacious that Nicholson, who had pleaded with Kabul for more police before the operation, sent them away once he received reports of their misdeeds.

The effort to install local government swiftly fared no better. The British-run reconstruction office in Lashkar Gah recruited seven elders originally from Marja who promised to return and rally their neighbors to support the operation. The Marines transported them to a staging base in the desert, but when it came time to deploy, they were too afraid to budge. U.S. and British diplomats had spent six months cajoling Karzai's administration to assign to the district sixteen representatives from key ministries, including education, health, justice, and agriculture. All they got was a district governor who had spent four years in a German prison for attempting to stab his stepson to death.

The ex-con, Haji Zahir, agreed to live in a tent on a Marine base and project the face of Afghan government. Although he possessed no budget or ability to summon help from the ministries, and had a fondness for lengthy siestas, he met a parade of supplicants every day, welcoming them inside his canvas house, which he had decorated with rugs and pillows. He struck the right tone, telling residents they had to cooperate with the Marines and the government if they wanted better security. But when Eikenberry came for a visit, his staff sent word in advance that he was not to be photographed with Zahir because of his checkered past. Upon arrival, the ambassador walked past the district governor without so much as a handshake. Then he embraced a former police chief widely regarded as a corrupt pedophile. Marja residents couldn't understand what message the top American diplomat in Afghanistan was trying to send them.

Eager to distract everyone from the absence of civil administration and the stabber turned district governor, Eikenberry and McChrystal persuaded Karzai to take a victory lap in Marja. The president arrived about a month into the operation with SMA and former police chief Abdul Rahman Jan in tow. At a meeting with several hundred residents crammed into a mosque, Karzai stood, smiled, and delivered a series of platitudes about how his administration was restoring security in the country. When it was time for the attendees to speak, Karzai expected a hero's welcome. But the residents were in no mood for niceties. They were bursting with anger, not at the Taliban or the Marines but at Karzai and his henchmen: SMA, ARJ, and a local factotum who oversaw the collection of bribes.

"We will tell you that the warlords who ruled us for the past eight years, those people whose hands are red with the people's blood—those people who killed hundreds—they are still ruling over this nation," thundered Haji Abdul Aziz, a prominent elder. "For so many years, there were only promises.... The people have run out of patience."

One man yelled at the president for allowing "hoodlums and criminals" to run Marja. Another accused the factotum of stealing his opium. Yet another said he was afraid that ARJ's policemen, who preyed on young boys, would be allowed to roam the area again. "You sent these people here!" the man screamed at Karzai.

To mollify the crowd, the president promised to make Marja an independent district—it had previously been part of Nad Ali, the other Little America farming community that had been carved out of the desert in the 1950s. Then he asked about Haji Zahir.

"Are you happy with him?"

The residents cheered. The Americans might have been squeamish about Zahir, but the residents weren't. Despite his criminal record, they regarded him as a far better option than Karzai's men, who had never spent a day in jail for their crimes.

After a few weeks, the Taliban crept back. Not in the same numbers as before, but they fielded enough fighters to create chaos. They shot at Marine patrols and planted new bombs in the roads. And they owned the night. They killed residents who signed up to work for the government, and they beat up farmers who accepted U.S. handouts. When I returned in late May, three months after the operation had begun, Marja had grown more violent and deadly than it had been in the first month. Although the Marines had expanded the areas they patrolled and had commenced several reconstruction projects, every step forward was matched by at least a half step backward.

Two-thirds of the stalls in the main bazaar had reopened, but the area's only baker had fled shortly before I arrived because insurgents had kidnapped his son in retaliation for selling to the Marines and the police. Men had begun to allow their burqa-clad wives to venture out of their homes, but when female Marines attempted to gather local women for a meeting, not a single person showed up. The Afghan government finally had assigned ten of the sixteen ministry representatives, but most of them were spending their days in Lashkar Gah, twenty miles to the northeast. USAID had offered to hire 10,000 residents for day-labor projects to clean the irrigation canals, but only 1,200 people had enrolled because of Taliban intimidation.

The Marines began to take extreme measures. To make it more difficult for Talibs to sneak back in, the Americans banned all motorcycles in the district, even though two-wheeled vehicles were the primary mode of transportation for most people. The Marines even blew up footbridges across the far western and eastern canals. Nicholson and his officers wished they could have leaned on a handful of tribal leaders to influence the population as they had done in Nawa, but Marja had no such chieftains. The vacuum was a legacy of the social engineering during the Little America days. Because the king's men had wanted Marja and Nad Ali to be modern, posttribal societies, they had mixed together families from dozens of tribes to live there. Most of the villagers were followers, not leaders, and when the new settlers had arrived and found themselves cut off by hundreds of miles from their chiefs, they had looked to the government for direction. Almost six decades later, the descendants of the original Marja residents had grown thoroughly disillusioned with Kabul. They didn't want the government to lead them, and they had no elders with enough stature to hold the place together.

A week before my return trip to Marja, McChrystal flew in from Kabul to see the problems for himself. As he sat in a sweltering tent and listened to Marine officers' assessments of the situation, he grew agitated.

"You've got to be patient," Lieutenant Colonel Brian Christmas told the general. "We've only been here for ninety days."

"How many days do you think we have before we run out of support from the international community?" McChrystal fired back. Side conversations ceased. Silence enveloped the room.

"I can't tell you, sir," Christmas replied.

"I'm telling you," McChrystal snapped. "We don't have as many days as we'd like."

Later that day, in a meeting at the reconstruction office in Lashkar Gah, McChrystal criticized the two-star British general in charge of southern Afghanistan for not sending more troops to secure Marja. "Had we put more force in there, we could have locked that place down better," he said.

The British general, Nick Carter, insisted that more forces
would not have accelerated a Taliban defeat. "This is about
convincing people," he said. He suggested that McChrystal's
outsized expectations were a mistake. "I think what's going to
make the difference, whether we marketed it right or not at the
beginning, is time," he said.

McChrystal was unconvinced. Marja, which had the same
population as Nawa, had been flooded with more than twice as
many U.S. troops and almost ten times as many Afghan forces.
There were more U.S. and British resources available for reconstruction and development. But security was improving far
less quickly. American and British diplomats in the reconstruction office had written off the success in Nawa as an anomaly,
although Marja was also an outlier, given its history as a Taliban sanctuary and the extent to which residents profited from
the lawlessness by growing poppy. The diplomats believed the
process of stabilization could not always be accelerated with
more coalition inputs, especially when the Afghan government
was not doing its part.

When Carter tried once again to counsel patience, McChrystal lost his cool. Obama's July 2011 deadline was looming. He
needed the Marines to take care of Marja quickly so he could
turn their attention to Taliban havens in other parts of the
country.

"You don't feel it here," he told the British general. But seen
from elsewhere, said McChrystal, who had just returned from
Washington, "this is a bleeding ulcer."

After my May trip to Marja, I went to see Kael Weston at Camp
Leatherneck. His air-conditioned office was a welcome respite
from the 125-degree temperature outside, but he didn't want to
talk within earshot of his fellow Americans. He asked me to go
for a walk with him.

The problem with Marja, he said as we strode through the
sand, was not just McChrystal's unattainable expectations. It
was the surge itself. The commitment of 30,000 additional
men and women in uniform required an iconic battle, one
that would justify the military's argument to Obama that more
troops could quickly reverse Taliban momentum and more

civilian resources could compensate for the Afghan government's ineptitude. But to Weston, what it proved instead was
that Karl Eikenberry had been right when he had written in his
November 2009 cable that the Afghan government lacked the
willingness and capacity to seize the opportunity provided by
American troops.

"We set ourselves up for an impossible model in the ninth
year of the war," he said. "We created our own strategic failure."

8

Search and Destroy

AT CAMP LEATHERNECK, the Marine headquarters in Helmand, everyone seemed to be working all the time. The minimum shift schedule for enlisted personnel was twelve hours a day, seven days a week. Officers usually put in sixteen- to eighteen-hour days. On Sundays, the officers were allowed to report for duty around noon. They could go to chapel or, as most did, just sleep late.

If they had spare time, there was no place to go except the gym. Save for a tiny PX where a Marine could grab a bag of Fritos or a tin of Skoal, the base had no amenities—no recreation room to watch a movie on a big-screen television, no Burger King or Pizza Hut for an afternoon snack. There wasn't even a place to get a cup of coffee if the chow hall was closed. The only diversion was a tent that contained a few grimy computers, but they connected to the Internet with the languor of dial-up modems. The tent lacked air-conditioning and smelled like musty socks, so troops sent their wives and girlfriends only the shortest of missives. Nobody needed to update his Facebook status. Every day was the same: hot, dusty, and dangerous. The ascetic environment did not bother Larry Nicholson. In fact, it pleased him. His principal ambition for Leatherneck was that it not emulate the giant NATO base on the grounds of Kandahar's airport, which had become the Afghan version of Baghdad's Green Zone.

Although it lacked Saddam's marble-walled palace and resort-size pool, the Kandahar Airfield furnished plenty of amusements to steal the time and focus of coalition troops. The principal distraction was a square-shaped wooden boardwalk built by the Canadians, who had been the base's principal occupants until large contingents of Americans started arriving in 2009. Each side was two hundred meters long. Shops and eateries lined the outer perimeter. Green Beans Coffee—it advertised "a Cup of Joe for a Joe"—served up quadruple-shot iced lattes. Around the corner was a gyro stand—Gyros for Heroes—an ice cream shop, and a burger joint. A handful of lucky Afghan merchants were allowed to operate stores, most of which sold gaudy trinkets and overpriced carpets that soldiers nonetheless purchased so they could show friends back home they had been to Afghanistan even if they had never stepped off the base.

Every NATO member with troops in the country was allocated real estate along the boardwalk. The Italians built the Mamma Mia Pizzeria. The French set up a café that sold smoked salmon sandwiches on mini baguettes. The Canadians brought Tim Hortons—their version of Dunkin' Donuts—and at any given time, it seemed as if at least a quarter of all the Canadians on the base were waiting in line for a beignet and a double-double (a coffee with two sugars and two shots of cream). The Dutch had a bar that offered nonalcoholic beer—the base was dry—and French fries with mayonnaise. The Germans established what they called an "Extreme Deutscher PX" that offered all manner of tough-guy paraphernalia: long hunting knives, brass knuckles, and camouflage outfits that looked like a cross between Chewbacca and a shrub. They offered an assortment of patches—an American flag with the words WE'RE GONNA FREE THE SHIT OUT OF YOU was a favorite—and polo shirts that depicted a man holding a rifle like a baseball bat above the words MAJOR LEAGUE INFIDEL. The German shopkeepers lacked any sense of irony about their merchandise, but everyone browsing the goods knew that, of all the NATO members in Afghanistan, the Germans were the most risk averse. They rarely left their bases. No German in Afghanistan would ever need a shrub suit.

The boardwalk's announcement boards were the guide to leisure-time pursuits elsewhere on the airfield. There was a Texas Hold 'Em competition on Tuesdays, salsa dancing on Wednesdays, and a discussion session of the Christian self-help author Rick Warren's book *The Purpose Driven Life* on Thursdays. Other signs warned soldiers to "Be Careful What You Say on the Boardwalk," lest they be overheard by a Taliban sympathizer among the Afghan laborers, who were required to wear black armbands around their shalwar kameez identifying them as garrison workers. World War II–era security posters had been altered with Photoshop to depict GIs holding BlackBerrys.

On the boardwalk, the Americans had opened a Burger King, a Pizza Hut, and a Subway. The American contribution to this military carnival also included a giant PX a quarter mile away that stocked surplus Operation Iraqi Freedom identification badge lanyards and Operation Enduring Freedom teddy bears. If you were feeling really flush, you could buy a new Harley-Davidson motorcycle at the PX—the distributor promised the lowest prices around—for delivery upon your return to the States.

When McChrystal took over, he wanted to shut down every business along the boardwalk. He ate one meal a day and spent no time relaxing; he didn't understand why others couldn't live the same way. But he soon discovered that his clout as a four-star general was limited. Although he was the top NATO commander in the country, he couldn't force other nations to close their shops. In the end, all he was able to torpedo were the three American fast-food outlets, which were run under a U.S. Army contract. Within months, they had been replaced by a Nathan's hot dog stall, a Kentucky Fried Chicken stand, and a brick-and-mortar TGI Friday's, where Bangladeshi waiters sporting flair served burgers and fajitas. The eateries were franchises that obtained direct contracts with a NATO office that did not report to McChrystal. Instead of wasting fifteen minutes at Burger King, troops began spending an hour waiting for a table at TGI Friday's and then another hour or two eating and gabbing.

The boardwalk offered plenty of after-dinner diversions too. In the center was a sea of sand on which a volleyball net had been erected. In the corner next to the Tim Hortons, the

Canadians had constructed a street hockey rink with a concrete floor and walls. Crowds would gather every evening to watch and play. On Thursday nights, a disc jockey would set up loudspeakers and blare AC/DC and Queen during breaks in the action.

As I took in the revelry one night, I chatted with an American soldier who was munching on a cheeseburger and fries. "The war feels so far away," he said.

The next day, I met Nisar Ahmed, who lived not more than ten miles from the Kandahar Airfield. A few weeks earlier, a neatly folded letter had been placed under the front gate of his family's house. It was addressed to his father, a gray-bearded schoolteacher who could not have been prouder that his son had graduated from Kandahar University and then secured a well-paying job as a field assistant for the United Nations Development Program.

> This is the last warning. Keep your son away from this work. . . . We know your son is working for infidels. If something happens to him, do not complain.

Two hours after Nisar's father found the letter in the courtyard, after they had discussed their options and concluded that they had no faith in the local police to protect them, Nisar called his boss at the United Nations and resigned. His decision—too insignificant to be counted on NATO's weekly security assessment—was another small fissure in the slow and quiet collapse of Afghanistan's second largest city.

In deciding to send Nicholson's nearly 11,000-strong Marine brigade to Helmand in early 2009, U.S. commanders had failed to grasp the extent of Taliban activity in Kandahar city. Because very few NATO troops were stationed there, the insurgents were fighting a different war. Instead of deploying roadside bombs and suicide attacks, they used paper and ink—or a bullet when the recipient of a letter did not comply with the warning it contained. Instead of driving around in their trademark white pickup trucks, clad in black turbans, they operated in the dark, prosecuting their intimidation campaign with beatings and traffic checkpoints meant to show residents that they were everywhere. Their goal was not to blow up everything and everybody but to weaken the government, security forces, and relief agencies so they could one day assert full control over the area. "Nobody in this city feels safe," Nisar told me as he whiled away an afternoon in his home after his resignation. "The Taliban do not show their faces during the day, but everyone knows they are in charge."

Because of Jim Conway's insistence that his Marines remain in Helmand, the responsibility for sending additional troops to Kandahar province fell to the U.S. Army. The Army's force generation command didn't have many options—there were 120,000 soldiers in Iraq and almost 45,000 in other parts of Afghanistan. Any unit that wasn't deployed was either resting or preparing to relieve teams in the field. Of course, rotation schedules could have been shuffled around, but Kandahar wasn't a priority for the Army, which was far more focused on eastern Afghanistan, where U.S. soldiers had been operating since late 2001. As top Army commanders cast about for spare troops to go to Kandahar, they settled on a brigade that had never deployed to a war zone and had spent the previous year preparing for a tour in Iraq. The unit's commander, Colonel Harry Tunnell, got the message about his new mission while he and his soldiers were conducting their last major exercise before shipping off to Iraq.

Like Nicholson, Tunnell had been gravely wounded in Iraq, where he led a battalion of paratroopers with the 173rd Airborne Brigade. In October 2003, his convoy was ambushed by insurgents near the city of Kirkuk. He was shot through the leg when he stepped out of his Humvee. He was evacuated to Germany and then to Walter Reed Army Medical Center in Washington, where he began a long rehabilitation that involved multiple surgeries. Although he eventually regained the ability to walk, running long distances was out of the question. That would have been a career ender for most officers, but the Army didn't want to lose Tunnell. He was among the very few African-American infantry battalion commanders, and his aggressiveness on the battlefield had led senior officers to predict that he would eventually become a general. He was allowed to substitute the running portion of his annual physical fitness test with a bicycle ride.

In 2007, he was given command of a newly formed unit—the Fifth Brigade of the Second Infantry Division. The 3,800-strong contingent was equipped with what was then the Army's newest combat vehicle, the Stryker, an eight-wheeled armored transporter that can carry eleven soldiers and travel up to sixty miles per hour. Strykers offered much better protection to the occupants, and contained far more sophisticated computer systems, than the Humvees the Army had used during the first five years of the Iraq War. But they had one major design flaw: Their hulls, which were flat, could not deflect the force of bombs buried in the road. As Tunnell was forming his brigade, the Army replaced Humvees in other units heading to Iraq and Afghanistan with MRAPs, heavy trucks that had V-shaped hulls that could diffuse roadside bomb explosions. But Tunnell's brigade got only a few. The Army had invested billions of dollars in designing and building the Stryker, and the Pentagon brass wanted to see it in action.

With little time to instill cohesion in a team of soldiers who had never worked together, Tunnell had drilled them repeatedly and aggressively. But he also encouraged his officers to seek guidance outside the military bubble. A young captain spent a few months studying small-business economics at the University of Washington. Another officer took a weeklong executive program on negotiation at Harvard. Tunnell himself went to an MIT seminar on innovation.

Despite his emphasis on education, Tunnell had a dim view of the intellectual underpinnings of counterinsurgency theory. He didn't think insurgencies were defeated by protecting villages and winning over residents through reconstruction and development projects. He believed that the top priority was to kill the bad guys. As he had convalesced in 2005 at the Army War College, he had written a short book about his experiences in Iraq that included a spirited prebuttal to the COIN fever that would sweep the military a few years later:

Military leaders must stay focused on the destruction of the enemy. It is virtually impossible to convince any committed terrorist who hates America to change his or her point of view—they simply must be attacked

relentlessly. . . . It is appropriate for military units to
develop goals that include appreciating local culture,
improving quality of life for the populace, and promoting good governance whenever these concepts improve
access to the enemy. However, if the pursuit of them
does not advance one's knowledge of threats and a
unit's capability to maintain the offensive, then they
are of little practical value as tactical or operational
objectives. Destruction of the enemy force must remain
the most important step to defeating terrorists and
insurgents.

By the time Tunnell took over the brigade, every other
infantry commander preparing to go to Iraq or Afghanistan
was using General Petraeus's COIN manual as his lodestar. But
not Tunnell. He told his soldiers that their approach to security operations would be drawn from an Army manual that
outlined counterguerrilla operations, which had long been
superseded by Petraeus's playbook. Instead of emphasizing
the protection of civilians, it instructed commanders to "give
priority to destroying the guerrilla forces." He called his unit
the "Destroyer Brigade" and ordered that its vehicles be painted
with the motto SEARCH AND DESTROY. When the brigade was at
the National Training Center in Fort Irwin, California, officers
there grew concerned about Tunnell's aggressive approach, but
more senior Army commanders did not force him to abandon
it. And selecting another brigade for the Kandahar mission was
out of the question—the Army's force generation command
was emphatic: No other units were available for an Afghanistan rotation.

The counterguerrilla orientation influenced preparations.
Tunnell boasted that his soldiers expended more ammunition
during training than any other brigade headed to Afghanistan.
In order to get higher scores than their peers at combat exer-
cises, he left more experienced officers in command of platoons instead of using the opportunity to train newly arrived
second lieutenants, who would have to take charge once they
got to Afghanistan. One lieutenant in the brigade told me that

the first time he spoke to his entire platoon over the radio was when it was in combat.

One of the lieutenant's responsibilities was to disburse money for small reconstruction projects. Such outlays were a priority for Petraeus, who called cash his most important weapons system. But the lieutenant never received any training on how to requisition funds or how to properly distribute them. "Almost all of our training focused on combat," he said. "All of the other stuff—learning about the culture, the language, the plan for reconstruction—that was an afterthought."

Tunnell's brigade set up its headquarters at the recreation-packed Kandahar Airfield in August 2009—almost four months after Nicholson's Marines had landed in Helmand. Instead of concentrating near the city, which was a priority for McChrystal, the brigade's four battalions were sent in different directions by Mart de Kruif, the Dutch general who ran the NATO headquarters in Kandahar at the time. He said he had Taliban problems everywhere and did not possess enough force to deal with all of them. With the Marines augmenting the British, neighboring Helmand had almost 20,000 foreign troops. Kandahar province, which was larger and more important, had fewer than 10,000. "The prize was Kandahar city, but we didn't act like it," said Tunnell's deputy, Lieutenant Colonel Karl Slaughenhaupt.

The Canadians, who had been the principal NATO force in Kandahar until the Strykers arrived, convinced de Kruif that the districts near the city were relatively stable. Some of McChrystal's aides did not believe the Canadians, whom they assumed were either ignorant of the extent of Taliban infiltration around the city or in denial. The aides thought most of the incoming forces should be placed in the districts of Zhari and Arghandab. Zhari, located directly west of the city, was covered with vineyards. Arghandab was a belt of lush pomegranate groves and dense cornfields to the northwest of the city. Both were saturated with insurgents. But in the interest of ensuring harmony among NATO members, McChrystal chose not to challenge the Stryker deployments. The one eight-hundred-strong Stryker battalion designated for central Kandahar province was instead sent to a district north of Arghandab, Shah Wali Kot, which was of far lower strategic value.

For centuries, Arghandab had been key terrain for anyone seeking to control the city. It is dominated by the Alikozai tribe, whose former chief, Mullah Naqib, determined who could pass through unimpeded. The Soviets were not welcomed, but hundreds of mujahideen fighters were, and they terrorized the Communists from redoubts within the orchards. In the 1990s, Naqib buckled to the Taliban, but in 2001, Hamid Karzai had persuaded him to switch sides. It was the main reason Karzai was able to roll into Kandahar that December. When Naqib died in 2007, Karzai anointed one of the chief's sons, Karimullah, the new Alikozai leader. Many Alikozai were surprised by the choice. Karimullah was young and lacked stature in the tribe. They figured that other members of Naqib's family would have made a better chief. Some accused Karzai, a member of the rival Populzai tribe, of using his office to select a weakling who would do the bidding of the president's half brother Ahmed Wali, the chairman of Kandahar's provincial council. Karzai had his man, but it was a hollow victory. Karimullah lacked the influence to keep his fellow Alikozai in line. The Taliban sensed an opening and surged into Arghandab over the following months. Many Alikozai men joined the insurgency. Others fled into the city.

By the time Tunnell's brigade arrived in August 2009, Arghandab was playing the same role for the Taliban as it had for the mujahideen in the 1980s—it was a land of bunkers, weapons caches, and bomb-making factories. After the Talibs blew up a wall of Kandahar's main prison and freed more than a thousand inmates in 2008, many escapees sought refuge in Arghandab, where they rejoined the insurgency.

Top Canadian officers told Tunnell's staff that no more than thirty to forty insurgents were in the district. The Stryker battalion in Shah Wali Kot, the 1-17 Infantry, soon learned how wrong the Canadians were. On their first patrol into Arghandab, they were pummeled with gunfire and lost a Stryker to a roadside bomb. A week later, during a mission to guard polling sites for the presidential election, Sergeant Troy Tom stepped on a mine while crossing a footbridge. The blast was so massive that Tom, a strapping twenty-one-year-old Navajo from New Mexico, disappeared entirely.

His platoon mates heard the explosion, but they had spread themselves so far apart that they did not see what occurred. Some thought Tom might have been kidnapped, prompting the battalion commander to declare him missing and push more men into the area to search. Soon thereafter, a soldier looking for Tom stepped on another large bomb, and he too disappeared. With two soldiers gone, Tunnell dispatched his fourth battalion, which had been designated as a rapid reaction force for all of southern Afghanistan, into Arghandab to help with the search. It devolved into a forty-hour firefight with insurgents, many of whom operated in dozen-man squads as the Americans did. Although the soldiers eventually recovered some remains of both missing men, five more comrades were wounded. Among them was twenty-five-year-old Lieutenant Dan Berschinski, a 2007 West Point graduate who lost his legs to a mine.

Tunnell decided to rewrite his battle plan. Based on Canadian reports, he had assumed Shah Wali Kot was the principal Taliban sanctuary north of Kandahar. But the fighting in Arghandab indicated otherwise. His intelligence officers soon estimated that there were between three hundred and four hundred enemy fighters in the area. In late August, Tunnell devoted half his forces to a two-battalion operation intended to clear insurgents from the northern part of the district. The 1-17 was to focus on a trio of villages not far from where Tom had been killed. Another battalion was to flush insurgents out of the south.

On the second week of the operation, I met with Lieutenant Colonel Patrick Gaydon, an artillery officer who had been put in charge of the Stryker brigade's special troops battalion, which was responsible for governance, reconstruction, and development. After he spent an hour telling me about the universities at which his fellow officers had taken classes before deploying and the sophisticated computer network that allowed soldiers to send and receive vast quantities of data while in the field,

I mentioned that I would be heading to Arghandab in two days to attend a meeting of local elders. Gaydon asked how I was getting there. I told him the general who was Tunnell's boss had arranged a flight. Gaydon was delighted; it meant he would have a chance to get there as well. Gaydon's unit had been in Afghanistan for a month, but it had not yet received any vehicles suitable for travel beyond the Kandahar Airfield. Because his team's mission was not to kill bad guys, it was at the end of the list for supplies.

I was astounded. Given his focus on government and reconstruction, Gaydon seemed like the officer who really needed to attend the *shura*. Over in the Marine areas, Larry Nicholson had insisted that his battalion commanders hold districtwide *shura*s within forty-eight hours of their arrival in Nawa and other parts of the central Helmand River Valley. But Tunnell did not regard community meetings as a priority for his operation. The brigade's State Department political adviser, Todd Greentree, had to meet with Tunnell three times to persuade him to authorize the *shura*. His ability to flout COIN, despite McChrystal's unambiguous embrace of it, revealed the lack of control the supposedly disciplined U.S. military had over officers who were scattered across a vast country and sometimes reported to non-American generals. Tunnell was fighting the war he wanted to fight, and nobody stood in his way.

Gaydon spent the day after our meeting drafting a speech he would deliver to the crowd of turbaned elders. "I want you to know that we are undertaking this military operation so that we can create an environment where we can work shoulder-to-shoulder with district leaders, elders, and the people of Arghandab over the long term," he wrote. But the morning we were supposed to leave, we learned our flight had been canceled. A delegation of visiting members of Congress wanted to fly around the south, and our helicopter had been reassigned as an airborne tour bus. We settled for an early breakfast in the chow hall with Greentree, who fumed over an omelet and hash browns that the brigade was missing an opportunity to win over residents and gird them against Taliban intimidation. "This is really, really bad," he said.

He couldn't understand why a few vehicles could not have

been diverted to transport them to the meeting. "Is this the most important thing we could have done in the operation today? Absolutely."

Gaydon tried to put the best spin on it. The *shura* would go on, he said. He planned to have an officer in Arghandab read the speech he had written. At least Tunnell will be there, I said consolingly. He's the one who matters. The Afghans always want to talk to the man in charge.

"Tunnell won't be attending," Greentree said. "He said he'll be too busy directing the combat operations."

The next day, I asked Greentree how it had gone. Fine, he said, for the first thirty minutes. Then two AH-64 Apache attack helicopters strafed a nearby building and the attendees fled.

The following months would yield more missteps. Tunnell's soldiers once drove a Stryker with loudspeakers through a village during an insurgent's funeral, announcing "This is what happens when you fight us." At a meeting with State Department officials, one Stryker officer dismissed a request that the brigade focus more on development, saying, "Come on, buddy, we're just here to rack 'em and stack 'em." The word around the Kandahar Airfield was that Tunnell had told his men that by the time they were done with their tour, the Afghans "will be praying to Mecca ten times a day." The brigade spent almost nothing from a multimillion-dollar military account for reconstruction projects during its first three months. And when a company commander posted on the wall of his base a quote from McChrystal's COIN guidance—"sporadically moving into an area for a few hours or even a few days solely to search for the enemy and then leave does little good, and may do much harm"—a senior officer ordered him to take it down. Not long after, Tunnell reassigned that company commander to a desk job.

Senior military officials at the Kandahar Airfield and at NATO headquarters in Kabul grew alarmed. Their concern extended well beyond Tunnell's rejection of COIN strategy. The 1-17 seemed to be making tactical mistakes. It quickly pulled out of areas it assaulted, which allowed insurgents to return. But its most egregious sin, the officials said, was using Strykers in places where its soldiers should have been walking. Barreling through the district in a vehicle that afforded the driver only a narrow slit of a window meant the soldiers couldn't scan the ground for bombs as effectively as they could if they were on foot.

Stryker after Stryker hit roadside bombs. Sometimes there would be a fatality. If the vehicle's occupants were lucky, there would be just a bunch of broken bones and concussions. But the insurgents began to adapt by building bigger and bigger bombs. In late October, when a Stryker rolled over one buried in the banks of the Arghandab River, seven soldiers and their interpreter died.

The second-ranking U.S. commander in Afghanistan, Lieutenant General David Rodriguez, raised the question of whether Tunnell should be relieved of his position. But the top U.S. general in Kandahar, Mick Nicholson, told Rodriguez he thought Tunnell could change. A few months later, Nicholson confided to colleagues that he regretted not having pushed for Tunnell's removal.

Some officers who worked for Tunnell told me the brigade had been thrust into an untenable position. Its four battalions were dispersed across a huge swath of southern Afghanistan, often forcing them to remain in their vehicles for drive-by patrols instead of bedding down in villages and walking the beat. Their area was crawling with far more insurgents than they had expected. And every time they thought they were gaining traction, senior commanders upended their mission. In mid-September, de Kruif ordered the second battalion that had participated in the Arghandab operation to move to the far western part of Kandahar province to replace a departing U.S. Army unit that had been working for the Canadians. That left the 1-17 responsible for all of Arghandab.

With so many insurgents holed up in Arghandab, Tunnell's men needed to take forceful action. But they failed to offer enough carrots with their sticks, and they failed to grasp the political winds within the NATO headquarters. Had Tunnell been just as tough but described his methods as COIN—instead of counterguerrilla operations—he would have run into less trouble with his superiors.

In November, British Major General Nick Carter took charge of southern Afghanistan from de Kruif. He immediately concluded that the Stryker battalion was the wrong unit for Arghandab. He pushed it back to Shah Wali Kot and brought in a battalion of the 82nd Airborne Division, which had been among the 4,000 soldiers sent to help train the country's army. (Despite the Pentagon's claims to the White House that the trainers were essential to build the Afghan army, they wound up doing little training. Most of them had been sent to fight insurgents in the western part of the country.)

By then, twenty-one soldiers from the 1-17 had been killed in Arghandab. It was the highest death toll of any U.S. Army battalion in Afghanistan.

Two months after the Stryker brigade returned home to Washington State, five soldiers from the battalion Tunnell had sent to far western Kandahar province were charged with murdering unarmed Afghans for sport and keeping their fingers as trophies. A subsequent Army investigation by a one-star general absolved Tunnell of any direct blame for the killings. By then Tunnell had relinquished command of the brigade. Had he still been on the job, he should have been relieved of command, the general determined, in part because of "his failure to follow instructions and intent."

Tunnell's stubbornness cost the United States a critical chance to pacify key areas around the most important city in southern Afghanistan during the first year of Obama's presidency. "We had a great opportunity," Mick Nicholson told a fellow general. "Sadly, we lost a year."

After the Strykers had been in Arghandab for a few weeks, McChrystal knew he needed more troops to improve security in Kandahar city and its immediate environs. He made it his top priority for 2010 and ordered the first wave of Army infantry units to arrive under the 30,000-troop surge to head there. But after the unrealistic expectations he had announced for Marja, he lowballed Kandahar. There would be no claims of government in a box or catastrophic success. Journalists would not be invited right away. He even wanted his subordinates to stop calling it an operation. "There won't be a D-Day that is climactic," he said. He urged Nick Carter, who had counseled patience in Marja, to heed his own advice: Counterinsurgency operations rarely had a decisive moment that could be scripted—there was no hill to seize or flag to plant in Kandahar. If all went well, security would improve slowly, like a rising tide. Better to let people see the difference than proclaim victory.

Because the Army's surge troops would not arrive in Kandahar until June—six months after the initial Marine surge forces landed in Helmand—McChrystal wanted to use the first half of the year to reshape the politics of the city and province. Two of his most trusted advisers, intelligence chief Michael Flynn and former Kandahar resident Sarah Chayes, told him in late 2009 that the only way to clean up the place was to oust Ahmed Wali Karzai, who had become the strongest of the strongmen lording over southern Afghanistan. Although Ahmed Wali had an important official role as chairman of the Kandahar provincial council, his real influence derived from an elaborate web of business interests, as well as a long-running relationship with the CIA, which had kept previous U.S. military commanders and diplomats from questioning his behavior. McChrystal wasn't dissuaded by the CIA connection; he knew the agency better than any other commander. His aides figured he'd be able to get Langley to cut Ahmed Wali loose.

Ahmed Wali was stockier and had less gray hair than the president, but there was no doubt he was a Karzai. He had Hamid's long forehead, pointed nose, and frowning lips. But he was even savvier. While Hamid had remained in Pakistan during the Soviet occupation, Ahmed Wali had decamped to the United States, where he had opened a successful Afghan restaurant in Chicago. He had returned to Pakistan in late 2001, as Hamid was taking off for Afghanistan on a motorcycle. In the initial division of spoils, Hamid had wanted to give the governorship of Kandahar to Mullah Naqib, the Alikozai leader who had helped liberate the city and who would have ensured an influential role for Ahmed Wali, but American officials had insisted that the post go to a Karzai family rival, Gul Agha Sherzai of the Barakzai tribe, because he had worked with U.S. Special Operations forces. Ahmed Wali did not pack up—he knew that controlling Kandahar was vital for the family. He exploited his brother's connections with the U.S. military and the CIA to steer contracts for construction projects and private security services to relatives and cronies. After the president reassigned Sherzai to a province in the east and appointed a weakling as governor, Ahmed Wali became the unrivaled center of power in Kandahar. The Americans came to him for intelligence and help with operating an anti-Taliban paramilitary organization called the Kandahar Strike Force—in exchange for a monthly fee. If U.S. officials wanted to build something, they often used companies with which he was connected. And if fellow Afghans wanted to do business in the area, they had to give him a cut. He ran for the provincial council in 2005 and, to the surprise of nobody in Kandahar, was elected chairman.

His appetite for power kept growing. He commandeered land that belonged to the Afghan army on the eastern fringe of the city to construct a gated community of mansions with wide, tree-lined boulevards. He orchestrated the forgery of thousands of ballots on his brother's behalf during the 2009 presidential election. His influence over the police and various private security firms meant that he often was the first stop when the United States, Canada, or any other country wanted to provide development assistance. He decided which Afghan businessmen would profit from the projects and which residents would benefit from the aid. In a December 2009 cable, a U.S. Embassy official called Ahmed Wali "the kingpin of Kandahar." His modus operandi was simple: He rewarded his friends and froze out his rivals. Those who got fat loved him dearly, and those who didn't usually cast their lot with the insurgency. But those defections actually helped Ahmed Wali. As insurgent attacks increased, Canada and the United States sent in additional troops and reconstruction dollars, which put even more money into his coffers.

Instead of seeking his removal on the basis of corruption or conspiracy, which could have tarnished the Afghan president and would have required a capacity for forensic investigation the U.S. military did not then possess, American officials focused on allegations that Ahmed Wali was connected to drug smuggling. When an American diplomat or a visiting member of Congress wanted to take the president to task, he or she often mentioned Ahmed Wali and drugs without citing any specific evidence.

When McChrystal delicately brought up Ahmed Wali in a discussion with the Afghan president in early 2010, Karzai demanded clear proof of wrongdoing. McChrystal told his intelligence team to do a deep dive on Ahmed Wali and present Karzai with whatever they could find. In early March, McChrystal met with his top aides to review the evidence. They had not been able to find any smoking guns. Either Ahmed Wali was not involved in drug trafficking, or he did a masterful job of covering his tracks. Faced with a lack of proof, McChrystal reversed course. He told his staff that they would have to live with Ahmed Wali, but he instructed them to work with the embassy to lay down a new set of rules. Among them was a demand that Ahmed Wali not meddle in that year's parliamentary elections and in the appointment of district governors. Intelligence chief Flynn met with Ahmed Wali and delivered a blunt warning: His activities would be closely monitored by the military, and U.S. officials would pounce on any indication of misbehavior.

McChrystal reasoned that coming to an understanding with Ahmed Wali would remove a sore point in his relationship with President Karzai, whose support was essential for the Kandahar mission. Some of the general's aides began to think Ahmed Wali could be persuaded to act in the best interests of his country. "He's like a thief who already has filled nine bags of loot," one of them told me. "We're hoping he'll realize this is not the moment to fill the tenth bag."

In early April, McChrystal and President Karzai traveled to Kandahar together. American officials saw it as an opportunity for Karzai to urge elders to support the upcoming security operations and to publicly moderate his increasingly strident rhetoric against the United States. Tensions had been growing over the previous months, culminating three days earlier when he had accused Western nations of perpetrating the fraud that had denied him an outright victory in the August 2009 election. In the same outburst, he warned NATO nations that they risked being seen by Afghans as invaders rather than saviors. His comments had prompted an unhappy phone call to him from Secretary of State Clinton, but it seemed to do little good. The following day, he upped the ante in a meeting with members of Parliament. "If you and the international community pressure me more," he said, "I swear that I am going to join the Taliban."

McChrystal and Karzai flew from Kabul to the Kandahar Airfield in an Air Force C-130 Hercules cargo plane equipped with an air-conditioned pod that included a desk and sofa. They then helicoptered to one of Ahmed Wali's palaces, where 1,200 men had jammed into a stuffy, low-ceilinged basement hall to hear the president speak.

"Afghanistan will be fixed when its people trust that their president is independent and not a puppet," he said. "We have to demonstrate our sovereignty. We have to demonstrate that we are standing up for our values."

Clearly, conciliation was not on his agenda. A half hour later, he asked the attendees whether they were happy about U.S. plans to improve security. The details were secret, but everyone knew more troops were headed their way. An irritable murmur echoed across the vast hall.

"Listen to me carefully: Until you're happy and satisfied, we will not conduct this operation," he said. The room rang with applause.

Karzai's stance revealed a fundamental disagreement over America's war strategy. U.S. officers and diplomats argued that tribal rivalries, an inequitable distribution of power at the local level, and the government's failure to provide even the most basic services were all factors that were pushing many Afghans into the arms of the Taliban. They believed that the remedy was a comprehensive counterinsurgency campaign. But in Karzai's eyes, the principal problem was the infiltration of militants from Pakistan, and he wanted U.S. and NATO forces to focus on the border. By mucking around in the districts of Kandahar and Helmand, the United States and its coalition partners were disrupting what he believed was a natural system of self-regulating Pashtun governance. Through all of his flare-ups, Karzai "is sending us a message," a senior U.S. military official told me. "And that message is: I don't believe in counterinsurgency."

The Americans ignored Karzai. McChrystal and his bosses were not willing to give up on COIN, even if the leader of the sovereign nation in which they were fighting had clearly done so. They would push into the districts around Kandahar and, they hoped, show him how protecting the people could improve security. The State Department readily agreed to help. For Eikenberry, who had diagnosed the Afghan government's essential problems in his cable during the White House strategy review, focusing on districts was a viable solution the Americans could implement. And it would allow him to regain some influence in Kabul after so firmly placing himself in the losing camp over the surge.

Under Eikenberry's direction, the embassy decided to steer the bulk of its development assistance directly to districts in the south and east instead of channeling it through the central government in Kabul, which rarely allowed funds to trickle down to the people. New reconstruction programs worth hundreds of millions of dollars would provide short-term jobs and agriculture aid in towns and villages. The embassy also established district-level stabilization teams, made up of a State Department representative, a USAID officer, and sometimes an expert from the U.S. Department of Agriculture, that were supposed to work with military units conducting COIN operations. Clinton was thrilled by the prospect: A civilian surge would occur in tandem with the military's, and it would demonstrate the value of having U.S. diplomats and development experts stationed side by side with soldiers and Marines.

Getting American civilians to the districts, however, was only the first step. What the Afghans really needed, in the view of almost every U.S. official involved in the war, was more Afghan civil servants at the local level. They wanted what Governor Mangal had promised the residents of Nawa soon after the Marines had arrived there: reopened schools, a functioning health clinic, a clerk to issue identification cards, and agricultural assistance. But Mangal and his fellow governors lacked the power to provide any of those services. Under Afghanistan's constitution, the power to allocate government workers and funding rested in Kabul—and therein lay the problem. Despite constant prodding, the relevant ministries failed to select people for local jobs, and when they did, those people often failed to report for duty. The pay was terrible, and if government workers showed their faces in many southern districts, they would be marked for assassination.

Eikenberry came up with an answer on an airplane flight in late 2009 with Jelani Popal, the head of the country's local governance directorate. He offered to have the U.S. government pay monthly bonuses to Afghan civil servants to work in dangerous districts—just as the State Department was doing for its employees in Afghanistan. Popal was intrigued. The plan was eventually named the District Delivery Program, and it also included funding to house and transport civil servants. All the Afghans had to do was select needy districts, assess their requirements, and identify personnel to fill the jobs. It was another stab at government in a box.

The initiative thrilled U.S. military commanders, none more than Dave Rodriguez. He recognized that the Afghan government's deficiency was a potential deal breaker for McChrystal's COIN strategy. To help the embassy, Rodriguez assigned several of his officers to spend their days at the Afghan ministries most involved in local government. Although most of them did not speak Dari or Pashto and they wore camouflage uniforms that discomfited many Afghan ministry workers, Rodriguez was confident that his efforts would transform the bureaucracy in Kabul.

Kandahar was supposed to be the program's showcase. USAID officers determined that the city and the surrounding districts required three hundred civil servants. The local governance directorate put out the call for applicants in Kabul and Kandahar, emphasizing the salary bonus. When nobody expressed interest, it dropped the requirement of a high school diploma. It got four applicants. Few people wanted to work in Kandahar given the lack of security, and most potential employees did not possess basic reading, writing, and math

skills. Eikenberry might have grasped the Afghan government's predicament before many others in the new administration, but his prescription was totally unrealistic.

Eikenberry refused to give up. The embassy drafted a list
of ten steps it wanted Karzai to take in support of the Kandahar operation. Among them were ordering his ministries
to expedite appointments to the districts and to place a high
priority on the delivery of services in the Kandahar area. To
track progress, the embassy convened a video conference every
Saturday with military and USAID officers in Kandahar. They
talked about the same issues week after week. By mid-October,
three months into the effort, the participants were still "gravely
concerned about the poor and declining capacity" of Kandahar
city's government, according to the notes of a person who sat
through the session.

Part of the problem seemed to be communication. When one
embassy staffer raised the ten-step list with a senior Afghan
official involved in local government, he told her he had never
heard of it. But the disconnect was even wider than the sharing
of paper. Before one of the meetings, embassy official Patricia
McNerney distributed a six-item agenda. Four of the six began
with the word "push" followed by a part of the Afghan government. Few in the embassy seemed to grasp the message in
their own documents: The problem was about more than just
salaries and security. Karzai's administration was not a willing
partner in America's grand plans to build local governments.

With civil service recruitment stalled, the Americans
focused on working with Kandahar's governor, its mayor, and
the district governors around the city. In Arghandab, they lavished resources and praise on Haji Abdul Jabar, an imperious
sixty-eight-year-old former mujahideen commander turned
district governor who was the sole, brave face of civil administration in the area. Every day, he received a parade of visitors
in his modest office, which abutted an Army base. Everyone
who saw him came with a complaint. *The Americans damaged
my property. Someone is squatting on my land. My son needs a
job.* Sometimes Abdul Jabar listened patiently and promised a
solution. Sometimes he dismissed the petitioner with a wave
of his hand.

When he was killed in a car bombing in June 2010, several military officers and diplomats initially blamed the Taliban. But an investigation revealed that he had been skimming U.S. funds for reconstruction projects in his district and residents had grown angry when they didn't receive a cut.

"It was a mob hit," a USAID official in Kandahar told me. "We saw him as a white knight, but we were getting played the whole time."

Unable to tell friend from foe, the Americans opted to do more of the governing themselves. That required legions of civilians who knew how to run a country.

9

Deadwood

WHEN RICHARD HOLBROOKE became the Obama administration's Afghanistan point man in January 2009, Summer Coish was keen to join his civilian operation. She had the requisite credentials: a master's in public health and experience working on foreign development projects. For the previous five years, she had been splitting her time between New York and Kazakhstan, where she and a friend had started a glossy biannual magazine about Central Asia. Although she dug a little deeper into her savings to print each issue of *Steppe,* the publishing venture had swelled the list of contacts on her mobile phone. She knew more Afghan entrepreneurs—from the founder of the country's most successful television station to the owner of the largest bottled-drinks company—than anyone else seeking a job with USAID.

She had met Holbrooke at a conference in Kazakhstan, but she didn't have his phone number. She was sure he'd remember her—she was tall and striking, with long blond hair and a fondness for dangle earrings acquired in far-off bazaars—but if she called his office cold, she figured the message would never get through. So she did a little Internet sleuthing and found his address on Manhattan's Upper West Side. She scribbled a note and attached it to the latest issue of *Steppe,* whose cover fortuitously featured a black-and-white photograph of a smiling Afghan farmer in his wheat field. It was the sort of carefree, slice-of-life scene from Afghanistan that magazines never seemed to print. She thought it would appeal to Holbrooke. She took the subway to his building on a Sunday and left her package with his doorman. At 11:30 that night, her phone rang. She didn't recognize the number on her caller ID but picked up anyway. "I've been reading your magazine all day," Holbrooke said. "Let's talk."

Instead of populating his new office at the State Department with risk-averse career Foreign Service officers whose Afghan expertise rarely extended beyond a few years, Holbrooke looked elsewhere for talent. He poached one of the country's foremost Afghanistan scholars, Barney Rubin of New York University. He lured Iranian-American professor Vali Nasr, who had lived in Pakistan as a doctoral student, and Kabul-born Rina Amiri, who headed Afghanistan programs at George Soros's Open Society Institute. He even recruited Ronan Farrow, the child-prodigy son of Woody Allen and Mia Farrow, to build links with nongovernmental organizations in Afghanistan and Pakistan.

Coish was just the sort of person he desired for his Washington team. But she wanted to live in Afghanistan, so he introduced her to Eikenberry. He brought her to the swearing-in ceremony for the new USAID director in Kabul, who happened to be an old friend of Coish's from Kazakhstan. They talked about possible assignments for her and settled on a position in Kabul coordinating donations from other nations. It seemed a good fit with Holbrooke's goal of increasing international support for the reconstruction of Afghanistan. She began packing her leather valise.

Then she got her first dose of State Department bureaucracy. Although Holbrooke wanted her to get started right away, USAID insisted that she fill out a voluminous stack of security clearance forms that required her to list all of her travel outside the United States and every "foreign contact" she had had in the previous eight years—no easy feat for someone who had lived overseas for much of that time. The documentation was mandatory not just for those reading secret cables but for anyone seeking a development job in Afghanistan. One senior USAID official told me that the forms required so much

information that some applicants spent three months completing them. And those who had the toughest time—because of
extensive travel in developing countries—were just the sorts
of experienced people USAID needed. Even to prosecute a war
with stakes as high as those in Afghanistan, where time was of
the essence, the government couldn't cut through its own red
tape.

Coish, a native of South Carolina, was deemed a "counterterrorism threat" because she had set up a foreign bank account
for *Steppe.* A retired police officer from rural North Carolina
working as a contract investigator for the government grilled
her for two days. "This is a real concern," the investigator said
about the bank account. "What if some rich sheik wanted to
influence you by depositing a lot of money into the account?"

Coish explained that there were no sheiks in Afghanistan.
Then the investigator asked her if she had ever visited a foreign embassy. Many times, she said. The investigator wanted
to know why. To get visas, Coish replied. The investigator, who
had only ever traveled out of the country to Baja California,
seemed flummoxed. "How do you get a visa?" (Once Coish got
to Kabul, she discovered that some of her colleagues apparently
had similar questions, even though they all possessed Afghan
visas in their black diplomatic passports. The embassy's con-
sular section sought to provide answers. If "you want to know
what a visa is, how to apply for a passport, and much more, this
is the seminar for you," the section wrote in an e-mail inviting
staffers to an hour-long briefing.)

It took four months for Coish to receive her clearance. She
then went to Washington to attend a series of USAID and State
Department briefings that seemed designed for people who
had never traveled outside the United States. It included an
admonition to limit consumption of fatty foods at the embassy
chow hall. "Do you want to come home chunky or hunky?" she
was asked. When she got to Kabul, she discovered it was a false
choice: Everything in the buffet was greasy and crispy. She
also was told repeatedly not to wear sunglasses while talking
to Afghans. "It was the key guidance they thought would get
you far in Afghanistan," she said. "They had no idea that a lot
of men in Kabul actually wear sunglasses."

After her training session, USAID's human resources department continued to slow roll the process. She spent a month in a $300-a-night hotel room waiting for the agency to issue her a diplomatic passport. Finally, fourteen months after she had delivered the magazine to Holbrooke, she received authorization to travel to Kabul. If the war in Afghanistan was a priority, lots of people in Washington seemed not to know—or care.

When she arrived, she expected to work with a team of fellow Americans committed to helping rebuild Afghanistan, and she assumed she'd be able to spend her evenings socializing with her Afghan friends to form public-private partnerships. Long gone were the days when the U.S. government had assembled postwar reconstruction teams based on political fidelity, as the Bush administration had during the first year in Iraq. Holbrooke was recruiting the best and brightest in Washington. She believed the same standards would apply in Kabul.

Within a day, she saw she'd been dreaming. She divided most of the people she met in the highly fortified embassy and USAID compound into three camps: those who had come to Afghanistan because they wanted to make a lot of money—with hazard pay and bonuses, some staffers earned as much as $300,000 a year; those who were getting their tickets punched for a promotion or a posting to a comfortable embassy in Western Europe; and those who were seeking to escape a divorce, a foreclosed home, or some other personal calamity. "It's rare that you ever hear someone say they're here because they want to help the Afghans," she told me after she had been there for a few months.

Everyone seemed bent on departure. One itching-to-go staffer designed an Excel spreadsheet he called the Circle of Freedom. You entered the date you arrived and the date you were scheduled to leave, and it told you, down to the second, how much time you had left in Kabul. A USAID employee took to listing his time to freedom in the signature line of his e-mail messages.

Set on a closed street off a traffic circle named for the assassinated Northern Alliance leader Ahmed Shah Massoud, America's diplomatic compound in Kabul was ringed by tall walls topped with razor wire. Rifle-toting Nepalese guards—Ghurkas for hire—patrolled the perimeter and manned three separate checkpoints everyone had to pass through before entering the embassy grounds. All employees wore identification badges around their necks. Blue cards were reserved for Americans with security clearances. The Afghan support staff had yellow ones that restricted their movements and subjected them to additional screening. When USAID administrator Rajiv Shah came to Kabul for a visit, he thanked the Afghan staff for their bravery and commitment during a town hall meeting in the embassy atrium. They never heard his words because guards barred yellow-badged Afghan staffers from attending the event.

As far as prisons went, the compound wasn't all that grim. There were a swimming pool, a bar called the Duck and Cover, and an Afghan-run café that served sandwiches and smoothies. A small convenience store stocked potato chips, candy bars, and lots of alcohol. The senior staff lived in apartments with kitchens, living rooms, and flat-screen televisions. Coish got a "hooch"—a trailer containing a twin bed, a small desk and armoire, a bathroom, and a telephone with a Maryland area code. The trailer was surrounded with sandbags. To accommodate the influx of new civilians, the hooches were stacked on top of each other, with metal ladders and catwalks to access the second story. When she arrived, she was assigned one on the ground floor. Those were coveted because they were deemed safer in case of a mortar attack. But once she saw the top level, she told the officials in charge of housing that she would grow depressed if she did not have exposure to direct sunlight. What she really wanted was a view. On the ground floor, all she saw were the walls. From the second story, she could gaze over the dusty, teeming city and think, for the briefest of moments, that she didn't live in the twenty-first-century version of Little America.

Once she started her job, she began to understand why her colleagues had no great love for their work. Meetings consumed much of the day. Her boss expected her to be at her desk until ten at night to draft memos, cables, and talking points for senior officials to read at meetings with Afghans.

Nobody wanted her to go out and talk to her Afghan contacts or to soak up the country. They simply wanted responses to their e-mails right away. Much of what she was asked to do could have been accomplished back in Washington—at far less cost to American taxpayers. But then she wouldn't have been counted as part of the civilian surge.

Most of Coish's colleagues also spent all day in their cubicles, hunched over computers. Embassy rules prevented Americans from leaving the compound unless they had official business—a meeting with an Afghan government official, dinner with a European diplomat, a visit to a U.S.-funded development project—and even then they had to obtain permission from the security office, which allotted the armored cars in the motor pool. Restaurants and offices had to be on a list of approved locations. Staffers had to identify the people with whom they were meeting and then submit reports upon their return to the embassy compound detailing the substance of their discussions with any citizens of countries listed on the State Department's Security Environment Threat List, which, of course, included Afghanistan. Coish had enough friends outside the embassy to know that the regulations were needlessly onerous. American aid workers and journalists regularly drove around in unarmored Toyota Corollas. Being kidnapped or shot always was a possibility, but Kabul was far safer than Baghdad, especially if you kept a low profile. If it wouldn't have been a firing offense, she would have summoned a taxi to pick her up from Massoud Circle and take her for a night on the town. Every evening brought another invitation: an exhibition at an art gallery, drinks at a journalist's house, dinner with an Afghan tycoon, a party hosted by expatriates working for nongovernmental organizations. She figured all of them were places to glean information. She eventually managed to leave nearly every night, but doing so often required creative obfuscation on her security forms to get an exit pass and an embassy vehicle.

If her vehicle ever struck pedestrians or another car, the security office did not want her driver to stop and check on those who had been hit. "Attempt to put as much space between yourself and the accident site as possible," the office urged.

The most powerful person on the embassy compound was not the ambassador but the head of the security office. His goal was to ensure that nobody working for the embassy was killed or wounded, which resulted in a near-zero-risk policy that kept diplomats and USAID officers from doing their jobs most effectively. Meetings and trips could be canceled, often with little notice, if the officer deemed the journey too danger-ous, even if it was of vital importance. Reward was rarely bal-anced against risk. To several staffers, it seemed as if those in the security office didn't share everyone else's goal of winning the war against the Taliban. The security office "has turned us into women and children on the *Titanic*," one embassy official groused to me.

A near-daily flurry of alarmist warnings from the secu-rity office sowed fear among embassy staffers: A suicide car bomber was driving around the city looking for Americans to target; a crowd of disabled veterans was protesting in the circle, causing dangerous traffic jams; Afghans posing as visa seekers planned to attack one of the checkpoints. The security office sent embassywide e-mails urging everyone to keep a copy of the DS-3088 Bomb Threat Report Form near their telephones. "In the event that a threatening call is received," the office wrote, the employee "should calmly begin taking notes on the form, obtaining as much information as possible and asking the questions contained therein." Some staffers took to travel-ing from the embassy to the USAID compound by an under-ground tunnel, even though the street was blocked off for two hundred yards in either direction. Most of Coish's colleagues assumed that she was risking near-certain death or abduction by hopping the wall every night. An FBI agent whom she met in the dining hall became so concerned about her travels that he eventually grabbed her mobile phone, pulled out the bat-tery, and copied down the serial number—so his buddies could track her if she was kidnapped.

For those who lacked paranoia or Coish's gift for bending the rules, there were furloughs every few months sponsored by the embassy's morale officer. The offers came by e-mail. One began with the tantalizing subject line "Magical Mystery Excursion!" It opened with a picture of a caged dog and two other forlorn mutts.

Do you wonder what Afghanistan is really like?
Worried that you'll never see anything except the airport?
Are your only photographs of sandbags?
Then respond quickly.

It ended with three photos of frolicking dogs.

There were only fifteen spaces. All were claimed within a minute. The destination, it turned out, was Babur Gardens, a historic park in Kabul that hundreds of Afghan families strolled through every weekend. The embassy personnel were escorted by Filipino contract security guards.

With off-campus trips a rarity, Coish's colleagues sought to have fun within the compound. Their e-mail in-boxes filled up with announcements of upcoming diversions:

RAMBO IN AFGHANISTAN. A screening of *Rambo III* at the Duck and Cover. "Wear a headband for $1 off drinks."

FIRST MEETING OF THE KABUL FLY FISHING FORUM. "Preliminary research reveals there are trout fishing opportunities in Afghanistan." [Of course, no embassy staffer was allowed off the compound for a fishing trip.]

WINE & SWINE PARTY. Held at the quarters of the Marines who guarded the embassy, the festivities would begin with afternoon volleyball matches and swimming. They advertised that "North Carolina BBQ experts" would be brought in "to cook these porkers." [Apparently nobody bothered to consider the cultural offense of roasting a pig in a Muslim country.]

HOLIDAY CRAFT MAKING! "No talent is necessary! Just come and enjoy the day with holiday crafts, music, and sweets! Please bring scissors, tape, and glue sticks if you have them."

THE BIGGEST LOSER. A weight loss contest for those who
were growing chunky instead of hunky from the fried
food dished up in the cafeteria.

The amusements grew tiresome after a while. Some staffers retreated to their trailers to watch movies on their laptops.
Others grew homesick and despondent. The embassy health
clinic doled out increasing quantities of antidepressant pills,
and when a State Department psychiatrist arrived in February
2010 for a monthlong visit, there was a rush to make appointments.

The most common salve, however, was booze. For those
not lucky enough to be invited to a private party in one of
the apartments, the Duck and Cover—whose logo featured a
duck wearing a combat helmet perched atop sandbags—was
the place to go. On Thursday nights, staffers crammed shoulder to shoulder in the pub, downing cans of Heineken, glasses
of cheap Australian white wine, and bottles of hard lemonade.
The place remained hopping until last call at two in the morning, when everyone stumbled back to his or her hooch.

But such nights were tame compared with Mardi Gras in
2010, when the embassy's social committee threw the party
that almost ended all parties. Hundreds of revelers, including
thick-necked security contractors, raggedy aid workers, and
suit-wearing diplomats from other countries, packed into a
tent next to the main embassy office building. The organizers
had procured more than enough liquor, but the partygoers had
access to only two restrooms. The queue for the toilets grew so
long that inebriated attendees began to relieve themselves elsewhere. The deputy Turkish ambassador urinated on the wall of
the chancery building. So did two American men who worked
at the embassy. A female staffer pulled off her underwear and
squatted on a patch of grass near the flagpole.

Eikenberry couldn't do anything about the Turk, but both
of the American men were sent home. When the woman was
hauled into her supervisor's office the following day and told
she would be disciplined, she claimed to have a small bladder and threatened to lodge an Americans with Disabilities
Act complaint. She was allowed to finish her tour in Kabul.

The following week, the word came down that there would be no more blow-out parties until the Marine Corps birthday ball that fall, and alcohol purchases at the embassy convenience store would be limited to two bottles of wine or one bottle of spirits per person per day.

Coish may have hated her job, but she was lucky to have a specific assignment before she arrived. Many people who were sent to Afghanistan as part of the civilian surge had no idea what they would be doing until they reached Kabul and waited around, often for a few weeks, for marching orders from supervisors at the embassy or the USAID mission. The allocations were random. People who wanted to work in the field found themselves sitting in a Kabul office, and those who had expected hot showers, air-conditioning, and fresh food wound up in tents on forward operating bases, eating meals out of a bag.

The civilian surge was supposed to place more diplomats and USAID officers in southern districts where recently deployed U.S. troops were conducting counterinsurgency operations. But most of the new arrivals wound up staying in Kabul. By late 2010, more than two-thirds of the 1,100 civilian U.S. government employees in Afghanistan were stationed in the capital to feed the mushrooming bureaucracy at the embassy and the USAID mission. Although there were plenty of Afghans in the city with whom to collaborate—placing American advisers in key ministries could have accelerated the District Delivery Program—most embassy and USAID staffers were required to sit at their desks. When Coish asked to work at the Ministry of Rural Rehabilitation and Development, which was a key player in reconstruction programs, her boss released her for only three days a week, and even that came with a condition—that she come in to the USAID office those evenings to draft memos and proofread cables.

It was the ninth year of America's war in Afghanistan, but it often felt like the ninth version of the first year, save for the massive expansion of the compound. Most staffers stayed for only a year, and 90 percent of them arrived and departed over the summer—because that's what Foreign Service officers do everywhere else in the world. By late August, the embassy and

USAID mission had a whole new crop of people who lacked institutional memory. To Coish, who arrived in April and witnessed the 2010 summer transition, "It was as if someone had pushed a giant reset button on the entire place."

From the outset, the civilian surge was bedeviled by a lack of initiative and creativity in Washington. Instead of scouring the United States for top talent to fill the crucial, well-paying jobs that were a key element of Obama's national security agenda, those responsible for hiring first turned to State Department and USAID officers in other parts of the world. But the best of them had already served in Iraq or Afghanistan. Many of those who signed up were too new to have done a tour in a war zone or too lackluster to have better career options. The personnel office also sought out retirees. A seventy-nine-year-old man was sent to the reconstruction team office in Kandahar.

USAID eventually agreed to hire outsiders for yearlong tours in Afghanistan. But the human resources team did not call up experts in private companies, universities, and nonprofit organizations. It waited for résumés to come over the transom. Most were from contractors who had worked in Iraq, often on wasteful projects that had accomplished little.

The result was almost as embarrassing as the first year of the Iraq occupation, when the Coalition Provisional Authority had given a twenty-four-year-old who had never worked in finance the job of reopening Baghdad's stock exchange. The USAID field officer sent to Musa Qala was reassigned after she got into a fight with the Marines because they would not give her an air-conditioned trailer. Nawa, which was one of the safest districts in Helmand province, could not hold down a State Department representative. The first one went on leave and never returned. So did the second one, but not before revealing to colleagues that he did not know the term ANSF, the commonly used acronym for the Afghan national security forces. The third one, who had been fired from his previous job as a town manager in Virginia, stayed.

"We're past the B Team," said Marc Chretien, a senior State Department official in Helmand. "We're at Team C."

Like Kael Weston, Chretien had served in Iraq with the

Civil engineer Paul Jones, who worked for Morrison-Knudsen, traveled from California to Afghanistan in 1951 to oversee the construction of irrigation canals in parts of Helmand Province. Six
decades later, U.S. Marines would fight the Taliban in the same
places. *(From* Afghanistan Venture *by Paul Jones)*

"Little America" in Afghanistan

WHEREVER progress and a changing earth might beckon is home to the men and their families who make heavy construction their living. These are a people as cosmopolitan as their trade, for construction knows no boundaries. These are a people who forever are adopting new friends and new ways of life, then moving on. These are the missionaries of progress.

So it is, half-a-world away in Afghanistan, where a small group of American supervisors for Morrison-Knudsen Afghanistan, Inc., are directing the building of a broad series of dams and irrigation canals under the most extensive program of public works ever undertaken in the history of this ancient Asiatic kingdom (*The Em-Kayan*, April).

Before M-KA began setting up its national headquarters at Kandahar in 1946, only some 125 Americans had ever before visited the remote country in its entire history. Now, with their neat homes and gardens, the M-KA families have established themselves in Afghanistan with all the "temporary permanency" that construction families have anywhere. Their homes at Kandahar, as shown in the accompanying photographs, are well-built, oil-heated in the winter and air-conditioned in the summer. Single men are quartered in well-furnished barrack rooms. For the wives, what with the pleasant Afghanistan climate, it is a perennial race each spring to plant the most prolific and attractive gardens around their homes.

Despite being 12,000 miles away from the U.S., Em Kayans in Afghanistan have a full selection at the company commissary of familiar stateside canned and packaged goods. At the Afghan bazaars in Kandahar, housewives can supplement their menus with excellent fruits and melons that abound in Afghanistan. The country is predominantly agricultural, producing sizable quantities of such fruits, cereals and vegetables. The fat-tailed sheep furnishes the Afghans

ABOVE, panoramic view of part of the residential area of Em Kayans at Kandahar, showing their neat homes and pleasant yards. BELOW, Afghan musicians performing during entertainment for Em Kayans.

BELOW, formerly the palace of an Afghan king, this handsome structure serves as the Morrison-Knudsen Afghanistan, Inc., hospital at Kandahar.

11

A page from the May 1951 issue of the giant American construction firm Morrison-Knudsen's corporate magazine. The company was hired by the royal government in Kabul to dig irrigation canals and build two dams in a grand attempt to modernize southern Afghanistan.

Lawrence and Bettina Odle, whose father worked for an American development agency, lounge in the Lashkar Gah town pool with their mother, Helga, in 1956. It was the only pool in Afghanistan where men and women could swim together. The town also had the country's only coed high school. *(Courtesy of Bettina Odle Nordby)*

Abdul Kayeum, the vice president of Afghanistan's Helmand Valley Authority, and his American-born wife, Joan, relax with a bottle of wine inside their house in Lashkar Gah in 1966. The town, built in the style of an American subdivision, was home to the Americans who worked in Helmand and a few English-speaking Afghan families. Before long, Afghans began to call the town Little America. *(Courtesy of Bettina Odle Nordby)*

An Afghan soldier walks through the war-ravaged town of Now Zad in Helmand Province in 2010.

Brigadier General Larry Nicholson, center, the commander of the Second Marine Expeditionary Brigade, talks to Marine officers at Patrol Base Jaker on June 29, 2009, three days before the start of a major operation.

A canal in Helmand Province constructed by American engineers in the 1950s

General Stanley McChrystal, the top U.S. and NATO
commander in Afghanistan from June 2009 to June 2010
*(Nikki Kahn/*The Washington Post*)*

Marines cross an American-built canal in Nawa district in 2009.

President Obama meets with his war cabinet in the White House Situation Room on October 9, 2009, to discuss Stan McChrystal's request for additional forces. *(Pete Souza/The White House)*

Marines walk through a flattened bazaar in the town of Marja in February 2010. The destruction had been caused by a 2008 U.S. Special Operations raid and air strike.

Larry Nicholson and his political commissar, Kael Weston, talk next to a canal in Marja in February 2010.

Afghan president Hamid Karzai speaks to elders in Kandahar in April 2010.

Marine Lance Corporal Rick Centanni, who postponed college to deploy to Afghanistan, spent his days driving an eight-wheeled light armored vehicle in southern Helmand Province. *(Courtesy of Jon Centanni)*

Farmers in Nawa district participate in a canal-cleaning project funded by the U.S. Agency for International Development in 2010. Development experts criticized the agency for pouring too much money, too quickly, into southern Afghanistan.

Afghan border police chief Abdul Razziq was accused of rampant corruption and other crimes, but U.S. commanders decided to work closely with him because they needed his help to fight the Taliban and ensure safe passage for military supplies.

General David Petraeus, the top U.S. and NATO commander in Afghanistan from July 2010 to July 2011 *(U.S. Department of Defense)*

Summer Coish went to Kabul in 2010 to work for USAID but quickly grew frustrated with security restrictions that prevented her from interacting with Afghans outside the heavily fortified U.S. Embassy compound. *(Nad Photography)*

Doug Lute, the deputy national security advisor for Afghanistan and Pakistan *(U.S. Department of Defense)*

Carter Malkasian, the State Department representative in Helmand's Garmser district, was unusually effective because he—unlike most of his colleagues—learned to speak fluent Pashto and stayed in the field for two years.

Karl Eikenberry, the U.S. ambassador
to Afghanistan from June 2009 to July
2011 *(U.S. Department of Defense)*

Veteran diplomat Richard Holbrooke
was the Obama administration's special representative to Afghanistan and
Pakistan until his death in December
2010. *(U.S. Department of Defense)*

Taliban attacks claimed the lives of more than 100 British soldiers in Helmand's Sangin district from 2006 to 2010. In the fall of 2010, after Americans replaced the British in the district, 29 U.S. Marines were killed and 30 others lost both legs.

U.S. Army Brigadier General Ken Dahl sought to improve coordination with the State Department and USAID, but his overtures were rebuffed.

USAID mismanaged efforts to repair a hydropower station at the Kajaki Dam, which could have provided much-needed electricity to Kandahar, the country's second-largest city.

Marines walk through the bazaar in the town of Lakari in July 2011. About 225 Marines were stationed in and around Lakari, despite more pressing security concerns in other parts of Afghanistan.

Marines and had been personally asked by a senior general to serve in Afghanistan. But in almost every other way, the two men couldn't have been more different. Chretien was stout and salty-tongued. He chain-smoked Marlboro Reds and wore Tommy Bahama silk Hawaiian shirts. He was as conservative as Weston was liberal. After fifteen years working for the federal government and two terms serving as a state representative in New Hampshire, he had become senior counsel to a Republican-led congressional oversight committee where he had helped lead investigations into former president Bill Clinton's fund-raising. In Iraq, he had doled out cash to encourage Sunni tribesmen in Anbar province to rise up against al-Qaeda militants. In Afghanistan, he wanted to reintegrate former Taliban fighters, but with the insurgents showing little interest in laying down their arms, he moved on to other challenges. He helped organize the initial deployment of American and British civilians to Marja, and then he served as a political adviser to a Marine general, just as Weston had done with Larry Nicholson.

When Chretien was in his adviser incarnation, I accompanied him on a trip to Marja in May 2010 to observe how the civilians there were performing. There were five of them—one from State, two from USAID, one from the U.S. Department of Agriculture, and, because it was in Helmand, one stabilization adviser from the British Foreign and Commonwealth Office. Given the stakes in Marja—it was just a week after McChrystal's "bleeding ulcer" comment—they should all have been stars. One of the USAID men, a young New Englander, was indeed a model of dynamism and creativity. But the other USAID staffer seemed lost in the heat and dust. Chretien and I observed him one morning as he woke late and then did his laundry and puttered around. While he wandered the base, we chatted with a stream of residents who had come to see Haji Zahir, the ex-con district governor. One of them was the district health director, whom we peppered with questions about the state of Marja's clinics. That evening, we told the lost USAID officer about our conversation and asked him for his thoughts about the health director. He sheepishly admitted that he had

never met the man. In his three weeks in Marja, he had not yet
left the base, even though the Marines were driving and walking around every day.

When he returned to Camp Leatherneck, Chretien sent a
note to the embassy about the staffing problems in Helmand.
"It seems our best and brightest have burned out long ago and
we're getting the straphangers these days," he wrote. "Or as one
wag put it, 'they're just along for the chow.' No need to go into
details here—let's just say that there's enough deadwood here
that it's becoming a fire hazard."

The lost USAID worker left within a few months. And he
wasn't alone. Forty percent of U.S. government civilians who
were assigned to Helmand from July 2009 to June 2010 did
not last six months. The churn complicated efforts to increase
the number of civilians in the field. By late 2010, USAID was
hiring twenty new people a month to go to Afghanistan, but it
was losing seventeen.

It was not just rank-and-file civilians who did not acquit
themselves well. The Marines mocked Andrew Erickson, who
became the top State Department official in Helmand after
Weston and Chretien went home, for trying to win respect
by wearing his version of a uniform: polo shirts embroidered
with his name and title. His staff had other reasons to roll their
eyes. While everyone else was focused on Taliban infiltration,
he started his own war—against poor prose. He sent subordinates e-mails upbraiding them over grammatical mistakes in
memos:

> NEVER, NEVER, NEVER SAY: "He told Andrew and I."
> SAY: "He told Andrew and me." If he told me, he didn't
>   tell I. If he told us both, he told you and me. Or Tom
>   and me. Get it? People have this thing in their brains
>   but it's syntactically erroneous and it drives me
>   bananas. Also, he didn't give Andrew and I. He gave
>   me. And he gave Andrew and me. Got it?

His dealings with those around him could seem tone deaf.
In February 2011, Erickson, who had been State's deputy director for narcotics affairs in Bogotá before coming to Afghani-

stan, flew in two Colombian women for a twelve-day visit. He wanted them to share their views about the reintegration of FARC militants in their country. But they spoke no English, and no Marine battalion wanted to host them. Eventually Erickson sent the women to Kabul to hold workshops with Afghan officials. One of their initial meetings was with Farhadullah Farhad, the deputy director of the Afghan program to reconcile with insurgents. He listened to them talk through an interpreter for an hour before putting a stop to the session. "Our problems are very different," he said as he got up to leave. "But I love to hear the sound of Spanish."

Erickson's counterpart in Kandahar, Andrew Haviland, also dug trenches for himself. During his first meeting with Kandahar governor Tooryalai Wesa, Haviland boasted about how he had forged a close relationship with one of Wesa's predecessors, the strongman Gul Agha Sherzai, the longtime rival of the Karzai family. A little background reading would have revealed that Wesa hated Sherzai, who was constantly meddling in the province. Then Haviland lectured Wesa about the need to work with powerful tribal chieftains in Kandahar, though many other American officials had been urging the governor to do the opposite. Infuriated, Wesa threw Haviland out of his office. "I never want to see him here again," Wesa subsequently told a one-star Army general in Kandahar.

Haviland then proceeded to demolish his relationship with the military. Prior to his arrival, the top general in Kandahar had removed a chain-link fence between the military and civilian headquarters buildings on the Kandahar Airfield. But when the civilians moved into a new building fifty yards away, the regional security officer at the embassy in Kabul ordered that a new fence be erected. The gates were equipped with combination locks, and military officers on the general's command staff, who possessed higher-level security clearances than many of the civilians, assumed that they would get the code so they could easily interact with one another. But Haviland refused to divulge it. And he made his subordinates sign nondisclosure agreements subjecting them to sanctions if they shared the numbers. "Forget about everyone working together to fix Afghanistan. He wanted to be separate," one civilian who worked there told me. "It was not just embarrassing. It was idiotic."

Some thrived in the midst of the deadwood. One was in Garmser, the district south of Nawa along the Helmand River. His name was Carter Malkasian, but everyone there called him Carter Sahib. He was the only foreign official in the country who I ever heard widely referred to as a *sahib,* an Urdu salutation once used to address British colonial officials that Afghans employed as a term of honor and respect.

The adoration stemmed from his unfailing politeness (he greeted people in the traditional Pashtun way, holding their hands for several minutes as a series of welcomes and praises to God were exchanged), his willingness to take risks (he often traveled in an Afghan police pickup truck instead of in an American armored vehicle with a squad of Marines), and his command of Pashto, the language of southern Afghanistan (he conversed fluently, often engaging in rapid-fire debates with gray-bearded elders). He was the State Department's representative in Garmser, and his job description called for him to provide political advice to U.S. troops, mentor the fledgling Afghan government, and supervise reconstruction projects. But the rail-thin thirty-six-year-old forged his own marching orders, even if it meant bucking the State Department's rules—and that made him uncommonly effective.

Seeing his role as more a proconsul than an adviser, he single-handedly cajoled influential tribal leaders and mullahs to return to the district, correctly betting that their presence would lead others to follow. He won the trust of skeptical residents through countless meetings and roadside conversations, pressing them to reject the insurgency and support their government. He also shaped the Marine campaign in Garmser in a way no civilian had in other parts of the country. He served as a counselor to five successive battalion commanders, influencing decisions about when to use force and helping them calibrate it with a political engagement strategy. He built such credibility with the Marines that if he urged a different course of action than the one they were planning, they almost always complied. Larry Nicholson was among his biggest fans. He thought the Americans needed a Carter Malkasian in every district of Afghanistan.

Malkasian was not like most of the others selected by State and USAID. He asked to work in the field, not stay in Kabul. He lived in a trailer on a dusty forward operating base, and his meals consisted of whatever fare was being served to the grunts, if he wasn't eating goat with Afghans. What really set him apart was his desire to live in a remote district for two consecutive years—very few State personnel did that—and his tendency to flout the regional security officer's rules. He regularly ventured around the district with the police chief, putting his security in the hands of rifle-toting Afghans—a potential firing offense if his bosses in Kabul ever discovered it. "The only way the Afghans will trust you is if you show that you trust them," he told me.

When a mob of more than a thousand angry men descended upon a small U.S. outpost in January 2010 because of rumors that some Marines had desecrated a Koran, Malkasian walked out of the protected base to talk to the group. Placing himself in extreme danger, he sat down with the leaders, seeking to convince them that there was no truth to the allegation and that they had been whipped into a frenzy by Taliban propagandists. Even so, he promised to have the Afghan government investigate the claims. The leaders eventually relented and ordered those assembled to disperse.

Malkasian spent two hours every morning and an hour every evening studying Pashto, and he engaged interpreters on the base in conversation at every opportunity. The result was interaction with Afghans to a degree that almost no other American official in the south was capable of. During one of my trips to Garmser, two elders came to the district center to seek permission—and funding—to establish a team of armed men to defend their village from insurgents. Their first visit was not to the Marine battalion commander or the police chief but to Carter Sahib. Malkasian, whose soft-spoken manner belied fierce negotiating skills, knew his price before the meeting: He would give the elders authority for the village defenders if they committed to sending some of their men to the police academy in the capital of Helmand province, which would demonstrate a commitment to the government. The elders were reluctant.

"It's very dangerous where we are," one of them said.

"If it is that dangerous, then you need all the equipment the real police can bring," Malkasian shot back in Pashto, without the awkward pauses that are a feature of interpreted conversations.

"We do not have enough men to give to the police," the elder said. The other elder said he worried that any men they sent to the police would be deployed in other areas, which would not help their village.

Malkasian gripped the first elder's hand and looked into his eyes. "They may be taken to another place for an operation, but they will return," he said. "They will be trained well, and they will be part of the government."

His assurances did the trick. A few minutes later, all of them walked over to see Omar Jan, the police chief. A deal was struck: The elders pledged to send five men to the police academy in exchange for permission to set up a fifteen-man village defense force.

Many Afghans came to view Malkasian as a friend. He was not a uniformed Marine, nor was he a self-serving Afghan government official. And he never seemed to leave. He took just two and a half months of vacation in the almost two years he spent in Afghanistan, one of which was for the birth of his daughter. The State Department's leave policy allowed him to take almost twice as many days away, but he regarded it as bad form to be gone that long. Malkasian's skill in saying no also endeared him to Garmser residents. If someone interrupted him in the middle of a conversation, he did not ignore the offender or lecture him about proper meeting procedure. He would quote a Pashto proverb. "If your father owns the mill," he often said, "you still have to wait in line."

Malkasian had earned a doctorate in the history of war at Oxford, where his dissertation had focused on the Korean and Vietnam conflicts and why, as he put it, "people fight long, grueling wars." He spent his first year out of school teaching at Loyola Marymount University in Los Angeles. He seemed headed for a comfortable life as a professor when he talked to an uncle who had been a Navy doctor attached to a Marine battalion in Vietnam that had sustained the highest casualty rate in the war and had come to be known as the "Walking Dead." The uncle was on his deathbed, and he admonished Malkasian to experience war if he was going to write about it. Soon thereafter, he joined the Center for Naval Analysis, a military-affiliated think tank in Virginia that offered the opportunity to visit U.S. forces in the field. That led to an assignment in Kuwait as the Iraq War was commencing and then a yearlong posting with the Marines in Anbar province starting in 2004. He went back to Iraq in 2006, and the following year he spent five months on a provincial reconstruction team in eastern Afghanistan's Kunar province, where he got to engage directly with Afghans and work with fellow Americans in solving problems.

When the opportunity arose to return to Afghanistan in 2009, he put up his hand. Once selected, he made only one request. "I specifically asked for somewhere that would have fighting," he said. As soon as Nicholson and Weston heard Malkasian was headed to Afghanistan, they pulled strings to get him sent to Garmser, which was then the most intense battleground for the Marines. It was not an obvious assignment for a slightly nerdy war-zone academic, but his Iraq experience had convinced the Marines he could handle it.

Although those who had served in Iraq were sometimes loath to draw on their experiences and use them in Afghanistan—it was frowned upon because people too often took the wrong lessons—Malkasian had no reservations about applying what he had learned elsewhere. When the Taliban started targeting elders and government officials in Garmser, he decided not to remain uninvolved, as he had when similar killings had occurred in Anbar. Instead, he reached out to contacts in Lashkar Gah to ask them to encourage other elders to return to Garmser in a sign of defiance of insurgent intimidation. And he urged the police chief to travel around the district to reassure residents. "If an elder gets killed, you can't sit back and write about it," he said. "My job was to mobilize the people to stand up to the Taliban."

In his last weeks in Garmser, he repeatedly told residents that they would not be abandoned by the United States and that the Marines would not leave until the Afghan army and police were "very strong." But he could not make the same promise about the State Department. The embassy had told him that it had no plans to fill his position once he departed.

To Summer Coish, the biggest problem with the civilian surge wasn't the quality of the people. It was the lack of a plan.

Her repeated complaints about being assigned mindless work led the deputy director of the USAID mission to send her to the Kandahar Airfield in June 2010 to tackle a high-priority crisis. The Kandahar security operation was starting soon, and military commanders kept asking USAID's senior representative on the base for the agency's development strategy for the province. But USAID didn't have one. Coish's job was to work with a colleague to draft it.

Before she departed Kabul, she talked to Afghan development officials. The minister of rural development urged her to propose that USAID move its Kandahar office from the sealed-off base to the city so Afghans could interact with American reconstruction officials. She thought it was a great idea but knew it wouldn't fly—the embassy's security officer would never allow the office to be located off the base.

She assumed her bosses were exaggerating the lack of a strategy. There were probably documents that simply needed to be updated, she thought, and turned into a flashy Power-Point presentation. But when she got to Kandahar, all she found was a handful of reports written by contractors about agriculture, irrigation, and electricity challenges. "Not one of them was practical."

Coish's assignment was to identify longer-term development initiatives that could be implemented once the initial wave of day-labor projects and other quick-impact assistance efforts ended. She and her colleague met with USAID officials on the airfield, and they talked to military officers working on reconstruction projects. The two groups were focused on similar issues, and they weren't coordinating. And then she sought out Afghan development officials in Kandahar. They told her the Americans rarely consulted them.

In all of her discussions, nobody questioned the wisdom of pouring so many resources into building district-level administration. It seemed clear that there were not enough skilled people to fill the jobs, and there was no way the Kabul government would be able to afford the District Delivery Program bonuses once U.S. funding ended in 2014. And why were the Americans expending so much effort to create a local government center in Arghandab when residents could drive into Kandahar city in fifteen minutes? They headed into the city to shop, so why couldn't they do the same to see a judge?

Coish figured it would take four to five months to come up with a sound strategy. But two weeks after she arrived in Kandahar, she got a call from Kabul. "We need that strategy right away," she was told. Coish and her colleague rushed back and cobbled together a bare-bones presentation. They determined that agriculture was the primary driver of economic growth and recommended that USAID focus its resources on increasing farm production, processing crops into value-added products such as juices, and expanding export opportunities. It was all pretty obvious stuff, but she expected to return to Kandahar to flesh out an implementation plan. By then, though, the summertime exodus had begun in Kabul. All of USAID's senior directors left. The new team wasn't interested in finishing the strategy, and they told Coish she couldn't return to Kandahar. They needed warm bodies to fill the cubicles in Kabul.

Soon thereafter, she was asked to evaluate her job performance in Afghanistan. Coish had stayed so busy that she barely managed to get four hours of sleep a night, but when she tried to think of how she had helped the Afghan people—or her fellow Americans—"I couldn't come up with anything worthwhile that I had done."

10

Burn Rate

WHEN I RETURNED TO HELMAND in April 2010, Larry Nicholson told me to travel to Nawa again. "You have to see the change," he gushed. "It's a boomtown."

Walking through the bazaar there a few days later, I understood why he had wanted me to visit. Turbaned men—and a few burqa-clad women escorted by their husbands—thronged the chock-a-block strip of shops to gawk at, haggle over, and buy up imported merchandise that had never before been sold in Nawa: shiny motorcycles and modern mobile phones from China, recently released Bollywood video discs from India, and bolts of brightly colored cloth from Pakistan. I had assumed that Nawa, like the rest of southern Afghanistan, was dirt poor, but everyone seemed to have money to burn. Intrigued, I chatted with merchants offering modern wares. They were local farmers who had plowed their savings into their start-ups. Esmat Nanai had begun by purchasing one new 125 cc Pamir motorcycle in Lashkar Gah and bringing it back to Nawa to sell. He had used the proceeds from that first sale to buy two more. By the time I got there, he had a half dozen, each with an asking price of 43,000 Pakistani rupees—about $500. He said business was brisk. How, I asked, could the farmers of Nawa afford such costly items? Many of them, even small-scale poppy growers, would have been lucky to make that much money in a year after subtracting expenses. "The projects," Esmat said as he turned his attention to a prospective customer.

I received a fuller answer next door, at Nawa's new ice cream

parlor. The owner, Mahmud Wali, who could see the perspi-
ration on my forehead, beckoned me over, shouting, "It's the
season for ice cream!" He had set up four plastic tables under
an awning, each decorated with a bouquet of plastic flowers
and a two-liter bottle of impostor cola called Pebsi. Behind the
counter were a soft-serve machine and a freezer, and out back a
generator growled as it worked to keep his cream iced. He had
bought all of this with a small-business grant from the Marines
and a contribution from his brother, whose wallet was bulg-
ing after serving as a foreman on a series of USAID-funded
day-labor projects. Those projects had provided the seed capital for most of the new businesses and the money for residents
to go shopping. "Nawa has ice cream because of cash-for-work,"
he proclaimed.

The success in Nawa was being driven by AVIPA, the agricultural voucher program whose one-year budget had been
doubled to $300 million by Richard Holbrooke. It was car-
pet bombing the district with U.S. dollars. Residents received
generous handouts—shiny red tractors, hand tools, and water
pumps. They were "sold" bags of seed and fertilizer for a fraction of their retail cost. And while they waited for the crops
to germinate, they got paid to clear out reeds and muck from
irrigation canals. The day-labor opportunities were so plentiful that everyone who wanted a job could get one. International Relief & Development, the contractor hired by USAID
to implement the program, was on track to spend $30 million
in Nawa during the one-year program. That worked out to
$400 for every man, woman, and child in the district. Although
nobody had precise economic data, the infusion almost certainly tripled or quadrupled the local economy.

Cleaning ditches became as lucrative as serving as a Taliban
gun for hire, and it was far safer. Unlike neighboring Marja,
where insurgent attacks were a daily occurrence, the ready
availability of employment kept Nawa largely free of violence.
It also provided an economic jolt that went well beyond the
bazaar. New brick factories appeared on fields near the district center to meet the demand from people who wanted to
expand their homes. Traders from Pakistan began plying the
main road to hawk housewares and electronics. Residents who

had fled began returning to avail themselves of the massive U.S.-funded stimulus. The acronym AVIPA quickly entered the Pashto lexicon in Nawa, and it stood for free money. "AVIPA is a very, very good program," said the district governor, Abdul Manaf. "The result has been great."

AVIPA seemed to be a wonder drug. Everyone was thrilled—residents, the district governor, the Marines, and USAID officials. Everyone except Scott Dempsey and Ian Purves, the two Western civilians who knew the most about reconstruction in Nawa. They made up the district stabilization team, and they saw a dark side to the cash surge. Already it was fueling tensions and rivalries within the community, and they predicted more vexing problems: The seed distribution was going to generate far more crops than farmers would be able to sell, and the plentiful day labor was raising public expectations for assistance that the Afghan government would not be able to meet once American contributions inevitably ebbed. The ice cream and motorcycle shops were great, but AVIPA was too focused on immediate gratification. It was doing little to build an agricultural economy that would generate lasting income to maintain those establishments. Before long, they reasoned, the district would face a steep decline.

Dempsey was an unlikely critic. As a USAID field officer, he represented an agency that had become obsessed with spending, despite its initial reservations about Holbrooke's expansion of the AVIPA budget. The officials running USAID in the early days of the Obama administration soon recognized that the best way to demonstrate progress to Congress and avoid the wrath of the State Department was to burn through its budget. Dempsey's bosses wanted him to look on approvingly as International Relief & Development contractors dumped money into the district—and that would have been the sensible thing for him to do if he had wanted a career in the agency. But the twenty-six-year-old Dempsey had a more nuanced view. He had grown up in a middle-class, Irish Catholic family in Buffalo that didn't squander money. He had enlisted in the Marine reserves right after the September 11, 2001, attacks, and upon graduating from the University of Maryland, he had gone to Fallujah in 2005 as part of a civil affairs detachment that had worked on reconstruction projects and compensated Iraqis for property damaged in the fighting but also sought not to upend the local economy with American payouts. He understood that cash was an important weapon of war but that, like any weapon, it had to be deployed judiciously.

While in Fallujah, he had become fast friends with Kael Weston, who lived on the same base he did and shared his liberal politics. When Dempsey had returned to New York, he'd worked on Eliot Spitzer's gubernatorial campaign, and then he joined the William J. Clinton Foundation, where he was an aide to the former president. In 2008, he quit to ride his bike from Buffalo to Seattle. When Obama won the presidency, Dempsey knew that more Americans would be headed to Afghanistan. He sought to join them, to do something patriotic and put the skills he'd acquired in Fallujah to use. But he didn't want to be a grunt. He applied for a job at USAID, and when he said he was willing to join the Marines in Helmand, the agency happily fast-tracked his paperwork. In July 2009, he boarded a helicopter to Patrol Base Jaker. When he landed, a Marine major introduced himself and told Dempsey, "You're the DST"—the district stabilization team.

USAID didn't have a plan for him. He was the first member of the civilian surge to arrive in Helmand. His superiors told him to work with Purves, a stabilization adviser employed by the British government, and assist the Marines with reconstruction activities, but they gave him no budget or specific responsibilities.

Then came AVIPA. It was meant to be the principal USAID effort to support the military's new counterinsurgency operations in the south. Dempsey initially regarded it as America's first and best chance to ensure that the security gains in Nawa would last. The Americans would win over residents and give them a shot at a better life.

In the fall of 2009, an International Relief & Development site manager came to Nawa to explain the program to Dempsey and Purves. The manager said the firm planned to spend almost $30 million in the district, $18 million of which would be devoted to day-labor projects. Dempsey and Purves looked at each other in disbelief. It was a tsunami of money.

Dempsey tried to object, but the manager wasn't interested. "It's our job to spend this," he said.

Under the terms of International Relief & Development's agreement with USAID, the $300 million had to be spent in one year. Holbrooke expected projects to commence across Helmand and Kandahar, and he wanted the work to focus on helping farmers grow new crops and get them to market. But only a few districts in the provinces were deemed safe enough by USAID for reconstruction. Instead of scaling back the program, the agency directed International Relief & Development to spend more money in the few places it could. And that meant lots of day labor, because it was the fastest way to shovel money out the door.

Although Dempsey worked for USAID, he lacked the authority to shape the program in Nawa. That power rested with an USAID bureaucrat at the Kandahar Airfield who had no background in farming. And even her ability to mold the work was limited: To get the projects started quickly, the agency gave International Relief & Development the $300 million under a "cooperative agreement" instead of issuing a contract to do the work, which would have taken longer. A cooperative agreement limits the government's ability to dictate changes once a project starts.

But Dempsey refused to remain an idle observer. When the firm started paying laborers $6 a day instead of the $5 it had promised—in an attempt to maximize spending that risked creating further distortions in the local economy—he complained so vociferously that his boss went to Helmand's governor and asked him to intervene with the company. But even a wage of $5 a day caused problems. At one point that fall, schools in the district suddenly closed. Teachers had become day laborers because the pay was better.

The push to spend money inevitably led to dubious projects and waste. In Kandahar, farmers were given far more handouts than they needed, according to a confidential evaluation conducted by an agricultural adviser working for International Relief & Development. "Instead of distributing one package of seeds and fertilizer per farmer, those who could be found ended up walking away with six packages, perhaps more than any one individual could possibly contemplate planting," the evaluation stated. The farmers who hit the jackpot took tons of seed and scores of free tractors to neighboring Pakistan and sold them for cash. In Helmand, fears of oversaturation were realized: The firm gave away so many watermelon seeds, and farmers grew so many of them, that the price of watermelons plummeted. Some farmers actually threw their watermelons away. In Nawa, the company gave out bags and bags of corn seed in the spring of 2010, even though farmers usually had no trouble acquiring them from local merchants. When Dempsey had arrived the previous summer, the district's fields had been blanketed with ten-foot-tall cornstalks.

The seed distributions paled in comparison to an imbroglio over water pumps. International Relief & Development spent several million dollars to buy thousands of gasoline-operated pumps, which it planned to give away to farmers across central Helmand. But when provincial leaders got word of the plan, they howled. The pumps, they argued, would suck the canals down to the mud, leaving farmers downstream high and dry. Since the pumps couldn't be returned, they were left in warehouses to gather dust.

The cash-burning venture that riled Dempsey most was the distribution of metal frames and plastic sheeting so farmers could assemble small, greenhouse-like tunnels in their fields in which to grow vegetables during the winter. It was a smart idea, but by the time the material was ready to pass out in Nawa, farmers had already planted their winter crops. Dempsey wanted to cancel the distribution, but International Relief & Development insisted on doling out the goods. Much of the material went to waste, although a few creative farmers turned the plastic sheeting into windows. He wrote yet another missive to his bosses: "I'm concerned that dollars spent is the metric for AVIPA's success without fully ground truthing each district's specific needs." But once again he was told to back down. "There were plenty of people at AID who knew it was a stupid program, but nobody wanted to rock the boat," he told me later. "Nobody wanted to stand up to Washington."

William Slocum, a senior program officer at International Relief & Development, insisted to me that AVIPA was effective.

He said the program had provided 5.4 million days of labor to unemployed men and generated an estimated $200 million in additional income for farmers across the south. But he also admitted it had been too much money for too small an area in too short a time. "Trying to spend $300 million in one year was not realistic," he said.

Although Dempsey found the waste galling, he was more concerned about the culture of dependency that the handouts were fostering. Most of the day-labor projects involved clearing irrigation canals and drainage ditches constructed during the Little America days. Before AVIPA, farmers had dredged the waterways themselves while they waited for their crops to mature. It was part of the unofficial social contract in the irrigated lands of southern Afghanistan: Neighbors helped one another maintain the arteries that sustained their farmland. By giving money to farmers to do what they had previously done for free, Dempsey believed, International Relief & Development was destroying the social fabric of Nawa. In Kandahar province, Governor Tooryalai Wesa, who holds a doctorate in agricultural economics, was livid when he heard that the firm was paying farmers in Arghandab district to prune their pomegranate trees. "In my childhood, everyone was cleaning the canals. They were pruning their trees. Nobody was paying them," Wesa huffed to me. "IRD is killing the culture here."

In Nawa, the most dependent resident was the district governor, Abdul Manaf, a stout and garrulous former mayor of Lashkar Gah who was seeking to rehabilitate himself after being accused of corruption. Manaf's strategy was simple: He positioned himself as the front man for America's largesse. He happily announced the day-labor projects and the seed handouts. It thrilled the Marines and USAID. They figured that locals would think their government was finally helping them.

None of it fooled Nawa residents. They knew the Americans were paying for it and Manaf was their stooge. But they were willing to embrace Manaf if the cash flowed. So he kept asking the Marines and USAID to spend. Whenever he wanted something, he went to the Americans, even when it was something as trivial as a new fabric awning for stalls in the market. Although for centuries Afghans had fashioned shades out of straw, the Marines agreed to pay for fancy fabric because they didn't want to disappoint Manaf. I asked him once why he didn't ask his own government for help. He laughed. "The government in Kabul doesn't do anything for us," he said. "The people here support me and Governor Mangal. We should give them something in return."

Unlike in most other government buildings in Afghanistan, there was no portrait of President Karzai on the whitewashed walls of Manaf's office. Instead, he displayed a photograph with Bill McCollough, the initial Marine battalion commander in the district. Marine officers loved it, but the Afghan government soon wrote off Nawa as an American enclave and began channeling its resources elsewhere. When the principal of a high school in the district asked the provincial department of education for notebooks for his pupils, he was told to seek them from the Marines.

The only thing Manaf could not get, though he tried repeatedly, was the opportunity to host Dempsey for a sleepover. With his broad shoulders, brilliant smile, and sandy hair, Dempsey was an attractive fellow. Women did double takes when he walked through the embassy compound. He was flattered by Manaf's overtures, but he was not interrested in an overweight, fiftyish Afghan district chief whose beard dripped with grease from his dinner. His designs were on a fetching female USAID staffer at the Kandahar Airfield.

Dempsey eventually got the girl, but he never got USAID to change its approach to development. Instead of focusing on short-term projects—USAID called it "stabilization"—he wanted to do with reconstruction dollars what Kael Weston thought should be done with troop levels: a go-long strategy. Dempsey believed AVIPA funds should have been spread out over ten years and aimed at helping farmers transition to growing fruits, nuts, and other crops that would have improved the quality of their lives. "It would have made far more sense," he said, "but it was politically untenable."

The cash spigot was in Washington. Afghan reconstruction funds ballooned to $4.1 billion for the fiscal year beginning in October 2009, and much of it was earmarked for USAID, which was eager to spend every penny. If USAID didn't use all of its budget, it would have a difficult time asking Congress for as much—or more—the next year. In Kabul, USAID officials assiduously tracked their "burn rate." In mid-2010, they were thrilled when it reached $340 million per month. The figure became a point of pride and was mentioned repeatedly in internal meetings as a sign of progress.

To maintain the spending, USAID needed more programs that were as large as AVIPA. It authorized a $600 million effort to improve municipal governments across the country that required the contractor it chose to implement "performance-based" budgeting systems within two years, a complicated accountability rubric that even most U.S. cities did not have. There was a $140 million initiative to help settle property disputes—widely regarded as a primary source of local conflicts—by training Afghans to appraise and value land. The agency also planned to spend $475 million to help reconstruct areas in the wake of counterinsurgency operations, $450 million for an agriculture follow-up to AVIPA, $225 million for a clean-water program, and $750 million for increasing electricity production.

The reliance on massive projects meant sacrificing Holbrooke's desire to direct much of the money through Afghan government ministries and local aid organizations. Most of the new work would have to go to giant American development contractors that could employ lots of people and spend lots of money quickly. Of course, many of those hired were not Afghans but Americans and other foreigners, who commanded steep salaries, ample rest breaks, and comfortable accommodations. They also required protection. Under the new programs, thousands of private security guards descended upon Afghanistan and sucked up a large portion of the reconstruction budget. A senior USAID official told me that security, management, and overhead costs had grown to almost 70 percent of the value of most contracts by late 2010. That meant only 30 cents on the dollar was going to help the Afghans.

In many cases, the real figure was even less. The big development firms relied on layers of subcontractors, each of which took a cut. Bribes had to be paid, sometimes to government officials and sometimes to the Taliban. Handing out cash to insurgents to keep them from attacking projects was a common practice. The contractors cared more about finishing their work—and getting paid—than about keeping their funds out of enemy hands. The government payouts were equally disturbing. Instead of demanding large wads of bills, local chieftains sought to control the flow of business and money. In Kandahar, contractors working for USAID and the NATO military command were forced to rely on subcontractors—for security, transportation, construction, and other services—that were linked via patronage networks to the extended Karzai family or its principal rival, former governor Gul Agha Sherzai. The linkages were often not apparent to American contracting officers cloistered at the USAID compounds in Kabul and the Kandahar Airfield. Some of the connections were revealed by a military task force starting in late 2010, but by then millions and millions of dollars had flowed through those corrupt networks. Much of the money wound up in the gleaming desert metropolis of Dubai, parked in bank accounts of Afghan politicians and warlords, out of the reach of U.S. authorities.

Some USAID staffers and contractors tried, as Dempsey did, to warn their superiors about the dangers of pumping so much money into Afghanistan. Others quietly seethed. They knew USAID officials would not take kindly to the criticism. They figured that trying to work within the system to help Afghans was better than getting blackballed.

Before long, alarming reports began arriving at USAID's Washington headquarters. One involved another project run by International Relief & Development—a $500 million initiative to construct 1,500 kilometers of all-weather gravel roads in the south and east. The goal, as described by USAID, was to "increase stability and security in these areas by facilitating trade, improving access to goods and services, and fostering interdependence between neighboring villages and provinces." After the firm had spent $270 million, USAID discovered that only 160 kilometers of roads had been built to international standards. Agency leaders in Washington were aghast that staff in the field had not sounded the alarm sooner. "It was galling," the senior USAID official told me. "We needed a contracting officer who had been around long enough to know this was bullshit."

In January 2010, three weeks before the Marines pushed into Marja, Colonel Randy Newman, one of Larry Nicholson's subordinate commanders, asked his staff to organize a briefing about agriculture in the district with the smartest guy they could find. The call went to Wes Harris, a sturdy, mustachioed agricultural extension agent from southeastern Georgia who was the U.S. Department of Agriculture representative at Nicholson's headquarters at Camp Leatherneck. He found himself in Helmand because Richard Holbrooke had prodded Agriculture Secretary Tom Vilsack to send farming specialists to Afghanistan. When the Agriculture Department had advertised the jobs, Harris had applied. Although the fifty-six-year-old had spent years assisting farmers on behalf of the University of Georgia and had regularly traveled to Washington to help the Agriculture Department draft the annual Farm Bill, he did not have any overseas experience. He didn't speak Pashto or know much about Afghan history. But when he talked to farmers—with the aid of an interpreter—they quickly found common ground. Harris had dirt under his fingernails. He knew more about farming than any USAID officer in Afghanistan, and because the soil and climate in Helmand were similar to those of southern Georgia, he had a keen sense of what would—and wouldn't—grow in the province.

Colonel Newman, a rangy infantryman who wore large glasses, had grown alarmed by satellite images indicating that Marja was blanketed with poppy, and he asked Harris for his thoughts on alternative crops. Harris had assembled twenty-one slides to illustrate his talk for the colonel and his senior staff, but it was the fifth one that piqued Newman's interest. Harris listed the income farmers made on a hectare of land from different crops, after the costs of seed, fertilizer, labor, and taxes were subtracted. Poppy, of course, was the most lucrative. But the closest competitor was a surprise to everyone in the room. It was cotton.

"Why aren't we doing that?" asked Newman, who had grown up on a farm in Indiana.

Harris had been in Afghanistan for only a month. He had not yet visited the cotton gin in Lashkar Gah or heard of Dick Scott's travails seven years earlier. "I think this is one of the ways forward," he said.

A USAID representative at the meeting reported Harris's comments to agency officials. An hour later, USAID sent an e-mail to Newman asserting that cotton was not a viable substitute for poppy because the government-run gin had lost $3 million in 2008. The claim seemed fishy to Harris. Based on the numbers he had crunched, there was no way the gin could have hemorrhaged that much money. Cotton was at record prices on the world market. There were also forty small, privately owned gins across the province. If cotton was so unprofitable, why did it interest so many local businessmen? He didn't have access to the gin's books to see for himself. But his subsequent conversations with USAID officials revealed what Scott had learned in the first years of the war: The agency hated cotton.

It wasn't until September—eight months later and well after the window to plant cottonseed that year—that Harris saw the spreadsheet that had provided the basis for the $3 million claim. It had been assembled by Rory Donohoe, the top USAID official in Helmand, who was not an agriculture expert. Harris soon spotted the problem: In converting expenses per kilogram to pounds, Donohoe had multiplied by 2.2 instead of dividing. And then Harris found another error: Donohoe had based his calculations on the world price for ginned lint cotton, not unginned seed cotton, which was how the gin compensated farmers—a mistake that had inflated costs by a factor of three. Harris was livid. The most viable alternative to poppy had been torpedoed by USAID because of a couple of flawed calculations. Was USAID so incompetent that nobody in the bureaucracy could recognize two simple mistakes? Harris wondered. Or was the agency playing fast and loose with the data to justify its long-standing aversion to cotton?

Either way, Harris figured he had his trump card. He identified the mistakes in an e-mail to the top Agriculture Department official at the embassy and waited for word that USAID was rescinding its opposition. Instead, USAID fired back with new arguments. Cotton requires too much water. Not so, said

Harris. Pakistan and Uzbekistan grow cotton more efficiently, and the competition would make it difficult for the Afghans to export their crop. "Who cares?" Harris responded. "It's something they know how to grow, and they're good at it." Afghan weavers and cloth merchants wanted to buy much of the gin's output; and, he noted, if foreign competition was so stiff, why were so many Pakistani buyers seeking Afghan cotton every year? USAID tried to argue that Afghan cotton was of inferior quality. Harris shipped samples back to the United States for analysis at the University of Georgia. Helmand cotton, he learned, "is as good as the cotton we produce."

When USAID claimed that cotton required government subsidies, he refrained from asking, "If we do it, why can't they?" World cotton prices were high enough to make the crop profitable without any help from Kabul. The only handout the farmers expected was minor—just free seeds from the processed cotton. There was also the potential for microcredit: In the 1970s, the gin had provided farmers with cash advances so they could buy fertilizer; the money had been deducted from their payments when they brought in their bales. To Harris, there was no defensible economic argument against cotton.

Practical considerations also weighed in cotton's favor. All those melons and vegetables that farmers were growing with cut-rate AVIPA seeds had to be transported to markets before they spoiled. But most farmers didn't own trucks. They had to rent or borrow tractors and carts—if any were available—and then they had to hope that on the rutted dirt roads from their farms to the bazaars, their melons didn't turn into juice. Cotton needed no such tender care. Once picked, it could sit on farms for months. And there was no way to damage it, no matter how bad the roads. Harvesting cotton, like poppy, was labor intensive, providing employment for the same idle local men coveted by Taliban recruiters.

"We looked at cotton from every angle," Harris said. "It just made sense."

Finally USAID raised the Bumpers Amendment, the law that forbids the use of U.S. funds to help foreign cotton producers. Once again Harris had a rejoinder. The amendment, he

insisted, prohibits only activities that affect American exporters. "You cannot tell me that Afghan cotton is going to have
any significant impact on U.S. exports," he argued.

USAID still refused to help. But Harris would not give
up. He persuaded a Defense Department task force seeking
to improve Afghanistan's economy to purchase new parts
for the gin, and he persuaded the Marines—with Newman's
encouragement—to help farmers transport their cotton to
the gin for processing. The Marines even used their discretionary funds to buy a machine to compress cotton bales so
farmers could fit more into their tractor carts. The assistance
helped the gin restart in October 2010—it had been shuttered
for all of the previous year—and process five hundred tons
of cotton. Although it was a fraction of the plant's capacity,
the activity attracted the attention of farmers across the province. Afghans knew the value of cotton. The Pashto word for
it—*spinzar*—means "white gold."

With its antediluvian machinery, bloated workforce, and
cryptic accounting system, the gin was far from a model enter-
prise. The Ministry of Commerce and Industry, which owned
the facility, decided how much cotton it would buy from
farmers—and at what price—based on bids it received from
buyers before the growing season began. To Harris, this was
a backward system that didn't encourage farmers to blanket
their fields with cotton, but it was the product of necessity. The
gin lacked the capital to buy first and sell later; it was forced to
limit its purchases to what it was sure to sell.

Harris thought USAID's insistence that the gin be privatized
before it received American help was unrealistic. The ministry
was not inclined to sell a factory that brought the government
money, even if a pittance. Either the Americans could sit on
their hands and watch Afghans return to poppy, or they could ·
help generate more money for farmers and the cash-strapped
government in Kabul. To Harris it seemed an obvious choice.

He wanted to provide the gin with $1 million to expand
its purchases from farmers. With that kind of buying power,
he said, "all of northern Marja would have turned white" and
one-eighth of the farmland across the province would have

been covered with cotton. He imagined the gin operating at capacity, with convoys of trucks rolling up to collect processed bales.

The Marines loved his vision, but they couldn't swing a $1 million loan. Their discretionary funds from the Pentagon, which were intended to build schools and roads, had no provision for that level of assistance to an established factory. The one organization that had money for such projects was USAID. A million dollars was a rounding error in the overall AVIPA budget. But by then Harris knew there was no way the agency would help the gin.

"Everything was there to make it work except for a basic understanding of agriculture by AID's supposed experts," he grumbled upon his return to Georgia. "They cost us a huge opportunity."

President Obama's strategy depended upon the civilian experts at USAID making smart decisions to help the Afghans. But the agency kept making mistakes. Sometimes the cause was bureaucratic inertia. Sometimes it was a staffer who put his personal agenda over the national interest. The result was a gross failure to capitalize on security improvements, paid for by the lives and limbs of American troops, to build a sustainable economy for the farmers of southern Afghanistan.

Allies at War

AMERICAN MARINES AND BRITISH civilian advisers were waging two wars in the hilly northern half of Helmand province by mid-2010: They were fighting the Taliban—and each other.

The quarreling among the allies began with the arrival that spring of more Marine surge forces, but the tension had its roots in the summer of 2006, when British commanders had decided to establish platoon-sized outposts in the districts of Sangin and Musa Qala that the Taliban quickly besieged and nearly overran. Although the British response in each district was different, the outcome was similar. The following years were grim.

In Musa Qala, the first wave of British soldiers almost ran out of ammunition after three months of harrowing combat to fend off near-daily attempts to storm their platoon house. With no easy way to resupply them—it was too risky to drive convoys or fly dual-rotor Chinooks, the only helicopters the British had—desperate commanders accepted a dubious offer from a tribal leader in the district: If British troops would leave, the leader said, so would the insurgents, whereupon residents would take charge of security. The British departed the only way they could—in a convoy of local freight trucks.

The truce was short-lived, and by the following February, hundreds of Taliban fighters had recaptured the area, prompting the British, aided by the U.S. Army's 82nd Airborne Division, to conduct a massive operation in late 2007 to wrest back control of the district center. They succeeded in pushing the

Taliban out of town. Then the British stopped. They established front lines about four miles north and south of the town
center; everything beyond was insurgent country. President
Karzai, with the agreement of the British, appointed as district
governor a former Taliban commander, Mullah Salam, in an
attempt to reintegrate insurgents into peaceful society. But
only a few switched sides. The commander turned governor
proved to be mercurial and corrupt, and his drug-addled militia ran roughshod over the area's residents. Even so, British
military and civilian officials deemed the center of Musa Qala
stable. Life within the security bubble began returning to normal. Shops and schools reopened, and policemen came back
to work.

Sangin never rebounded. There was no deal to be made
there, so British commanders sent more forces. Still, they did
not have the manpower to establish a decisive advantage.
The insurgents set up bomb-making factories in a valley that
hugged the headwaters of the Helmand River and they struck
an informal mutual defense pact with drug barons who ran
a network of opium-processing labs in hillside hamlets. The
British commanders made matters worse by spreading their
troops across several small outposts along the valley, condemn-
ing them to a Sisyphean mission: They would clear insurgents
from small parts of the district, but then they had to move on.
The Taliban would seize them back, forcing the Brits to attack
the same areas again and again. Sangin's lush wheat fields and
dense poppy groves soon became killing fields. From 2006 to
2010, Taliban bombs and bullets in the district claimed the
lives of more than a hundred British troops—about a third of
the country's total war dead in that period.

Soon after the Musa Qala truce fell apart, the top U.S. and
NATO commander at the time, General Dan McNeill, told a
visiting American official that the British had "made a mess
of things in Helmand." In January 2009, Helmand's governor,
Gulab Mangal, made a brief visit to Sangin, where he discovered that insurgents were operating with impunity no more
than five hundred meters from the district center. Mangal was
incensed when British troops told him it wasn't safe to venture

to the bazaar—or anywhere farther than two hundred meters from the main British encampment. "Stop calling it the Sangin District and start calling it the Sangin Base. All you have done here is build a military camp next to the city," he complained. Mangal grew even angrier when the Afghan army commander in Sangin and the district governor told him that British troops "were searching compounds, walking on the roofs of homes, and treating the local population badly—including pointing weapons at people and going into areas where women were working," according to a U.S. State Department cable describing the visit.

The dissatisfaction with the British extended up to Kabul. In a November 2008 meeting with U.S. Ambassador Bill Wood, Foreign Minister Rangin Dadfar Spanta expressed disappointment that British troops did not fight as aggressively as American forces. A month later, Karzai questioned the effectiveness of the British during a meeting with senators John McCain, Joe Lieberman, and Lindsey Graham. He related an anecdote about a woman from Helmand who had asked him to "take the British away and give us back the Americans." Wood put it even more bluntly in a note to Defense Secretary Gates: "We and Karzai agree the British are not up to the task of securing Helmand."

British officials insisted that their problems in the province stemmed from a lack of manpower. Unlike the Canadians, who ceded parts of Kandahar province to the Americans in 2009 only grudgingly, British commanders were eager to give up responsibility for large swaths of Helmand. Their efforts in and around the Iraqi city of Basra were widely regarded as a fiasco, and top officials in Whitehall were petrified that Helmand would turn out the same way without American assistance. But to avoid losing face, the Ministry of Defense wanted a discreet bailout. The British sought a few thousand U.S. troops to help in the central and northern parts of the province. That would allow the British to hand off Garmser and Nawa and avoid dealing with Marja. They would concentrate on Lashkar Gah, the Little America community of Nad Ali, and the northern districts of Musa Qala and Sangin. The British also insisted on retaining control of the reconstruction office in Lashkar Gah, which took its orders from the Foreign Office in London, not the NATO headquarters in Kabul.

The decision to send the hard-charging Marines to Helmand instead of Kandahar upended British hopes for a delicate balance between the allies. Once Larry Nicholson's brigade arrived, there were more Americans than British in the province. Nicholson understood that the British were sensitive about needing an American rescue, and he sought to minimize friction. He met regularly with his British counterpart, and he welcomed a talented British diplomat to serve as a political adviser alongside Kael Weston. But Nicholson quickly grew irritated with the British approach to countering the insurgency. He abhorred the establishment of front lines that they did not cross, and he recoiled when he saw how Afghan soldiers were segregated in camps on British bases. He told his Marines that COIN required genuine partnership, not a vestigial colonial attitude toward the natives, and that meant eating and living together. What riled him the most, however, was the British reconstruction team. The team's members had their own views about which parts of the province merited military attention, and those did not always mesh with Nicholson's. That was to be expected, because the British had been trying to triage a shorthanded mission for three years. But the United States had injected 10,672 Marines into Helmand, and Nicholson wanted the voting rights that came with being a majority shareholder.

Tensions flared during the Marines' first operation—the push into Nawa, Garmser, and Khan Neshin. The Brits thought it was a fool's errand to travel deep into the Desert of Death and conduct a full-scale counterinsurgency mission in Khan Neshin. They voiced their objections to Nicholson, but he was unmoved. What mattered to him was that Governor Mangal wanted the Marines to head there. When State Department official Marc Chretien visited the reconstruction office two months after the operation commenced, feelings still were raw.

"Your Marines seem to have exceeded the ops plan," a British lieutenant colonel told him.

"Well, of course," Chretien replied. "They're Marines. They're dogs of war. It's what they do."

Chretien had been stationed in Iraq before Afghanistan. When he had informed a three-star British general who was visiting Anbar province that he was heading to Helmand, the general had said, "We want a marriage with you Yanks in Helmand, not a date rape." Chretien took the request to heart, and he repeated the quote to Colonel Mike Killion, Nicholson's top operations officer, before a meeting they had with the head of the reconstruction office in September 2009. Killion was an expletive-spewing, linebacker-sized Marine with a tin of snuff in his pocket who oversaw the brigade's daily combat missions. When his watch officer announced that Marines were in a TIC—troops in contact—he jumped up and became a wartime conductor, barking and gesticulating orders in his vast combat operations center, which was filled with Marines hunched over laptops and large video screens displaying live feeds from Predator drones. When all was quiet in the desert, he stewed in his plywood-walled office like a caged animal.

"Check," Killion said to Chretien as they walked in to meet with Hugh Powell, an Oxford-educated diplomat who ran the reconstruction office and was supposed to be of equal rank to Nicholson and the British general in the province. Powell, dressed in a pressed blue cotton shirt, had called the meeting to complain about a Taliban facilitator who had been detained by the Marines. The British insisted that he had switched his allegiance to the Afghan government. The Marines were skeptical. The man was on NATO's Joint Prioritized Effects List, the compendium of top insurgents to be killed or captured. It seemed to the Marines that the British were simply trying to free the man because he was one of their informers.

The meeting began with a series of pleasantries and then a bit of history. "Helmand was an idyllic place," Powell said, "and then you Marines arrived."

Killion believed the province had been overrun by the Taliban because of British appeasement. "Look, buddy, it's not hard to be idyllic if you're sitting on your ass," he growled. "We're here to win."

The meeting degenerated. So did the relationship. When the Marines pushed into Now Zad that December, Powell's succes-

sor, Lindy Cameron, refused to provide the same sort of reconstruction resources accorded to other districts in the province
because she didn't think it made sense to try to rebuild an
abandoned city. "They stiffed us," Nicholson seethed to me at
the time. "So much for all of us being on the same team."

Cameron had a legitimate argument, but the Marines didn't
want to hear it. They had written off the reconstruction office
as hopelessly disconnected from the war, a view that was reinforced by the frequent parties and social events that occurred
on the office's compound in Lashkar Gah. It wasn't as wild as
the U.S. Embassy in Kabul, but Nicholson's officers were never-
theless incredulous when they learned that the office had held
an alcohol-sodden "Lash Vegas Pimps and Hos" bash while the
Marines were struggling to pacify Marja.

Disagreements also erupted in Musa Qala after Marines
replaced British soldiers in early 2010. Within forty-eight
hours, the Americans had punched beyond the northern front
line and seized a town that had long been a Taliban stronghold.
Then Marine units began targeting insurgents well beyond the
old southern line. The Marines also leaned on the provincial
governor to replace Mullah Salam. "They didn't pursue the Taliban," the Marine commander in the district, Lieutenant Colonel Michael Manning, said of the British. "We'll go after them."

When I visited Musa Qala in July 2010, Manning made little
effort to conceal his frustration with the pace at which representatives from the reconstruction office were rebuilding the
area. Musa Qala's grand mosque, which had been destroyed in
the 2007 military operation, was supposed to have been fixed
two years earlier. It remained a giant hole in the ground. The
British had also pledged to construct a bridge over a riverbed
that floods every winter, forcing people to rely on ferries. "They
were here for four years," another Marine officer said as we
gazed over the still bridgeless river. "What did they do?"

Manning and I stepped into his office—it was a cell in a
former Taliban prison that had been turned into a base by the
British. He opened a trunk and pulled out a wooden sign on
which was scrawled, PROMISE EVERYTHING, DELIVER NOTHING.
Manning said he had found it in an encampment that British
military engineers had vacated.

British officials insisted that construction of the mosque and the bridge had been delayed because they had been teaching the Afghan government how to take charge of such projects itself. "The U.S. approach is focused on getting it done. Our focus is on building up the government to deliver," a British government official in Helmand told me. "The process is more important to us than to the Americans."

The British method also did not sit well with the Afghans, particularly Governor Mangal. Leaders of the reconstruction team wanted him to be a success—he was, after all, the Afghan face of their governance efforts—and they provided the provincial administration with a degree of assistance that far exceeded what American-run reconstruction offices did in other parts of the country. They even paid for his security detail and the costs of running his office because he received only a minuscule budget from Kabul. In exchange, they sought behind-the-scenes control that he found belittling. He had a difficult relationship with Powell, and matters only got worse when Cameron arrived. "She'd try to direct him and tell him what to do in front of other Pashtun males," said one U.S. diplomat who observed her interactions. "It crossed a line."

Mangal saw the Marines differently. Not only did Nicholson treat him with deference, but the Americans had manpower and firepower the British lacked, and they were willing to plant the flag in places such as Khan Neshin and Now Zad that the British had written off. "The Brits had bear-hugged Mangal so tightly that they almost suffocated him, but he knew who had the muscles," said Kael Weston. "Mangal couldn't get enough of the Marines."

The disputes between the allies soon expanded beyond who controlled the reconstruction agenda to a more fundamental difference over war strategy: The Marines were bent on expansion; the British were intent on retrenchment. By the spring of 2010, about 20,000 U.S. troops, mostly Marines, were stationed in Helmand, compared to about 9,000 British. The Marines wanted to push south to the town of Barham Chah on the Pakistani border, and west to neighboring Nimruz province, which abuts Iran. Neither foray seemed in keeping with General McChrystal's counterinsurgency mission.

Barham Chah was tiny, and the bad guys in whom the Marines were interested—insurgents and drug smugglers—often drove through the desert, bypassing the town. Nimruz was largely sand. The NATO command deemed it so strategically unimportant that it was one of just four provinces without a reconstruction team. But the Marines saw danger—and potential. Their intelligence reports indicated that Taliban fighters were using the northern part of the province to stage attacks in Helmand. Nicholson and his senior staff officers believed they could combat that threat by devoting American troops and resources to support the provincial government and its security forces. Nimruz's capital had twenty-four-hour-a-day electricity, courtesy of the Iranian power grid, which made it ripe for economic development. The province also had one of the country's most valuable trade routes: a paved highway that connected Iran with Afghanistan's national ring road. "If we're going to succeed here, we have to experiment and take risks," Nicholson said.

The opposition of senior U.S. and NATO commanders—one called Nimruz "the end of the earth"—did not dissuade the Marines. They began constructing a vast base on the province's northeastern edge. The original plans for the encampment envisaged two airstrips, an advanced combat hospital, a post office, a large convenience store, and rows of housing trailers stretching as far as the eye could see. Nicholson expected more than 3,000 Marines—one-tenth of the surge troops—to be based there by mid-2010. Among them would be a full infantry battalion to conduct operations in Nimruz. Although McChrystal opposed the growth of Marineistan, there was little he could do about it. The Marines did not report to him—operational control of Nicholson's brigade rested with a three-star Marine general at the U.S. Central Command—and they did not always seek permission before planting the flag on new patches of desert.

But the Marines' ambition did not factor in British fatigue. As British casualties mounted in 2009 despite the arrival of the Marines—that July was the bloodiest month yet for British forces in Helmand—the public's weak support for the war dipped further in the United Kingdom, prompting parliamentarians to escalate calls for a change in war strategy. Some in the ruling Labor Party called for a full-scale withdrawal by the end of the year. Prime Minister Gordon Brown managed to hold the line, but it was clear that Britain's stance in Helmand needed to shift if he wanted to prevent an outright revolt in his party. His government's first step was to inform the Obama administration that it would not increase forces, even nominally, in tandem with an American surge. "The cupboard is bare," a top British official told a senior American diplomat in London. Then the Defense Ministry instructed military commanders to work up secret plans to hand off Sangin and Musa Qala to the Americans and consolidate in less dangerous parts of the province.

Nicholson and Weston got an inkling of the British desire to give up Sangin in late 2009. It became clearer in December when Conservative leader David Cameron, who would become the next prime minister in a few months, visited Helmand. His countrymen, he said, were "spread too thinly." By then, 245 British soldiers had been killed in Afghanistan. Although it was less than a third of the U.S. war dead at the time, it amounted to a significantly greater proportion of the country's population. Another statistic also weighed on British leaders: Although they had 30 percent of the troops in Helmand, they were responsible for 70 percent of the population. Like McChrystal and Doug Lute at the White House, British officials believed that too many Marines were in insignificant places.

When Cameron met with Nicholson and Weston, the top British commander in Helmand, Brigadier General James Cowan, began laying the groundwork for the shift by emphasizing the British sacrifice. Cowan said he had recently asked the British field hospital next to Camp Leatherneck, which treated both Americans and British, how much blood it had transfused in the past month. The answer, Cowan reported, was that far more blood had been used on the Brits—because they had so many casualties—than on the Marines.

An awkward silence descended on the room. Cameron said nothing. After ten seconds, Weston spoke up. "There's been enough blood shed by all of us here," he said.

The following month, when Foreign Secretary David
Miliband visited Helmand, an aide passed him a note during
his meeting with Nicholson and Weston. Two more British
soldiers had been killed in Sangin. It was at that moment that
Weston grasped the stakes for both nations: The British could
no longer sustain those sorts of messages, but that would mean
more "fallen angel" notifications for Nicholson and his Marine
successors. As the meeting continued, it seemed to Weston
that Miliband was discreetly asking Nicholson to help Britain instead of raising the matter in a higher-profile way with
Hillary Clinton or Bob Gates. Soon thereafter, Weston drafted
a cable for Ambassador Eikenberry titled "U.S.-U.K. at a Cross-
roads." It argued that the United States needed to ease its closest ally out of the toughest parts of Helmand, not force the
British to stick it out. Eikenberry agreed, but the subject was too
sensitive for even a top secret cable, which would have been
viewed by hundreds of people within the American bureaucracy. The ambassador drafted a memo that he sent directly to
Clinton.

"We couldn't have a situation that made Basra look like
child's play," Weston told me later. "Helmand was much more
important in terms of British self-respect and the U.S.-U.K.
partnership. We had to help our best friends in the world."

Nicholson agreed to take on Musa Qala, but he had no desire
for Sangin. He already had Marja on his plate, and he wanted
to push on to Nimruz and Barham Chah. Officers on his staff
scoffed at the Brits. The point of the American surge, as they
saw it, was to move into places where there were no coalition
forces, not rescue the country with the second largest military
contingent in Afghanistan. But Weston knew—regardless of
the Marines' objections—that Americans would end up going
to Sangin, and he figured it made sense to start preparing.
Nicholson grew exasperated as Weston kept pressing the point.
"Kael," he admonished, "enough on Sangin."

British officers eventually decided to let the Marines, who
always seemed to be spoiling for a fight, find their own way
to Sangin. It happened early in the summer of 2010. After the
transfer in Musa Qala, the top British commander in Helmand

had agreed to place his troops in Sangin under the control of the Marines. Colonel Paul Kennedy, the top Marine field commander in northern Helmand, quickly concluded that he needed more forces there, so he diverted the new battalion that was supposed to head into Nimruz. Soon after the new battalion arrived in July, British officials informed the Americans that the British unit in Sangin would not be replaced when its tour finished early that October.

By concentrating in and around Lashkar Gah and the districts of Gereshk and Nad Ali, the British military would finally have enough combat power to perform a genuine protect-the-population counterinsurgency mission. Those were important areas, and improving British odds of getting them under control should have pleased the Marines. It did for a while, then both sides resumed bickering. This time, Sangin replaced Musa Qala as the principal point of friction. The Marines felt the British-run reconstruction office began paying less attention to Sangin once British forces departed the district. British officials denied the allegation, but they shouldn't have. Although the Marines believed Sangin was the most critical part of the province— because the fighting was so intense and so many of their comrades were getting killed and wounded up there—it wasn't. Lashkar Gah and Gereshk were far more populous and vital. But the Marines weren't all wrong: If they were going to succeed where the Brits had failed in Sangin, they required more than rifles and missiles; they needed meaningful resources for reconstruction.

The dispute once again illuminated how the two closest allies in Afghanistan failed to understand each other. Had the British not torpedoed their relationship with the Marines through unseemly deals and a nineteenth-century attitude toward the Afghans, and had the Marines not always equated British restraint with appeasement, the two militaries could have been true allies. The British could have emulated the American model of massing combat power to strike hard and fast. And the Marines could have grasped the British wisdom in picking only the most important fights. The result almost certainly would have been fewer body bags draped with the Union Jack or the Stars and Stripes.

12

Odd Man Out

IN THE SUMMER OF 2009, a new spirit of comity drifted over Great Massoud Road in Kabul, the closed-off boulevard separating the U.S. Embassy compound from the vast NATO headquarters that was the seat of American military power in the country. For the previous four years, neither side had been able to abide the other. The soldiers scoffed at the embassy's effort to institute a normal relationship with a country that was at war, while the diplomats believed the military had been preoccupied with Iraq at the expense of Afghanistan. Both were right. But everything changed after Obama took office and cranked open the spigot of troops and reconstruction dollars. In unguarded conversations over coffee on their respective sides of the street, diplomats praised Stan McChrystal for grasping the importance of improving governance and tackling corruption, and military officers told me they were thrilled that Karl Eikenberry was the ambassador. He was a former three-star general who had been the top U.S. commander in Afghanistan from 2002 to 2003, and they saw him as one of them, someone from outside the cautious, bureaucratic State Department mold who would marshal the necessary resources to win the war.

By the fall, the bonhomie had evaporated. The unraveling began with Eikenberry's cable calling into question McChrystal's rationale for the troop surge. McChrystal and his top deputies were livid, not because Eikenberry was so skeptical but because he had not shared the cable with them before he sent it to Secretary Clinton and the White House. Giving the military a heads-up, they felt, would have been collegial, and it might have resulted in a discussion that addressed some of the ambassador's concerns. From that moment on, many senior officers felt the embassy wasn't on their team.

Obama's decision to impose a deadline on the surge caused an even deeper rift. Mirroring the chasm between commanders and civilians in the president's war cabinet, many in the embassy quietly cheered the timetable, while officers across the street thought it was self-defeating. They laughed at arguments from the White House that setting a date on which troops would begin coming home would encourage the Afghan government to work harder. The problem, as the soldiers viewed it, was a lack of skills and resources, not will. Many in the military also believed that Obama's announcement of the date in his West Point address had simply encouraged the Taliban to hang on because they knew the Americans would start withdrawing in July 2011.

The clashing views stemmed from differing perceptions about American influence in Afghanistan. The military is an action-oriented culture—soldiers seize territory, kill people, build bridges—and commanders believed that with enough effort, they could stabilize the country and succeed where other empires, from the Mongols to the Russians, had failed. They also saw the Taliban—not just al-Qaeda—as a threat to the United States, even though Talib insurgents had domestic ambitions.

Those in the embassy compound hailed from the State Department's observe-and-report culture, and they were predisposed to dwell on the limits of American power instead of its transformative potential. In their eyes, Afghanistan needed to be fixed, but not at any cost. They tended to focus on the half-empty aspects of the situation there—Karzai's erratic behavior, the Afghan army's incompetence, the long-standing tribal rivalries—instead of sharing the military's COIN-infused optimism that all of those deficiencies could be cured with American money, training, and hand-holding.

After Eikenberry's cable was leaked in early 2010, which froze his already chilly relationship with Karzai, several officers in the headquarters were incredulous that the ambassador did not resign or that Hillary Clinton did not remove him. But Eikenberry had the White House's support. Jim Jones liked him, as did Joe Biden. Doug Lute was an old Army buddy. They weren't going to cut loose someone who had written a blunt cable, even if it had become public. It was more than loyalty, though. They agreed with him, and they regarded his views as an important counterweight to the military's glowing claims of progress. Like the July 2011 deadline, Eikenberry's continued presence in Kabul was a manifestation of Obama's growing skepticism that the surge would accomplish what McChrystal, Petraeus, and Mullen had promised.

As winter gave way to a pleasant Afghan spring, the military's frustration with the civilians in Kabul—and, by extension, those at the White House—only hardened. Eikenberry had wanted to rebuild his relationship with McChrystal's team, and he thought that he could do so by embracing the surge and addressing the problems he had outlined in his cable by concentrating on improving district-level government. But the bureaucracy foiled him. The State Department failed to dispatch quickly the additional personnel it had promised, and embassy managers were reluctant to send more staffers into the field. Although State was exhibiting its customary inertia, officers in the NATO command interpreted it as intransigence. USAID's delays in commencing new reconstruction programs—because it didn't have the staff to design and bid contracts quickly enough—elicited the same sentiments. "If we lose," said an American working for the NATO headquarters in Kabul, "it's going to be because of the civilians."

In my travels with McChrystal and my many visits to his headquarters, I picked up plenty of off-the-record consternation among his aides about Obama's deadline, Eikenberry's cable, and the embassy's foot-dragging, but I never heard it get personal. That June, however, an article appeared in *Rolling Stone* magazine that described McChrystal's entourage disparaging members of the president's war cabinet during a trip to Paris. One aide who was quoted called Jim Jones a "clown" who remained "stuck in 1985." A person whom the article described as "a member of the general's team" offered thoughts on Holbrooke: "The Boss says he's like a wounded animal. Holbrooke keeps hearing rumors that he's going to get fired, so that makes him dangerous. He's a brilliant guy, but he just comes in, pulls on a lever, whatever he can grasp onto. But this is COIN, and you can't just have someone yanking on shit." The coup de grâce was an exchange about Biden, who irked senior military officials perhaps more than any other top civilian in the administration because of his opposition to COIN:

"Are you asking about Vice President Biden?" McChrystal says with a laugh. "Who's that?"
"Biden?" suggests a top adviser. "Did you say: Bite Me?"

When Obama read the article, he was furious. He ordered McChrystal back to Washington. The two met the following day, and McChrystal offered his resignation. The president accepted it without hesitation. Thirty minutes later, he asked Petraeus to assume command of all U.S. and NATO forces in Afghanistan.

Selecting Petraeus to replace McChrystal pleased everyone in the war cabinet. Gates and Mullen, who feared a change in strategy, were relieved. The COIN fight would be led by the nation's most famous—and in their view most capable—general. Surge opponents had a wholly different reason to feel optimistic. Petraeus would be heading to Kabul as the hero of Iraq, and some believed that gave him an incentive to adjust the strategy there so he wouldn't sully his undefeated record. "If Dave Petraeus concludes that this isn't working, he is going to figure out a way to transition to something else," a top White House adviser told me shortly after the appointment was announced. "He might deny that he is doing it. He might insist it's consistent. But I can't see him at the end of the day being the guy who wants to be the captain going down with his ship."

Other surge skeptics in the White House quietly hoped Petraeus, the deftest general in the Army, would manage to achieve a few short-term battlefield victories. At least, they thought, he could leverage his relationships with journalists, pundits, and members of Congress—all of whom he had assiduously courted over the years—to create an image of improvement. Either way, they believed, it would allow Obama to begin aggressive troop withdrawals starting in July 2011. Even those most dubious of the surge recognized that the president couldn't tell the American people that the troop increase had not worked. That was too politically risky. The United States wasn't supposed to lose wars. He would need to draw down on a message of success.

Despite the optimism in Washington, the switch did little to heal civilian-military relations in Kabul. Eikenberry sought to forge a bond with Petraeus by meeting him in Europe and traveling with him into Kabul. On the flight, the ambassador told the general that Karzai seemed ready to endorse a controversial program championed by the U.S. military that would expand armed village-level defense forces. Petraeus raised the issue with Karzai at his first meeting with him as commander. The Afghan president "went through the roof," according to a person in attendance, and delivered a long lecture to Petraeus about Afghanistan's history of unruly militias. Petraeus and his aides faulted Eikenberry for misreading Karzai and creating an immediate rift between the president and the general.

But the public sniping between their camps stopped. Eikenberry instructed his staff to improve cooperation with the military, and Petraeus ordered his subordinates to cut the trash talk. He told them that he would be the only one speaking to the press. Everyone else was to shut up.

That they did when journalists with notebooks were around. When they weren't, the grousing resumed. And the dissatisfaction expanded to the White House. Petraeus's imperious style earned him the nickname "King David" among some on the National Security Council staff. Despite their reliance on him to craft a narrative of amelioration, they mocked his frequent references to Iraq—one aide counted more than two dozen utterances in a single hour—and they rolled their eyes at a PowerPoint slide he had developed to describe his path forward in Afghanistan. He called it the "Anaconda Strategy." It had a large circle in the center to depict the insurgency. Inside the circle were "insurgent needs"—weapons, money, safe havens, foreign fighters, popular support, and ideology. Outside the circle, with arrows pointing inward, were actions to be taken by coalition forces: counterterrorist operations, conventional operations,

Afghan conventional and special forces operations, village
defense forces, reconciliation, reintegration, governance, inclu-
sivity/transparency/anticorruption programs, biometrics, intelligence fusion, counternarcotics, surveillance/reconnaissance,
counterinsurgency in detention facilities, rehabilitation of
detainees, rule of law, education, basic services, jobs programs,
economic development, Pakistan engagement, border-crossing
point improvements, and strategic communications.

"Does he really think it's our mission to do all of this?" one
senior White House official snorted to me in the fall of 2010.
"It's laughable."

But Petraeus didn't just want to create the perception of
progress. He wanted a win.

The other festering rivalry among the teammates was Richard
Holbrooke versus the White House. The antipathy was visceral
and vicious, dwarfing the quarreling in Helmand and the nasti-
ness across Great Massoud Road. And it sabotaged America's
best chance for a peace deal to end the war.

From the moment Holbrooke became Obama's special representative for Afghanistan and Pakistan, his overriding goal
was to midwife a negotiated settlement among the Taliban, the
Afghan government, and the United States. He didn't need a
lengthy policy review to weigh the options facing the United
States. He had become convinced, even before Obama moved
into the White House, that the military's goal of defeating the
Taliban through a full-on counterinsurgency campaign would
be too costly and time-consuming, and the chances of success
were almost nil given the safe havens in Pakistan, the corruption of Karzai's government, and the sorry state of the Afghan
army. In his visits to Afghanistan as a private citizen, Holbrooke had traveled to villages and heard a widespread desire
among the Pashtuns to reconcile with their brothers and cousins who had taken up arms. To Holbrooke, brokering a deal
was the only viable American strategy.

He had more personal experience with war—and peace—
than anyone else in the upper reaches of the Obama administration. After serving in Vietnam for three years—first as a
USAID field officer in the Mekong Delta and then as an aide

in Saigon to ambassadors Maxwell Taylor and Henry Cabot Lodge, Jr.—he had joined the war staff in Lyndon Johnson's White House and witnessed a president being sucked deeper into a failing conflict based on deceptive assessments by his commanders. Johnson had appointed Holbrooke to the U.S. delegation to the 1968–69 Paris peace talks with North Vietnam when he was just twenty-seven years old. Although in the following decades Holbrooke had reached rarified heights in the worlds of diplomacy and banking, Vietnam had scarred him, as it had so many of his generation, and it was the prism through which he gazed at Afghanistan. In September 2010, he spoke about his Vietnam experience at a State Department conference on the American venture in Southeast Asia. To many in the audience, it seemed as if he were talking not about the past but about the present: "We fought bravely under very difficult conditions. But success was not achievable. Those who advocated more escalation or something called 'staying the course' were advocating something that would have led only to a greater and more costly disaster afterwards."

His most significant diplomatic achievement occurred at Wright-Patterson Air Force Base in Dayton, Ohio, in 1995, when he forged a deal among bitter rivals in the former Yugoslavia to end three years of bloody sectarian war that had killed roughly 100,000 people. The talks, which lasted twenty days, would not have happened if he had not spent three months shuttling among the principal Serbian, Croatian, and Muslim leaders to cajole, arm-twist, and threaten, while also green-lighting U.S.-led NATO air strikes. He had approached the dispute not as a principled ideologue but as a pragmatic mediator who kept his gaze constantly on what was possible. That same attitude drove his quest for peace in Afghanistan—as did his ego. He wanted to be the man who had ended two wars.

The prospect of a peace deal appealed to Obama. Less than two months after he took office, the president said he was open to seeking reconciliation with the Taliban, comparing such an effort to a U.S. initiative to work with former Sunni militants in Iraq who were willing to break with al-Qaeda. His comments alarmed top military and intelligence officials. Mullen and Petraeus thought it was too soon even to talk about talking. They wanted to implement a COIN strategy first and then talk, but only to Taliban leaders who wanted to surrender; they were reluctant to make any meaningful concessions to the enemy. CIA officials argued that the United States could not negotiate with the Taliban until its leadership denounced al-Qaeda—otherwise the nation would be making deals with terrorists. Hillary Clinton was also skeptical. Even Holbrooke, who wanted everything right away, agreed that it was too soon. Obama had just authorized 21,000 additional troops for the war. The Americans needed to pressure the Taliban and reestablish the U.S.-led coalition's momentum before he could sue for peace. But Holbrooke figured it was never too early to bend the ears of others within the administration about his goal. He started with Clinton. A few weeks after he took over, he invited Shamila Chaudhary, a bright but junior officer on the Pakistan desk, into a meeting with Clinton. It was a classic Holbrooke move—slashing through layers of bureaucracy so the boss could hear directly from a plugged-in Pakistani American in her employ. Chaudhary told Clinton that the United States should be speaking to a broader array of Pakistanis, including former president Nawaz Sharif. "Doesn't Nawaz talk to the Taliban?" Clinton asked. "Which Pakistani leader hasn't talked to the Taliban?" Chaudhary replied. Everyone in the room laughed, and Holbrooke shot Chaudhary a thumbs-up sign. It was exactly the message he wanted the secretary to hear.

Although Holbrooke had campaigned aggressively for Clinton during the Democratic primaries, he had hoped Obama would choose him to be secretary of state. A week after the election, he traveled to Chicago for an hour-long meeting with the president-elect. It was an awkward but cordial session that left Holbrooke with the clear impression that the job would not be his. When it went to Clinton—Obama had been influenced by the book *Team of Rivals,* about Abraham Lincoln's decision to include former political opponents in his cabinet—Holbrooke assumed he'd get a plum job. Obama had agreed to give Clinton wide latitude to assemble her team at the State Department, and Holbrooke was close to both Clintons, who were indebted to him for delivering peace in the Balkans, the most significant diplomatic breakthrough of Bill

Clinton's presidency. Clinton offered Holbrooke her toughest assignment: the job of handling Afghanistan and Pakistan and trying to broker peace under even longer odds.

Holbrooke was unwilling to be a mere "special envoy" in charge of coordinating outreach to the two nations. He wanted to be a "special representative" who would oversee all of the State Department's work on Afghanistan and Pakistan as well as coordinate diplomacy with all of the countries in the region. It would also help him assert his primacy over an eventual peace process. Clinton gave him the go-ahead.

Holbrooke took control of the department's Afghanistan and Pakistan offices, and he cherry-picked a few Foreign Service officers to work directly for him. But most of his staff were drawn from outside the State bureaucracy. He lured experts from universities and nongovernmental organizations. He also asked for—and received—representatives from the Pentagon, the CIA, and USAID, as well as the Treasury, Justice, Homeland Security, and Agriculture departments. He viewed his office as an all-star team, and he even held an event at a Washington hotel to publicly introduce the members. Many career officers at State were miffed, but Holbrooke didn't care. If he was going to fix Afghanistan, he'd have to break bureaucratic china.

Soon after becoming the special representative, Holbrooke insisted upon signing off on every significant nonmilitary initiative in both countries. But he was too peripatetic and distracted to focus on the paperwork he had created for himself. His staff was equally disorganized. His office consisted of a dozen experts focused on their own projects, with nobody to herd the flock. Contracts for multimillion-dollar USAID programs languished on his desk for months, as did documents that addressed dozens of pressing matters. Officials at USAID, the White House, and the embassy in Kabul grew frustrated—"His office was the antithesis of orderly process," one said—but Holbrooke did not care. Although he spoke in grand terms about the civilian surge and new reconstruction programs during press interviews, congressional testimony, and White House meetings, he didn't really believe in those efforts. His brain remained focused on the path to negotiation. It was a strategy that could have worked if he had not become embroiled in nasty, long-running disputes with two fellow civilians: Karl Eikenberry and Doug Lute.

Eikenberry should have been a natural ally. Holbrooke had helped to select him, and both men were dubious of counter-insurgency theory, President Karzai's true motivations, and the willingness of Pakistan to flush out insurgent sanctuaries. But Eikenberry was a former three-star general who was used to receiving orders and then being allowed to lead his troops. Holbrooke put him on a short leash, sending him dozens of e-mails and requests for information every day. Seemingly every night brought another get-out-of-bed phone call from Holbrooke, who loved to micromanage and expected everyone else to get by on as little sleep as he did. Eikenberry soon grew tired of Holbrooke's seven-thousand-mile-long screwdriver; he had a vast embassy to run and a complicated diplomatic relationship to oversee. When Holbrooke visited Afghanistan, the situation was even worse. He dressed down Eikenberry's subordinates and complained that they had set up too many meetings for him with English-speaking ministers instead of with "real Afghans" who could give him "a clear picture of why the Taliban is so strong." When embassy officials refused to heed his edicts, Holbrooke wasn't afraid to employ threats. "So let me ask you, what are you doing for your next assignment?" he said to one of Eikenberry's top deputies, suggesting that his career was in jeopardy. Eikenberry, who had a comfortable military pension and did not covet more work for the State Department, could afford to fight back. He told colleagues that Holbrooke's criticism of embassy staffers was creating "a terrible morale problem." He slow-rolled permission for Holbrooke's deputies to visit Afghanistan—they needed his approval to stay on the embassy compound—and when they did get there, he restricted their ability to travel and meet with Afghans. He also sent missives about Holbrooke, particularly regarding his strained relationship with Karzai, to the White House.

Those messages went to Lute, who was an old friend of Eikenberry and had his own reasons to dislike Holbrooke. Lute was an active-duty three-star general who had joined the Bush White House to serve as the Iraq and Afghanistan war czar.

He had direct access to Bush, the power to convene meetings of deputy cabinet secretaries, and a West Wing office, albeit in the basement. When Obama had assumed the presidency, he had decided to keep Lute around, in part because the general could provide the new National Security Council staff valuable insight into how the military operated—and he could let them know if his fellow generals were trying to pull a fast one on the new crop of civilians. But Holbrooke didn't think much of Lute. The diplomat saw the general as an unimaginative paper pusher. Lute spent much of his time organizing meetings and compiling data that showed how the war was being lost. He believed his work was of vital importance, and he thought that Holbrooke needed to follow his lead. He bristled at the attention journalists lavished upon Holbrooke, who spent more time hopping the globe than engaging in the mundane but important work of overseeing war policy. Lute's resentment grew with each request that Holbrooke's office ignored and each State Department memo that had to be revised by the NSC staff. Before long, the two men's staffs were in open warfare with each other. Lute's team would schedule key meetings when Holbrooke was out of town. When they didn't want him to travel to the region, they refused to allow him to use a military airplane. They even sought to limit the number of aides Holbrooke could take on his trips. Holbrooke retaliated by convening his own weekly interagency meetings on Afghanistan and Pakistan, traditionally the domain of the NSC. The Monday sessions, which he called his *shura,* riled Lute, who eventually began compiling a dossier of Holbrooke's supposed misdeeds.

Instead of trying to mediate the disputes with Eikenberry and Lute or making it clear to both that Holbrooke was the administration's point man on Afghanistan and Pakistan policy, senior officials at the White House let the fighting persist—and sometimes encouraged it. Holbrooke had no friends on Team Obama. Denis McDonough, then the NSC chief of staff, had been angered by Holbrooke's strong-arming of Democratic foreign policy experts to support Clinton during the 2008 primary. Susan Rice's dislike of Holbrooke dated back to the Clinton administration, when she had been the assistant secretary of state for African affairs and he, having become interested in the AIDS epidemic in the years after the Dayton Accords, tromped over her turf and criticized her performance. Ben Rhodes, the NSC's communications director, told colleagues that Holbrooke was the source of repeated leaks of sensitive matters to journalists. (Although Holbrooke enjoyed gossiping with reporters and he almost always spoke without authorization from the White House, I know from personal experience that he was not the source of nearly as many stories as the NSC thought he was.) Joe Biden's dislike of him stretched back to Bill Clinton's administration. Jim Jones, a former four-star Marine general and supreme allied commander in Europe, placed his sympathies with Lute and Eikenberry—they were, after all, fellow generals. Holbrooke's lack of organization and lust for the spotlight rankled Jones, as did his personality. Jones told NSC staffers that he found Holbrooke unctuous and prolix.

With frequent references to Vietnam and a flair for the dramatic, Holbrooke's style left him the odd man out among White House advisers. If Obama or Clinton was not at a meeting, Holbrooke insisted upon steering the discussion and dominating the conversation. He was a throwback to a time when Averell Harriman, Henry Kissinger, and George Kennan had held unrivaled sway over shaping policy, and he wanted the same influence on Obama's team. "He spoke like a man who just left talking to Kennan—and walked into 2009, still in black and white, with his hat on," said Vikram Singh, one of his top deputies. "Sometimes it was a bunch of bullshit, and sometimes it was a bunch of wisdom. But if you were this young crowd that came in with Barack Obama, it seemed cartoonish. You probably felt like this guy isn't serious. What's going on here? What is he trying to do? And he made you feel nervous and uncomfortable, and that was very detrimental to him. They weren't able to hear what he was saying because they were distracted by the mannerisms and the way he did things—and he couldn't figure that out."

The only one who could was Clinton. She tolerated his idiosyncrasies—his need to talk to her numerous times a day, to bounce around without a clear agenda—because she was confident that he'd deliver a breakthrough in Afghanistan. He insisted that great diplomacy was like jazz—you needed to improvise—and she was willing to let him riff. In return he never crossed her, even when he thought she was wrong.

In early 2010, Jones sought to oust Holbrooke. He summoned Holbrooke to the White House and discreetly noted the veteran diplomat's shortcomings over the previous year. Jones thought his message was clear, but Holbrooke wasn't sure what the national security advisor was driving at. After the meeting, he phoned his old friend Leslie Gelb, the former president of the Council on Foreign Relations. "He knew there were difficulties, but he didn't realize how serious they were," Gelb recalled.

It became clear to Holbrooke a few weeks later. That February, Jones sent Eikenberry a letter that sympathized with the ambassador's complaints about Holbrooke and suggested that he would be removed from his job soon. The letter came to Holbrooke's attention because Jones sent it not as a private note but as official correspondence on White House stationery, which is automatically copied to relevant agencies.

Shortly thereafter, Jones called Holbrooke in for another meeting. That time, he was far less ambiguous. He told Holbrooke that he should start thinking of his "exit strategy." After the meeting, Holbrooke's first call was not to Gelb but to Clinton, who was traveling in the Middle East. The following week, she went to see Obama armed with a list of Holbrooke's accomplishments that had been assembled by his staff.

"Mr. President, you can fire Richard Holbrooke over the objection of your secretary of state," she told Obama. But Jim Jones, she said, could not.

Obama backed down, but Jones and Lute didn't. They kept adding items to their dossier on Holbrooke. They even drafted a cover letter that called him ineffective because he had ruined his relationships with Karzai, Eikenberry, and officials in the Pakistani government. But Jones held off on giving it to the president, who did not seem ready to force the change upon Clinton. In the interim, he and Lute sought to put Holbrooke into a box.

Lute and other NSC staffers cooked up their most audacious plan to marginalize Holbrooke shortly before Karzai's visit to Washington in April 2010. They arranged for Holbrooke to be excluded from Obama's Oval Office meeting with the Afghan leader, and then they planned to give Obama talking points for the session that would slight Holbrooke. Among the lines they wanted the president to deliver to Karzai: *Everyone in this room represents me and has my trust.* The implication would be that Holbrooke, who would not be present, was not Obama's man, while Jones and Lute, who would be there, were people to whom Karzai should listen. The scheme was foiled at the last minute when Clinton insisted that Holbrooke attend the session.

With Clinton protecting him, Holbrooke spent far less time worrying about how to save his job than Lute spent trying to fire him. "Doug is out of his depth fighting with me," Holbrooke told one of his aides. "The White House can't afford to get rid of me."

Obama could have ordered a stop to the infighting, but he remained hands off, even though he favored a negotiated end to the war. His sympathies lay with his NSC staffers—Holbrooke's manic intensity was the antithesis of Obama's well-known "no drama" rule. So he kept his distance. He never granted Holbrooke a one-on-one session in the Oval Office, and when he traveled to Afghanistan in March 2010, he took more than a dozen staffers, but not Holbrooke, who was not even informed of the trip in advance. During the Situation Room sessions to discuss McChrystal's troop request, Obama kept his views about surging to himself, but he was far less sphinxlike about Holbrooke. At the start of one meeting, Holbrooke gravely compared the "momentous decision" Obama faced to what Lyndon Johnson had grappled with during the Vietnam War. The president cut him off. "Richard," Obama said, "do people really talk like that?"

The president's lack of support devastated Holbrooke's deeply loyal staff, who was just as skeptical of the military's counterinsurgency strategy as Lute and others in the White House were. "The tragedy of it all is that Richard's views about all of this stuff—about the surge, about Pakistan, and about reconciliation—were probably closer to the president's than anyone else in the administration," said Vali Nasr, a Tufts professor who was one of Holbrooke's senior advisers. "If the president had wanted to, he could have found a kindred spirit in Richard."

Even without the internal attacks, Holbrooke believed navigating a path to peace talks was going to be challenging. The Taliban was an atomized insurgency that lacked the necessary organization to pursue reconciliation. It had no office, mailing address, or formal structure. Its leader, the reclusive, one-eyed Mullah Omar, empowered subordinates to oversee the fighting. It was not clear whether Omar wanted to talk—in 2009, the Taliban appeared to be winning—or whether he and his fellow mullahs would be willing to accept American conditions for negotiations: that they renounce violence, break with al-Qaeda, and embrace the Afghan constitution. Even if they did, could Omar get his men to abide by a peace deal? Would the terms be acceptable to the Karzai government and the old Northern Alliance leaders? And what about neighboring powers? Pakistan's intelligence service, which was sheltering the Taliban's leadership, would almost certainly seek to manipulate—and scuttle—any negotiations. If Holbrooke's shoot-the-moon attempt at reconciliation was going to have any chance of success, the effort at least needed the backing of his fellow Americans, starting with the president. But the White House never issued a clear policy on reconciliation during the administration's first two years. Jones and Lute hated the thought of him once again basking in a Dayton-like spotlight, hogging the victory they all deserved to share. They wanted him out of the way, and then they would chart a path to peace.

The consequence was profound: The Obama White House failed to aggressively explore negotiations when it had the most boots on the battlefield. Promising leads were left to wither. And the military once again capitalized on civilian disunity to pursue its maximalist objectives.

In July 2009, King Abdullah of Saudi Arabia sent a personal message to Obama asking him to dispatch someone to meet with a group of Taliban emissaries who had been talking to the Saudi intelligence service. The Saudi intelligence chief had already met with the U.S. ambassador to Riyadh and the CIA station chief there to discuss the overture, but the Saudis deemed the discussions so promising that Abdullah asked his

ambassador to Washington, Adel Al-Jubeir, to discuss the matter directly with Jones. There were differing opinions among
Holbrooke's aides about whether the overture was as significant as the Saudis were claiming, but Holbrooke thought it was
worth pursuing. Instead, the offer languished at the NSC.

When Obama announced the surge, Holbrooke was not
deterred by the absence of a reconciliation policy. He figured
it was the moment to proceed full tilt toward negotiations,
and he sought to put reconciliation on the agenda for Karzai's
April 2010 visit to Washington—the same trip during which
Lute tried to exclude him from the Oval Office. To demonstrate
good faith, Holbrooke pushed to remove some Taliban leaders
from a United Nations sanctions list that froze their assets and
impeded their ability to travel, and he wanted to make it easier
for the Karzai government to begin talking to the Taliban by
abolishing a U.S. government blacklist that restricted whom
the Afghans could speak to without American permission.
Both moves were opposed by U.S. military and intelligence
officials.

The NSC expressed support for reconciliation that spring,
but with a twist: Lute favored a U.N. envoy to lead the effort.
His preferred candidate was former Algerian foreign minister
Lakhdar Brahimi, who had served as a U.N. special representative to Afghanistan. Lute's plan relegated Holbrooke to a support role. "It was driven by hatred," said an NSC staffer who
worked for Lute. "Doug wanted anybody but Richard."

It seemed a masterstroke, except that the Afghan and Pakistani governments despised the idea. Even a few Talibs in contact with foreign intelligence officials seemed baffled. Everyone
in the region wanted the United States to lead the effort. They
knew the United Nations was powerless.

Lute argued that Brahimi had Karzai's trust and that he could
deal with Iran and Pakistan in ways a U.S. diplomat couldn't.
There was also the opportunity to shift blame for failure. "If
this doesn't work," he told colleagues, "do we want to own it or
do we want the U.N. to?"

Clinton was furious with Lute. "We don't outsource our foreign policy," she declared to Holbrooke and his staff. Then she
went to Obama to kill the idea, giving him a memo outlining her

objections. She didn't stop there; she also urged Tom Donilon, who had replaced Jones as national security advisor, to rein in Lute. Donilon, who had been friendly with Holbrooke for years, promised her that he would address the issue. Holbrooke's staff hoped the tensions with the NSC would subside, but Lute soon resumed his efforts to find someone else to take charge of reconciliation. This time, however, he focused on Americans. Among his candidates were Thomas Pickering, a former ambassador to Russia, India, and the United Nations; and James Dobbins, a former assistant secretary of state who had served as a special envoy to Afghanistan during the George W. Bush administration.

Although others in the White House began to question Lute's effectiveness given his frayed relationship with not just the State Department but the Pentagon as well—Mullen and Petraeus viewed him as a quisling for opposing the surge—Lute remained valuable to Donilon and others at the NSC, who believed he kept the war trains running on time. Lute's frequent video conferences with commanders also helped to ensure that the military did not veer even further off the reservation. But Holbrooke was stung by Donilon's unwillingness to remove Lute. Holbrooke told his confidants that the new national security advisor was "only a friend half the time."

As Washington officials fought among themselves, a quiet shift was occurring at the NATO headquarters in Kabul. While other military leaders remained opposed to reconciliation, McChrystal began softening to the idea in the months before he was removed. His thinking was shaped by Christopher Kolenda, an astute Army colonel who had been working on a program to provide resettlement and job-training assistance to low-level insurgents who wanted to stop fighting. As Kolenda examined the reasons why Afghans were at war, he came to believe that a negotiated settlement was the only viable path forward. In December 2009, as others in the headquarters were giddy over Obama's decision to surge, Kolenda explained to McChrystal how Mullah Omar's annual messages at the Eid-al-Fitr holiday had become more sophisticated and moderate. The Taliban, he told the general, "is opening the aperture for a different outcome." He mapped out six key Taliban themes—including their participation in the government, political reform, human rights, and justice—to argue that both sides were not as far apart as many in the military believed. McChrystal was not immediately sold, but he was intrigued. He instructed Kolenda to keep working on it.

Kolenda figured that Holbrooke would be a natural ally and reached out to his staff, but he discovered that Holbrooke had not yet gamed out options or performed a rigorous analysis. Holbrooke raised the possibility of a limited NATO cease-fire in part of the country as an expression of American seriousness about reconciliation. To Kolenda and McChrystal, it seemed premature to put down America's guns, particularly without a comprehensive plan or explicit promises from senior Taliban leaders. Despite their differences, Holbrooke and McChrystal began talking regularly about ways to achieve reconciliation. As spring turned to summer, McChrystal became a believer. He realized that the United States would not be able to secure an outright military victory in Afghanistan, and the Afghan government would not be able to get an outright political victory, so a peace deal was the only real solution to the conflict. McChrystal didn't want to let up on the Taliban just yet, but he said he was ready to "clearly show them there's daylight if you go to it." He told his staff that he was "on board" with talking to the Taliban, and in early June, he directed Kolenda to prepare a briefing for Karzai on reconciliation.

Then McChrystal was fired. When Petraeus arrived in Kabul, he ordered a halt to the military's reconciliation activities. He told his subordinates that if the Americans applied enough military pressure, the insurgents would switch sides in droves. To some in the headquarters, it sounded as if he wanted to duplicate what had occurred in Iraq's Anbar province, when Sunni tribesmen had eventually decided to forsake al-Qaeda and side with the United States. Although Obama had mentioned the Sunni Awakening as a possible model in his first public comments on reconciliation, his views about a peace deal had evolved by the summer of 2010. He told his war cabinet that he was open to pursuing negotiations with the enemy, the likes of which never occurred in Iraq. Petraeus's approach was more akin to accepting a surrender from a rival under siege, not compromising with a still-potent adversary to end a war. Kolenda and several others doubted large numbers of Taliban fighters would opt to defect. "You had an industrial-size sanctuary in Pakistan and a radioactive government," said one senior officer who opposed the Petraeus approach. "None of the conditions for the Sunni Awakening existed in Afghanistan."

Kolenda sought to change Petraeus's mind. When he failed, he packed up and returned to the Pentagon, where he told a friend, "We're squandering our point of maximum leverage." The shift did not go unnoticed at the White House, but Lute and other NSC staffers were so consumed with trying to foil Holbrooke that they were unable to marshal the necessary support among the war cabinet to force Petraeus to shift course. Any proposals on reconciliation from the NSC were deemed dead on arrival in Holbrooke's office. Documents that went the other way suffered the same fate.

On a visit to Kabul in October 2010 for a civilian-military conference among U.S. and Afghan officials, Holbrooke sought to lobby Petraeus directly. The two men had a cordial relationship, largely because Holbrooke kept his true feelings to himself. He thought Petraeus's COIN strategy was silly, and he hated the way the general frequently referred to him as his "diplomatic wingman." ("His job should be to drop the bombs when I tell him to," Holbrooke once told his staff.)

"Dave, we need to talk about reconciliation," Holbrooke said to Petraeus as they got into an armored sport-utility vehicle, according to Holbrooke's recollection to his staff.

"Richard, that's a fifteen-second conversation," Petraeus replied. "Yes, eventually. But no. Not now."

13

A Bridge Too Far

ON A BRIGHT, crisp morning in late January 2010, Larry Nicholson journeyed to the end of his empire aboard an MV-22 Osprey, a newfangled flying contraption that lands like a helicopter but soars like an airplane. The arrival of an Osprey squadron at Camp Leatherneck the previous November had unnerved more than a few Marines—thirty of their brethren had been killed in several horrific crashes during the aircraft's development. But Nicholson and his senior officers were confident that the kinks had been ironed out. The snub-nosed, winged birds have two propellers that tilt into a horizontal position for takeoffs and landings; once aloft, the blades swing down so the Osprey can ascend to ten thousand feet and fly as fast as a plane. Compared to the Marines' other rotary-wing aircraft in Helmand—Vietnam War–era CH-53 Super Stallion helicopters that inevitably leaked hydraulic fluid on passengers—the Ospreys possessed far greater speed and range. They also fed the Marines' expansionist tendencies.

Nicholson headed 105 miles southwest to Taghaz, a forlorn oasis in the Desert of Death that consisted of several dozen mud-walled houses and a ramshackle bazaar along a narrow ribbon of marshlands and salt flats birthed by the southern Helmand River. Home to a few hundred farmers and a wintertime encampment of camel-borne nomads, the village had been written off as strategically irrelevant by the British. The Afghan government had a similar view; it had never sent a single civil servant to Taghaz. But the Marines had different ideas.

To them it was a critical crossing point along the river, and they had spare troops in the southern desert who were casting about for new tasks. A week earlier, Nicholson had dispatched a platoon of Marines to the area to glad-hand the locals, disrupt Taliban attempts to smuggle bomb-making supplies from Pakistan, and construct a crude outpost that would mark the expanding frontier of Marineistan. Taghaz was twenty-five miles downriver from Khan Neshin in the direction of Pakistan and Iran—the Marines' deployment there represented the deepest conventional-force foray into the sands of southwestern Afghanistan since 2001—and the general wanted to see it for himself.

In Afghanistan, Ospreys seemed to travel in both space and time. When Nicholson's aircraft alighted upon a dirt patch next to the bazaar, it was as if he had journeyed back centuries from the modern world at Leatherneck. Taghaz had no electricity or running water. Residents lived in adobe buildings that lacked windows and furniture. They cooked over open flames and relieved themselves in the fields. Nobody had a television or a mobile phone. Save for the odd motorcycle, the people of Taghaz lived as they had five hundred or even a thousand years before. The Marines could gaze at the ruins of a sandstone fortress constructed by Alexander the Great's army on a nearby escarpment and feel as if they had been transported to those ancient days. When they e-mailed letters home, the only comparisons that came to mind were images of the Old Testament from Sunday school. *This place*, many a Marine wrote to his wife or girlfriend, *is biblical.*

As Nicholson's Osprey touched down amid a giant dust cloud and a deafening roar—it was the first aircraft ever to land in the village—the locals came out to stare. In most towns along the river valley, young boys would wave as Nicholson walked by, and they would throng his aides as they handed out candy they had received in care packages. Merchants and old men loitering in the bazaar would offer pleasantries, and they often told the general that they were grateful for American efforts to beat back the Taliban. But when Nicholson and Kael Weston walked through the tiny Taghaz bazaar, there were no smiles or expressions of thanks. The residents glared.

The two men had never encountered such an icy reception in Afghanistan. It reminded them of their worst days in Fallujah. As Weston walked along a row of tumbledown stalls, he saw a message in the stone faces: *We don't want you here. We don't like you. Get the hell out.*

Weston was not an I-told-you-so guy—he'd never do that to his friend Larry—but what they faced in Taghaz reinforced his conviction that the Marines did not need to be there. He had voiced his opposition a few weeks earlier, when operations officers at Leatherneck had told him of the plans to push into Taghaz. At the time he couldn't be as passionate as he had been when he had criticized the Now Zad expedition because he had not been able to visit the place. He had based his objections on a map of Helmand. He told Nicholson that the village wasn't worth it. It had few residents, and it was literally in the middle of nowhere. He repeatedly cited the lack of an Afghan government presence. "If the Afghans aren't there," he asked Marines at the headquarters, "why should we go there?" To Nicholson and his senior officers, sweeping into Taghaz was an important counterinsurgency tactic, even if it appeared to be another case of Marine expansionism. Nicholson believed the Marines needed to be in places like Taghaz to discover Taliban redoubts and seize homemade bombs being smuggled from Pakistan. "If we want to protect Nawa and Garmser, we can't just stay there," he told his staff. "The key is to move every day—every day to a different position, so as the sun comes up, the enemy never knows where you're going to be."

As they walked through the bazaar, one of the Marines stationed there casually remarked that they had just discovered a roadside bomb near their outpost. It appeared to have been planted with the complicity of residents in the week since the Marines had arrived. To Weston, that revelation was even more ominous than their cold reception in the bazaar.

The outpost was almost as primitive as the surrounding village. The Marines lived in tents, ate field rations, and relieved themselves in plastic bags. There was no shower, weight room, or recreation center. Two car-sized canvas bladders held water and kerosene fuel to power their vehicles. Their command center consisted of a few computers inside a small metal shipping container. The place was smaller than a football field, and it was surrounded by razor wire and refrigerator-sized bins filled with dirt to keep out car bombs. It was just the sort of spartan encampment that Nicholson favored. With no distractions on base, the men would spend most of their time on patrol. "Every day, you've got to be hunting or helping," he told them in a rousing pep talk. The phrase had been coined by a company commander in Garmser, and Nicholson loved it so much that he'd taken to using it whenever he could. He wanted his Marines to be chasing bad guys and assisting the good people of Helmand with equal vigor.

After touring the outpost, Nicholson and his entourage trudged through a bog toward a larger base a few miles away. As Weston looked beyond the muck, he saw what appeared to be snow-flecked fields. When he walked over them, he realized the white powder was salt. It was the curse of the unfinished Little America project: Because farm drains upstream flowed into the river, the water turned salty and dirty by the time it reached Taghaz, which had naturally saline soil. The combination was disastrous. Weston spotted sprouts of green, but they were poppy shoots—the only crop that would grow on such inhospitable land. Back at Camp Leatherneck, agriculture expert Wes Harris grumbled that nobody had asked for his opinion before the Marines made promises to help the farmers of Taghaz and other communities in Khan Neshin district. If the Marines really wanted to assist them, he argued, "the best thing to do is send Greyhound buses down there and ship all those people somewhere else."

On the hike to the larger base, Weston strode to the front of the pack and kept pace with the junior Marine assigned to walk "point"—the most dangerous assignment in the group because he had to scan the ground for pressure-sensitive mines; if he missed spotting one, chances were he would step on it. Weston saw a chevron with crossed rifles on the grunt's body armor—the insignia of a lance corporal, the second lowest rank among enlisted Marines deployed in Afghanistan. It intrigued Weston the way a colonel's eagle or a general's star might draw the attention of other diplomats. He believed the best way to understand what was really happening on the ground was not to ask the staff officers; they were too eager to please and would varnish the truth. He gabbed with the lance corporals, who went on patrols and pulled guard duty; they saw everything, and, more often than not, they told it like they saw it.

The lance corporal said his name was Rick Centanni. He had been raised in Yorba Linda, California. Had he removed his Kevlar helmet and dark ballistic glasses and scrubbed a day's grime away, Weston would have seen the playful face of a nineteen-year-old who had just grown his first mustache. Centanni had thick eyebrows, deep-set eyes, and dark locks that had been buzzed into a Marine regulation high-and-tight. Weston noted they were leaving the higher-ranking "fat-ass Marines" in the dust. Centanni laughed. He had been a line-backer on the Esperanza High School varsity football team, and he was proud of maintaining his physique despite the fatty field rations and a grueling work schedule that interfered with regular workouts.

The mention of Yorba Linda—Richard Nixon's birthplace—piqued Weston's interest. He had family in Southern California. He asked Centanni about his hometown and how he had come to join the Corps. Centanni had enlisted as a Marine reservist as soon as he turned eighteen—he felt the pull to serve his nation—and had headed off to boot camp two weeks after graduating from high school in 2008. Although he had been accepted into a program that allowed him to arrange his training so he could enroll in college, he had decided to spend that fall on Marine duties. He was assigned to a reserve battalion based at Camp Pendleton that fielded eight-wheeled light armored vehicles. In early 2009, he received word that the battalion would be heading to Afghanistan that November. He could have begged off, saying he was in the college program. "I can't say no," he told his father, Jon Centanni. "The force is deploying, and I want to go."

Jon was a cop in Santa Ana who worked on an antigang task force, and Rick was his only son. When Rick was in grade school, Jon and his wife had split. She had moved to Arizona, leaving Jon to raise Rick by himself. He doted on his son, and he arranged his work schedule so he could coach Rick's baseball team for ten years. They played video games and enjoyed war movies together—*Full Metal Jacket* and *Platoon* were favorites. They remained close even when Rick became a teenager, and though they spent weekends watching football and working on high-horsepower pickup trucks, they weren't afraid to say "I love you" to each other. Rick didn't share all of those details with Weston, but he made it clear that he adored his father and wanted to wear a badge, too. Rick's dream was to join the California Highway Patrol.

He had enlisted with two friends from Esperanza, and all of them had been assigned to the same battalion. During training, the battalion's sergeant major, Robert Cottle, a veteran Los Angeles Police Department SWAT officer, had noticed Rick's last name on his uniform. He asked if he was Jon's son, and when Rick said yes, Cottle offered to make him his driver. Rick readily accepted. It meant he wouldn't have to spend his seven-month deployment on a tiny, out-of-the-way base, walking patrols and pulling all-night guard duty. He lived at the battalion headquarters, which was housed within a crumbling, earth-walled castle in Khan Neshin, and he got to go everywhere Cottle went, which was pretty much everywhere the battalion commander went. His days were spent crisscrossing the desert, visiting every Marine outpost across the district. And unlike Cottle, he actually got to see where they were going because he sat in front of the vehicle's only window.

In his spare time, he learned how to perform basic repairs on the armored vehicles, hoisted weights, and clowned around with his pals from Yorba Linda. One of his friends had a video camera, and he filmed short clips, which Rick sent to his father. The videos showed off his vehicle's uncomfortable interior, his tinkering with an engine, and a small plastic Christmas tree with colored lights that he and his buddies had set up in their tent.

Rick's first weeks in Helmand transformed him into a more serious and disciplined person. The deaths of comrades, and the responsibility of driving the battalion's senior enlisted man, yanked him into adulthood. April would bring his twentieth birthday. "When I get home," Rick told his father on a phone call, "I'm not going to be a teenager anymore."

When Weston and Centanni reached the larger base, Weston fished a silver-rimmed coin the size of a half dollar from his pocket and pressed it into Centanni's palm. It was the sort of token that generals in command routinely handed out to injured troops or those who had performed extraordinary service. The military ones were purchased by the Pentagon; they usually featured the unit's logo on one side and stars denoting the general's rank on the other. Weston's were embossed with the State Department's seal on the front and a map of Afghanistan on the back. He had ordered them from a mint in Washington State. The embassy had refused to provide staffers with funds for coins. The last shipment had cost Weston $560, but he regarded it as a small price to express his gratitude to young Americans who spent months living in the dirt.

He had come to view the coins as amulets since he had handed one to a Marine in Fallujah who was not much older than Centanni. A few days later, during the fierce battle to retake the city in November 2004, the Marine's platoon commander had been felled by a sniper. The young Marine had tried to resuscitate his leader, blowing into his mouth and compressing his chest, but the wound was too severe for the man to be saved. Weeks later, the Marine had run into Weston. He shook as he described what had happened. He told Weston he had drawn strength from the coin, which he had tucked into his flak vest. From then on, Weston came to share the belief that his coins were special. He handed out scores of them to Marines and soldiers in the worst neighborhoods of Iraq and Afghanistan. Several of the recipients had faced close calls, but none had died.

"This is a good-luck coin," he told Centanni. A half hour later, Weston and Nicholson boarded an Osprey for the return flight to Camp Leatherneck.

The next day, a thirteen-man squad from the Taghaz outpost walked through the bazaar. As they passed a stall where residents could make phone calls—the owner had rigged an antenna to pick up a far-off cellular signal—a man walked toward the Marines. Then he blew himself up.

The two Americans closest to the bomber, Lance Corporal Jeremy Kane and Navy Petty Officer Xin Qi, the platoon's corpsman, were killed almost instantly. A third member of the squad, twenty-five-year-old Sergeant David J. Smith, was gravely wounded. He was flown by helicopter to a field hospital and then on to the Army's medical center in Landstuhl, Germany. He died three days after the explosion. Like almost everyone else in the battalion, he was a reservist. He had served in Iraq and was pursuing a bachelor's degree in distribution and logistics at East Carolina University when he learned about the battalion's Afghanistan deployment. He had the same ability as Centanni to play the college card. Instead, he volunteered for the mission.

When Weston heard of the bombing, he felt sick. He was certain it was retribution for his visit with Nicholson. They had fired a shot across the bow of the insurgency by establishing an outpost there, walking through the bazaar, and showing up in a futuristic aircraft that flaunted American military might. To Weston, the bombing was the Taliban's response: *You can send the general here, but we're going to retaliate within twenty-four hours.*

Eleven days after the bombing, I accompanied Nicholson and Weston as they traveled to Khan Neshin for a memorial service at the castle. More than a hundred Marines stood at attention under a cloudless sky. They faced three pairs of boots. Behind each was a downturned rifle. Helmets sat atop the stocks, and dog tags hung from the grips. The chaplain offered a prayer, and then the dead men's buddies rose to speak. One recalled Smith's love of golf. Another praised Qi's devotion to duty. A third said Kane had been a fitness buff who was close to completing a degree in criminal justice. A fourth Marine rose to read from Psalm 23: *Yea, though I walk through the valley of the shadow of death, I will fear no evil: for thou art with me; thy rod and thy staff they comfort me.*

After the chaplain concluded the service, Nicholson and his sergeant major, Ernest Hoopii, walked up to the row of boots and knelt in prayer. As lower-ranking Marines followed, Nicholson led me up one of the parapets and along the south-facing wall. He gazed over a row of huts and marketplace stalls surrounded by green fields. "When we arrived in July, there was nobody here," he said. Seven months later, it wasn't thronged, but there were men milling about. The activity seemed robust enough to satisfy the general. To him, Khan Neshin was similar to Now Zad—a town that could be reborn if the Americans provided security and development assistance. This was his *Field of Dreams:* "If you build it," he said as he scanned the horizon, "they will come."

Almost two months later, on March 24, Weston got word that two more Marines had been killed in the Taghaz area when their light armored vehicle had driven over a roadside bomb. One of them was Cottle, the battalion's sergeant major. Weston didn't focus on the second name in the fallen-angel message. What concerned him and the rest of Nicholson's team was the recovery of the bodies. The explosion and resulting fire had been so intense that fellow Marines had to wait a half day before they could enter the vehicle.

A week later, Nicholson and Weston flew back to the castle for the memorial service. As Weston looked over the program booklet, he saw photographs of both Marines.

Oh, no, he thought. *It's Rick.*

Weston had talked to Centanni for less than a half hour, but the young Marine's death hit harder than any of the eighty-nine other American troopers who were killed in Helmand while he was Nicholson's political adviser. One of them, Sergeant Bill Cahir, was a good friend from Weston's Fallujah days. He was a fellow Democrat who had been a congressional staffer and a newspaper reporter before joining the Marine reserves in 2003. The forty-year-old Cahir specialized in postconflict reconstruction, and he had served two tours in Iraq before running unsuccessfully for Congress in Pennsylvania. Weston reeled when he learned that Cahir, whose wife was pregnant with twins, had been felled by a sniper in Nawa in August 2009. As painful as the news had been, Weston knew Cahir had been doing important work in an important place.

He could not draw the same solace from Centanni's death. He knew the Marines had to secure Nawa, but did they have to go all the way to Taghaz? He wished he had lobbied harder against the decision to establish bases there. If he could have turned back the clock, he would have walked into Nicholson's office, closed the door, and told him: *Over my dead Department of State body should we send platoons of Marines there.*

Taghaz. Khan Neshin. Barham Chah. To Weston, they all reminded him of the Kamchatka Peninsula in the board game Risk—a strategically insignificant area that you moved into only if you had a surfeit of plastic soldiers. He felt the same way about Now Zad, other rural communities in northern Helmand, and all of Nimruz province. One of his Marine friends, Sergeant Todd Bowers, told him that when they went into a remote village in northern Nimruz, one of the residents had begun speaking to them in Russian. The villagers had no idea that the Soviet occupation had ended twenty years earlier and that American troops had been in the country since 2001. "I looked at the village and thought: Who are the real bad eggs who are a threat to the United States?" Bowers said. "They didn't come from villages like this."

Sending Marines to remote hamlets to perform counterinsurgency was never supposed to be part of the overall American war plan. Obama didn't want full-blown COIN. He did not believe that every village and valley had to be pacified. He had ordered McChrystal to focus U.S. forces in the most important parts of the country. Other places could be ignored or dealt with by the Afghans when their army was strong enough. McChrystal and Petraeus agreed, but for a slightly different reason. Because Obama had not given them all of the troops they wanted, they had to triage. They didn't think it made sense to have so many Marines in Khan Neshin and Taghaz, and they certainly did not share the ambition of Marine commanders to push farther south. Had Afghanistan been a Risk board, they would have moved some of those men elsewhere: to Kandahar, to eastern Afghanistan. But the Marines were a package deal. It was as if the plastic game pieces in Helmand had been Krazy Glued together. Even four-star Army commanders couldn't break them up.

Weston didn't think Nicholson was being insubordinate in moving into Taghaz. Taking Kamchatka was a rational act if you had the troops. Weston believed the surge had put too many pieces on the Risk board. The problem had been compounded by the decision to send the Marine brigade to Helmand instead of Kandahar. The blame for those choices lay not with Nicholson but in Washington. To Weston, Nicholson was an aggressive commander who was using the resources at his disposal to secure his entire area of operations. Weston disagreed with some of Nicholson's moves, but the political adviser understood that the general was playing the generous hand he had been dealt. He wasn't going to keep his Marines sitting on bases.

There was no doubt in Weston's mind—or in mine—that Nicholson had used his forces to transform the central Helmand River Valley, evicting the Taliban from its sanctuaries and giving the Afghans another chance to make something of Little America. By the time they departed in mid-2010, Nawa had grown so quiet that Marines regularly walked around without their flak vests. Much of Garmser was safe enough for American civilians to commence reconstruction projects. Hundreds of families were returning to Now Zad. Even the bleeding ulcer of Marja was starting to heal. Nicholson's year in Helmand felt like the most dynamic and entrepreneurial period of the Afghan War. After years of drift, momentum was finally starting to swing America's way.

But was it sustainable? There were still too few competent Afghan soldiers and policemen. The Karzai administration was doing little to help build and sustain local government. I wondered whether, once the ephemera swept into the desert, the changes the Marines had ushered in would be enough to set Afghanistan on a path to stability.

Nicholson didn't obsess about how Helmand—or Afghanistan as a whole—would look in five or ten years. He had a twelve-month-long tour, and he was determined to pack as much as he could into each day. Weston called him a "grunt general." He hated the formalities that came with the job—welcoming visiting dignitaries, sitting through hours-long planning meetings, and presiding over ceremonies. He preferred to be out with the twenty-year-olds, walking on patrols and eating dodgy goat stew with village elders. He gave his colonels the same orders he gave the lance corporals: They had to be hunting or helping every day.

It was that ethos that had led him to Now Zad and then to

Taghaz. He saw problems, and he wanted to fix them. Weston sought to get Nicholson to focus on the probable instead of the possible. Governor Mangal wanted to hoist flags everywhere, but did he really have the capacity, without American and British assistance, to govern those places? Would the Afghan army and national police force send men to those places? Weston believed the answer to both questions was no. "There will never be a Marine bridge too far," he told Nicholson. "But there are places that are too far for the Afghans."

Nicholson was convinced that everything his Marines were doing would set Helmand on a path to eventual peace and prosperity. But he left the details to his successors. He would clear, hold, and start building. Handing off to the Afghans wasn't his responsibility.

In April 2010, Nicholson headed home. At a sunbaked outdoor ceremony at Camp Leatherneck to transfer authority to a fellow Marine general, Nicholson told the crowd, which included Governor Mangal and hundreds of American officers, that he was proud of what his brigade had accomplished over the previous year. "And we're even prouder of what the future holds for this great province."

Nicholson admitted to me that he had a soda-straw view of Afghanistan. "This is my place," he said of his part of Helmand, "and I'm going to do everything I can to make my piece work." He was happy to have so many troops at his disposal, but he also believed he deserved them. Although Helmand was home to only 4 percent of Afghanistan's people, it had the highest number of insurgent attacks of any province. He and his fellow Marines were convinced—despite the CIA's claims to the contrary—that the taxation, processing, and trafficking of opium, much of which was cultivated in Helmand, were the principal sources of funding for the Taliban. And even though Kandahar had greater strategic importance, Nicholson believed the city and its surrounding districts would never be secure unless insurgents were beaten back in Helmand.

Even if all of that were true—plenty of officers in Kabul and at the Pentagon questioned those assertions—the troop levels in Helmand still seemed high relative to those in Kandahar and parts of eastern Afghanistan deemed critical to the security of Kabul. Nobody doubted Nicholson's success. They just wondered, in the zero-sum calculus of troops on the battlefield, if he was too successful.

The Marine drive to vanquish the Taliban from every corner of Helmand was rooted in more than elevated troop levels. Many members of the military, from top generals to lowly privates, believed the Afghan insurgency posed a genuine threat to the United States. They argued that Taliban leaders retained deep links with al-Qaeda and that if the Talibs were left unchecked, they would once again seize control of the entire country, reinstitute extremist social policies, and welcome back al-Qaeda leaders who would plot new attacks on the American homeland. Many in the White House, the State Department, and the CIA disputed that contention, but the military stated it as proven fact. Some senior officers privately questioned the "if-then" logic—they wondered whether al-Qaeda would really seek to reconstitute itself in Afghanistan, whether some of the fighting was driven more by local tribal grievances than animus toward the United States—but they stuck to the script in public. The good-versus-evil narrative was the most straightforward way to explain the war to nineteen-year-old lance corporals. They couldn't tell young men who stood a fair chance of getting blown up that they were in Afghanistan to referee long-standing disputes between an unsavory government and tribesmen who felt marginalized. So they described the mission in a binary way: They were in Afghanistan to protect the Karzai government—and the decent, law-abiding people who supported it—from terrorists and religious zealots who wanted to attack the United States.

Framing the conflict that way drove a deep wedge between military leaders and civilian officials. It led many generals, not just Petraeus, to oppose the reconciliation sought by Holbrooke. They wanted to kill or capture as many bad guys as they could and then force the others to lay down their weapons. It also encouraged the military to embrace a counterinsurgency strategy that was far more expansive than many civilian officials thought necessary. Civilians were forced into the awkward role of counseling restraint, as the military had a generation earlier, before the fervor of COIN took hold.

Borrowed Items 16/04/2019 11:09
XXXXXX3089

Title	Due Date
le America : the war within war for Afghanistan	07/05/2019
e Custer album : a pictorial graphy of General George Custer	07/05/2019

ank you for using this unit

r Library Doesn't End Here
: free eBooks + eMagazines
w.tinyurl.com/ebook-emag
ask Staff for details

****
KE YOUR LIFE EASIER
****

ail notifications are sent 2 days before
date
staff to sign up for email.

The top commanders thought their civilian counterparts—
and much of the American public—simply did not grasp the
stakes. Four days after his son was killed by a mine in Sangin,
Marine Lieutenant General John Kelly, who would go on to
serve as the senior military adviser to defense secretaries Bob
Gates and Leon Panetta, delivered a speech to Marine veterans
in St. Louis. Grieving for his boy, he provided a window into
what many commanders privately thought but normally didn't
say:

> We are at war and like it or not, that is a fact. It is not
> Bush's war, and it is not Obama's war, it is our war and
> we can't run away from it. Even if we wanted to sur-
> render, there is no one to surrender to. Our enemy is
> savage, offers absolutely no quarter, and has a single
> focus and that is either kill every one of us here at home,
> or enslave us with a sick form of extremism that serves
> no God or purpose that decent men and women could
> ever grasp. St. Louis is as much at risk as is New York
> and Washington. Given the opportunity to do another
> 9/11, our merciless enemy would do it today, tomor-
> row, and every day thereafter. If, and most in the know
> predict that it is only a matter of time, he acquires
> nuclear, chemical, or biological weapons, these extrem-
> ists will use these weapons of mass murder against us
> without a moment's hesitation. These butchers we fight
> killed more than 3,000 innocents on 9/11. As horrible
> as that death toll was, consider for a moment that the
> monsters that organized those strikes against New York
> and Washington killed only 3,000 not because that was
> enough to make their sick and demented point, but
> because [they] couldn't figure out how to kill 30,000,
> or 300,000, or 30 million of us that terrible day. I don't
> know why they hate us, and I don't care. We have a say-
> ing in the Marine Corps, and that is, "No better friend,
> no worse enemy, than a U.S. Marine." We always hope
> for the first, friendship, but are certainly more than
> ready for the second. If it's death they want, it's death
> they will get. . . .

The problem is our enemy is not willing to let us go. Regardless of how much we wish this nightmare would go away, our enemy will stay forever on the offensive until he hurts us so badly we surrender, or we kill him first. To him, this is not about our friendship with Israel, or about territory, resources, jobs, or economic opportunity in the Middle East. No, it is about us as a people. About our freedom to worship any God we please in any way we want. It is about the worth of every man, and the worth of every woman, and their equality in the eyes of God and the law; of how we live our lives with our families, inside the privacy of our own homes. It's about the God-given rights of life, liberty, and the pursuit of happiness and that all men are created equal, that they are endowed by their Creator with certain inalienable rights. As Americans we hold these truths to be self-evident. He doesn't. We love what we have; he despises who we are. Our positions can never be reconciled. He cannot be deterred—only defeated. Compromise is out of the question.

In Yorba Linda, Jon Centanni shared those sentiments. His son had been buried with full honors at the Riverside National Cemetery: a flag-draped casket, Marine pallbearers in their dress blues, a twenty-one-gun salute, taps.

The funeral procession, escorted by a phalanx of police motorcycles and accompanied by hundreds of Jon's fellow law enforcement officers from across Southern California, rolled slowly through the city, passing all of Rick's childhood schools. As the white hearse drove by, neighbors waved American flags. Students at Esperanza High placed their hands over their hearts. WE LOVE OUR Y.L. HEROES, proclaimed a large yellow banner held by three girls.

"This is a global war on terror, and if we're not there, they're going to be right back here," Jon Centanni said to me as we sat in his garage and watched videos of Rick filmed by his buddies. "If we're not keeping them on the run, they're going to be right back here, finding some way to fly planes into buildings, blow up subways, whatever it is, just to create terror in the minds of Americans."

He showed me a photo of a shirtless Rick and pointed to a tattoo over his left pectoral: FOR THOSE I LOVE, I GIVE MY LIFE.

To whom was he referring? I asked.

"To our country," his father said. "He loved the United States."

Jon took a swig of Jack Daniel's and a drag on a Marlboro Light. We went into an adjoining room and stared at a shrine to Rick. His helmet rested atop a rifle. There was his football jersey, a four-foot-tall carved wooden eagle, and a poster of him. Visitors had left scores of patches, commemorative coins, and bumper stickers: AND ON THE EIGHTH DAY, GOD CREATED MARINES. MY SON FIGHTS FOR OUR FREEDOM.

"What do we do? Do we pull out of there?" Jon said. "The current government isn't ready to accept responsibility. They'll get overrun, and then we're right back where we were—if not worse, because nobody's going to trust us now. They're going to look at us like we were back in the eighties and went, 'All right, we're out of here.' This is something we need to keep moving forward with, whether it takes twenty-five years or fifty years."

Weston wanted to call Jon Centanni and offer his condolences, perhaps visit him and shake his hand, and place a coin on the shrine. Weston no longer referred to them as good-luck coins. Not after Rick's death.

He believed Rick was a hero who had served his nation with honor and courage, but he didn't know what he would say if the conversation turned to Taghaz. Had the mission there made America safer? Had it been essential to securing Afghanistan? He didn't think so, and he couldn't bear to say it to the grieving father of a dead Marine.

"We were killing, by and large, average Omars," Weston told me, using his favorite term for an Afghan everyman. "We weren't killing Mr. al-Qaeda."

Three months after Rick was killed, Weston headed home to southwestern Utah for good. He planned to unwind by taking long hikes in Zion National Park. All told, he had spent seven years on America's two war fronts.

Before he left Afghanistan, we went for a walk around Camp Leatherneck. As he gazed over the dusty expanse, he felt as if he had stepped onto the set of a sci-fi movie. When he had arrived, just a few dozen tents and plywood buildings had dotted the camp. The ground had been covered with a foot of 600-grit sand that, with a puff of wind, would coat every inch of his body. Just a year later, Leatherneck and an adjoining British encampment had together become the second largest city in Helmand. The two camps generated—and consumed—ten times the electricity that the rest of the province did. Metal-walled housing units and offices sprawled across the landscape as far as he could see. The chow hall had been moved into a structure as large as a circus big top. Tons of gravel had been spread around to reduce the dust. Looking to the east, Weston saw telescoping cranes with pincer arms hoisting metal shipping containers big enough to fit on eighteen-wheel trucks as if they were toy blocks, ferrying the cargo necessary for America to fight a modern war: air-conditioners, laptop computers, tins of Skoal to be sold at the PX, cardboard cartons packed with Priority Mail care packages from home. To the north were hundreds of hulking, mine-resistant trucks sprouting antennae and explosive detectors parked in ramrod-straight rows, waiting to be distributed to troops who hoped the half-inch-thick armor and V-shaped hulls would protect them from the blast of the home-made fertilizer bombs that speckled the dirt roads. Off in the distance, a convoy of tankers bearing fuel and water snaked across the lunar landscape.

"It's obscene," he said as he sipped from a small carton of grapefruit juice—made in Kuwait—that had been shipped to Pakistan and then hauled overland to Leatherneck at an exorbitant cost.

After a year in Afghanistan, Weston had grown despondent. Although he had supported Obama's deployment of 21,000 more forces early in his term, the president's subsequent decision to bow to his generals and approve a 30,000-troop surge had led to the needless expansion of Leatherneck and the incursion of Marine units to places they should have left alone. Weston had not come around to the view of many of his fellow Democrats that the United States should pack up and go. What he wanted was a lighter, more nimble American presence, one that was focused on killing big-fish Taliban, training the Afghan army, and supporting modest programs to improve the government.

"This place is an endurance test," he said as he took a pull from his juice box. "Your average Afghan thinks it's not about the number of soldiers and Marines. For them, the issue is who is going to be there five or ten years from now? Will it be us or the Taliban?"

The central assumptions on which Obama had predicated his surge seemed to have collapsed. The military had ignored his order to limit the counterinsurgency mission. Pakistan had failed to crack down on Taliban sanctuaries. President Karzai and his ministers in Kabul were corrupt and incompetent and could not deliver the basic local governance that Washington so desperately wanted. USAID was taking far longer than expected to create new employment and repair critical infrastructure.

Weston began walking back to his office. Ninety Marines and sailors from the brigade had been killed since their deployment had begun. Each was memorialized with a four-by-six-inch framed photo on the plywood wall leading to the combat operations center. Many had been blown up while engaging in the most prosaic of tasks: walking foot patrols, manning supply convoys, or simply driving from one base to another. One of them, Corporal Nicholas Uzenski, who had been fatally shot during a firefight in Now Zad in January 2010, had told his buddies he had signed a check before his deployment. "To the United States of America," he had written. "Paid in full."

To Weston the surge was a big bluff—a long-odds gamble that the Afghan government, the Taliban, and the Pakistanis would all behave differently with more American pieces on the Risk board.

"The bluff should have been called much earlier," he said as he passed the flagpole. "But only we can call our own bluff."

PART THREE

Triage

14

The Boss of the Border

HARD BY THE BORDER WITH PAKISTAN, the sand-swept city of Spin Boldak defied all notions of Afghanistan as a land of privation. Anything and everything could be acquired along the labyrinthine alleys of its sprawling bazaar—at prices that put Walmart and Costco to shame. Guns. Opium. Booze. Cuban cigars. French cologne. Gold and diamonds. Flat-screen televisions. Laptops with the newest microprocessors. DVDs of movies still playing in American cinemas. Chinese-made air-conditioners and refrigerators. Luxury sedans and sport-utility vehicles, with or without bulletproof glass and armor plating within the doors. All the market lacked was merchants and shoppers willing to pay taxes. Everyone was a smuggler.

The tax evasion scam was simple but extremely profitable. The merchandise was imported through Pakistan, where it was exempt from duties because it was intended for sale in Afghanistan. Customs inspectors working for the Kabul government were supposed to tax each inbound shipment, but that rarely occurred. Many drivers circumvented the official border crossing gate by driving a few miles east or west through the desert. Once the goods changed hands in the Spin Boldak bazaar, they were smuggled back into Pakistan and sometimes through the desert to Iran, depriving Islamabad and Tehran of tax revenue. Cars were the most lucrative because Pakistani duties on imported vehicles often amounted to more than the sale price.

When I visited Spin Boldak in July 2010, the Afghan side of the border appeared to be a free-for-all. Donkey carts and child porters weaved amid brightly painted, smoke-belching cargo trucks. Customs officers waved vehicles through with nary an inspection. Policemen refused to interdict vehicles that skirted the official crossing. But the frontier was far less dysfunctional than it seemed. Drugs and untaxed televisions moved with the efficiency of a FedEx package. The cops had orders to turn a blind eye toward certain trucks that bypassed the gate. Other convoys received police escorts through the desert. Bribes were assessed on almost every shipment.

The master of the racket was Abdul Razziq, an illiterate thirty-two-year-old border police colonel who had built himself into one of the most powerful warlords in the south. He commanded a force of 3,500 armed men. All that muscle gave him an unrivaled degree of influence and control over anything that crossed Afghanistan's southern border. His men decided which smugglers could pass and for how large a bribe. They also did their own share of trafficking. The ill-gotten gains went straight to Razziq. Those who crossed him often wound up in ditches, riddled with bullets. In 2006, he allegedly ordered the murder of a smuggling rival and fifteen of the man's friends.

Razziq had been born months before the first Soviet troops rolled into Afghanistan, and the tumult that engulfed his nation in the three decades that followed buoyed him to power. His uncle became a top lieutenant in an Achekzai tribal militia that fought the Soviets. But the group later switched sides and allied itself with the Communists in exchange for assistance in beating back the rival Noorzai tribe for control of border trade routes. When the Taliban sprouted after the Soviets left, their first major conquest was Spin Boldak, which they seized with the support of the Noorzai, who saw the radical Islamists as a better alternative to the Achekzai. Once the Talibs took the city, they killed Razziq's father and hanged his uncle from the barrel of a tank. Razziq and the rest of his family fled to Pakistan. In early November 2001, he assembled an Achekzai militia at the behest of Gul Agha Sherzai, the bearlike former governor of Kandahar who was working with U.S. Special Forces soldiers to liberate Kandahar from the Taliban. Young Razziq quickly earned a reputation as an aggressive but astute tactical leader. Once the Talibs fell and Sherzai claimed the governorship, Razziq set out to rebuild his family's influence in Spin Boldak. The following year, his bravery and lineage led fellow Achekzai to appoint him—at the age of twenty-three—the leader of the tribe's militia, which he used to consolidate control over the border. When the Karzai government sought to integrate militiamen into the uniformed security forces, Razziq jumped at the opportunity. He and several hundred of his men became members of the Afghan border police. They would eventually receive uniforms, vehicles, new weapons, and other equipment—much of it from the Americans. Most important, his anointment as the commander in Spin Boldak conferred legitimacy that allowed him even greater dominion over illicit activities along the frontier.

With his lanky frame, jet-black beard, and a boyish face that broke into broad, seemingly guileless grins, Razziq did not fit the image of most Afghan warlords. He looked like a rank-and-file policeman, not a commander. His behavior was atypical too. Though other warlords would have kept the border loot for themselves, squirreling it away in offshore bank accounts, Razziq shared the wealth. He fed the needy and supported influential elders, earning the adoration of many residents. Because he deemed the five hundred officers he had been allotted by the Interior Ministry insufficient, he plowed some of his border profits into expanding his force.

Razziq also funneled a healthy share of his spoils to his patrons in Kandahar and Kabul. Much of it went to people linked with the Karzai family. But Razziq played all the angles in the interest of self-preservation, much like a savvy Washington lobbyist: He paid off Noorzai leaders to keep them from disrupting operations along the border, and he sent cash to Gul Agha Sherzai, the Karzais' principal rival in the south. And Razziq didn't completely shut out the customs inspectors. They collected a nominal portion of duties—enough, he figured, to keep the Ministry of Finance happy. The whole scheme was illegal, but it ensured that he remained the strongman of Spin Boldak.

Razziq's stretch of the border may have been the most corrupt swath of southern Afghanistan, but it was also the safest. Driven by a visceral hatred of the Taliban dating back to the fall of Spin Boldak in 1994, he pursued insurgents with the same zeal he brought to smuggling. Ample funds allowed his men to buy equipment without waiting for budget allotments from Kabul or handouts from the Americans. He also commanded a remarkable degree of devotion among his ranks. Tribal fealty was part of the reason—many border policemen were fellow Achekzais—but Razziq also employed deft recruiting tactics. He drew some of his personnel from a refugee camp near the city, offering to protect their families in exchange for their loyalty. His men soon became the most effective—and aggressive—Afghan security force in Kandahar province. They conducted far more independent operations than any other Afghan police or army unit. They seized scores of Talibs many of whom tried to sneak in from Pakistan with thousands of pounds of ammonium nitrate fertilizer intended for the manufacture of homemade bombs.

For the first eight years of Razziq's reign in Spin Boldak, U.S. and NATO forces all but ignored him. The few American troops in the south focused on hunting down Taliban leaders who had decamped elsewhere. When the Canadians took over in Kandahar in early 2006, they lacked the manpower to establish anything more than a nominal presence at the border. But instead of maneuvering around him, the Canadians agreed to a request by Afghan officials to allow Razziq's men to assist in an operation that summer to oust Taliban fighters from Panjwai, a Noorzai-dominated district to the west of Kandahar. Worried that they would be slaughtered by Razziq and his fellow Achekzai militiamen, some Noorzais sided with the Taliban in self-defense. That alliance led Razziq to fulfill their fears. His men rampaged through the area, reportedly killing women and children. "After that, everyone was with the Taliban," said Ustaz Abdul Halim, a prominent Noorzai elder and former mujahideen commander. From then on, the Canadians insisted that Razziq confine his operations to the border. He complied and was left alone.

All that changed in the late summer of 2009. U.S. commanders sent a battalion of soldiers from Harry Tunnell's Stryker brigade to Spin Boldak to augment Razziq's efforts to interdict Taliban infiltrators. The battalion commander worked closely with Razziq, who possessed vital local intelligence, a desire to pursue insurgents, and a force that was almost ten times as large as the American contingent. But not everyone on the newly constructed U.S. base outside the city shared the commander's enthusiasm about the partnership. The military presence led the embassy to assign a stabilization team to the district, and its members grew concerned about Razziq's clout, which far surpassed that of the district governor, the local police chief, and every other Afghan official in the area. In Kabul, officials at the U.S. Embassy and NATO headquarters had similar worries. Intelligence assessments detailing his involvement in drug smuggling added to the alarm, as did reports that he countenanced widespread fraud in the presidential election that August by storing in his house overnight several ballot boxes that turned out to be stuffed with sheets identically marked for Karzai.

To General McChrystal's top aides, Razziq embodied the root cause of Afghanistan's instability. They believed that his disregard for laws and formal systems of power, his penchant for frontier justice, his willingness to liquidate tribal rivals, and his thirst for graft would eventually alienate and anger enough people that the events of 1994 would be repeated: The Taliban, with the support of non-Achekzai tribes, would take over the district. McChrystal believed that the success of his counterinsurgency strategy required bold steps to sideline warlords and build formal systems of government. Some of his advisers suggested several strongmen to push aside, including Ahmed Wali Karzai, but they advocated starting with Razziq. Though he was close to the Karzai family, it did not appear likely that the president would protect him at all costs.

When officers at the NATO regional headquarters in Kandahar heard of the plan, they were aghast. The top commander there, British Major General Nick Carter, thought the risks of removing Razziq were too grave for the uncertain reward of improved governance. In discussions with McChrystal and his senior staff, Carter cited Razziq's cooperation with international forces and his willingness to conduct independent operations against the Taliban, which few Afghan units were able or willing to do. If Razziq were removed, Carter wondered, what would happen to his armed men? They probably wouldn't work for anyone else. Would they turn into an outlaw militia? If that occurred, who would provide security along the border? The Stryker battalion had fewer than 400 soldiers in the district compared to Razziq's 3,500-strong force.

In December 2009, Carter was dealt a trump card with the announcement of Obama's 30,000-troop surge. The new forces would require mine-resistant vehicles and supplies to build bases. They'd need food and fuel, all of which would have to be trucked through Pakistan. That necessitated security along the border and on the highway from Spin Boldak to the Kandahar Airfield. NATO convoys had not hit a single roadside bomb on that road in the previous year. If Razziq was out of the picture, Carter argued, the resulting instability could hold up critical shipments and delay the start of surge operations.

That was the deciding factor for McChrystal. He said Razziq could stay. The following month, McChrystal relented on Ahmed Wali Karzai after learning that U.S. intelligence agencies lacked proof that he was involved in drug smuggling or other illegal activities.

The volte-face on Razziq and Ahmed Wali revealed the fundamental contradiction in the military's counterinsurgency strategy. It depended on persuading the Afghan people to support their government over the Taliban, but the United States did not have the time, resources, political will, or support from President Karzai to take the most essential first step in winning public trust: purging the corrupt strongmen and replacing them with competent, credible civil servants. Even if McChrystal had insisted on sacking the power brokers, it was too late in the game to make a difference. By 2010, Razziq and his fellow thugs across the country were part of an entrenched, kleptocratic system that stretched all the way to the top of the Afghan government. If he was removed, his replacement would almost certainly have been forced to run smuggling rings and shake down truck drivers because of demands for cash from superiors in Kabul. Fixing the system required more than firing people—the entire government would have to be overhauled.

Instead of admitting that the Afghan government was an insurmountable obstacle to executing the COIN strategy—that would have amounted to acknowledging the truth of Ambassador Eikenberry's cable criticizing the proposed surge—the military tried to have it both ways. COIN remained the order of the day, and the strongmen became part of the solution, not the problem. To reconcile the contradiction, the military sought to reform them, hoping that a combination of threats and incentives would encourage them to become more savory characters.

Their guinea pig would be Razziq.

"Come," Razziq said to me as he grabbed my hand and led me into the bazaar. "I show you my city."

As soon as people saw him, shouts of "Razziq is here!" echoed across the stalls. Within a minute, we were mobbed. He was a colonel in the border police, but everyone deferentially addressed him as "General Razziq."

"How are you?" he said to every store owner he passed. "Do you need any help?"

Young boys wanted his photograph. Gray-bearded men offered him tea. Shopkeepers refused to sell him anything; when he sought to buy me a bottle of the same faux French cologne he splashed on himself, the merchant insisted on giving it to him for free.

Spotting a man with a laptop under his arm, Razziq stopped and asked where he lived. The man said he was from Chaman, just across the Pakistani border. Razziq flashed a smile of recognition. "I know your uncle," he said. The politeness had a subtext: *I know how to find you if you cause trouble here.*

An old man shuffled up to Razziq and told him he had information about Taliban activity. "It's worth a lot to you," he said. Razziq told him to meet him in his office that afternoon.

A few minutes later, Razziq walked into an electronics shop fashioned out of a metal shipping container. The crowd swelled outside.

"Make sure nobody steals my stuff!" a merchant shouted to a friend.

"I'm here!" Razziq yelled back. "Don't worry!"

As he waded back into the throng and I struggled to keep up, I found myself next to Robert Waltemeyer, a colonel in the U.S.

Special Forces who had recently arrived in Spin Boldak. "You can see the enigma he presents," Waltemeyer said. "There are not a lot of Afghan officials who can walk through a crowd as freely as this. Right or wrong, if we're looking for an accepted Afghan leader, you can't deny we have one right here."

Waltemeyer was an old friend of McChrystal, and his job was to reform Razziq. Five months earlier, in February 2010, McChrystal and Carter had traveled to Spin Boldak and laid down a set of red lines for Razziq. They told him that he could no longer close the border at will—it had to remain open for a set number of hours each day—and they urged him to legitimize his business interests. They also instructed him to confine his operations to the Spin Boldak area and warned him that his activities would be coming under new scrutiny. To prevent the session from turning entirely admonitory, they praised his efforts to fight the Taliban and promised to provide more resources to train his force. A few months later, the Interior Ministry had appointed a brigadier general to oversee Razziq, and the NATO command sent Waltemeyer to serve as his mentor.

Razziq nodded and smiled when the Americans talked, but he wasn't about to change his stripes. He knew the Karzais would never remove him. He was too valuable to their wallets.

Soon after the commanders delivered the new rules, Carter returned to Spin Boldak with an exciting offer for Razziq: Because he was now an important person, did he want to learn to read and write, and perhaps even study English? Others in the room were dumbstruck by Carter's suggestion. The interpreter—an Afghan working for the U.S. Army—refused to convey the question. (That fall, another NATO officer would once again urge Razziq to learn to read and write. After the offer was translated, Razziq nodded but didn't make any promises. He didn't need those skills to acquire money and power.)

Several weeks later, Carter and his deputy, U.S. Marine Brigadier General Thomas Murray, brought the newly appointed Afghan brigadier general to meet Razziq in Spin Boldak. When Carter talked, Razziq appeared to listen attentively. But when the Afghan brigadier and two other senior Afghan officers, including the top army corps commander for the south, began to speak, Razziq turned to chat with Murray. He slapped the American general on the knee and poured him a cup of tea. Carter had wanted the three Afghan officers to lay down the law, but Razziq blew them off. Soon thereafter, U.S. officials heard that the Afghan brigadier had received a message from Kabul: *Don't mess with Razziq.*

When Waltemeyer had arrived, he'd presented Razziq with a "mentorship plan." After that first meeting, Razziq rarely returned Waltemeyer's phone calls. Conducting joint operations with U.S. troops, as he had been doing since the Stryker battalion arrived, was fine by Razziq, but he wasn't going to allow himself to be housebroken like a puppy. He scoffed when I asked him about the attempts to confine him to security patrolling along the border. "My duties are universal," he said.

Owen Kirby, the State Department representative in Spin Boldak, quickly came to see the futility of the reinvention effort. His superiors had told him to limit his dealings with Razziq and focus instead on working with the district governor and his staff. (An embassy memo instructed U.S. diplomats to avoid being photographed with "malign actors" such as Razziq and Ahmed Wali Karzai.) But the district governor wielded no power. When the provincial governor, Tooryalai Wesa, wanted something in Spin Boldak, he called Razziq, and when Kirby proposed initiatives to the district governor, his inevitable response was "Ask Razziq."

To Kirby, the reform effort was a waste of time. "Did we really think we could groom him into something better?" he asked. He believed that the United States had to choose between a counterinsurgency strategy that entailed a long-term nation-building effort—perhaps as long as two decades—or a more expedient solution that involved embracing Razziq and other strongmen. "Our problem is that we were attempting to do both and undermining each," he said.

The month after my visit to Spin Boldak, Governor Wesa called President Karzai to report that Taliban forces were blocking a road and searching cars in western Kandahar city. "Could you, Mr. President, order NATO to come and help us?" Wesa asked.

"Shame on you," Karzai replied. The president, who had issued a decree a few weeks earlier giving governors authority over Afghan security forces in their provinces, told Wesa to organize an Afghan response. "Go after them," Karzai said. "Don't wait for NATO."

Wesa cobbled together a few hundred Afghan soldiers and policemen and sent them into the Taliban-controlled area. The Afghan forces became trapped in a minefield, and five of them were killed trying to leave. "It was a gong show," said Bill Harris, the senior American official at the Kandahar reconstruction office.

Wesa was determined to try again, but for the next attempt he contacted Razziq for help. Carter could have objected on the grounds that Kandahar city was well beyond Razziq's authorized area of operations, but he didn't want to forestall a rare Afghan-led operation. His tacit approval was the end of the reform effort. With Obama's July 2011 deadline drawing ever closer, "we finally realized that we didn't have the time to do the full-spectrum COIN that we wanted to do," a senior U.S. officer told me. "If the Afghans wanted to step up, even if it ran counter to our best-laid plans, we couldn't let the perfect become the enemy of the good."

Razziq roared up from Spin Boldak with three hundred heavily armed men. A U.S. Special Operations team linked up with him to call in air strikes and medical evacuations, if they were needed. Unlike Afghan army units, many of which needed to be prodded and led into battle, Razziq's troops charged right in, arresting twenty insurgents and seizing scores of improvised explosive devices. Their aggressive tactics were effective, if unorthodox. When his men spotted a stolen Afghan police truck that they suspected was rigged with a bomb, they didn't wait for American ordnance-disposal technicians to arrive. They fired a rocket-propelled grenade at the truck, which ricocheted off the side and struck a nearby tree. The explosion dislodged a suicide bomber in white robes who had been hiding in the tree. He fell from the branches, landing on top of the truck and blowing it up.

The next month, Razziq's men helped U.S. troops flush insurgents from redoubts in Arghandab district. In seventy-two hours, his force captured fifty Taliban fighters, five large road-side bombs, and five hundred pounds of explosives. All they required from the Americans was some basic battlefield intelligence reports and modest air support.

As McChrystal and the military softened their stance on corruption, the U.S. Embassy headed in the opposite direction. To counter concern within Obama's war cabinet during the surge debate that government malfeasance would doom a counterinsurgency strategy, Hillary Clinton had urged Karzai to do more to tackle graft. She warned that increases in U.S. aid would depend on the introduction of new anticorruption measures and offered to send agents from the Federal Bureau of Investigation and the Drug Enforcement Administration to Afghanistan to help apprehend and prosecute offenders. Although Karzai resented the prospect of American investigators snooping through his government, he didn't want to throttle back foreign assistance. Three days before his second-term inaugural ceremony, several of his top ministers announced the creation of two new antigraft agencies. One of them, the Major Crimes Task Force, would be mentored by the FBI and Britain's Serious and Organised Crime Agency. The other, the Special Investigative Unit, would be coached by the DEA. Unlike other civilian agencies, which refused to send their best people to Afghanistan, the DEA had made the mission a top priority. Afghanistan was, after all, the source of much of the world's heroin. The agency dispatched some of its most talented field officers to the country, and it brought Afghan investigators to its training center in Quantico, Virginia. "We were told to clean up the Afghan government," one senior DEA agent told me, "so that's what we set out to do."

The get-tough approach fit with Eikenberry's view of how to fix Afghanistan. Building district-level government was only part of the plan; a crackdown on malign influences was also required. Even after McChrystal had decided to back down on Razziq and Ahmed Wali Karzai, Eikenberry instructed his field officers to keep up the pressure. "We were supposed to block and check the warlords," said Bill Harris. "We were supposed to get in their faces."

Although the American personnel would effectively be conducting the investigations and building the cases behind the scenes, U.S. officials assumed Karzai would tolerate the two countergraft agencies because they were headed by Afghans and housed within his government. That proved true until the agencies arrested one of Karzai's aides, Mohammed Zia Salehi, on bribery charges after a wiretap revealed that he had solicited a new car worth $10,000 in exchange for impeding an investigation of a money-exchange firm that had allegedly funneled $3 billion in undeclared cash out of the country. Although the agencies had notified the country's attorney general and interior minister about the impending arrest, the anticorruption teams did not provide advance warning to the president or his senior staff because American officials worried that Salehi, a top official in Karzai's national security council, would be tipped off and flee the country. Afghan agents surrounded the aide's five-story apartment building at 5 a.m. and demanded that he surrender. Before Salehi came out, he phoned a friend at the National Directorate of Security, the country's intelligence agency, which dispatched its own agents to the house in an attempt to prevent the arrest. The American-led anticorruption squad eventually got its man, but not for long. When Karzai learned of the arrest, he was incensed and ordered the attorney general to release Salehi. By 6 p.m. that day, the presidential aide was on his way home.

Karzai blasted the early morning arrest as a heavy-handed tactic "exactly reminiscent of the Soviet presence" in his country. Within weeks, he restricted foreign involvement in the two anticorruption agencies and directed that their personnel no longer receive the salary enhancements from the U.S. government that were essential to recruiting skilled investigators.

The raid and its aftermath provoked a fierce debate within the U.S. government. Senior military officials were livid that Americans involved in the arrest had not consulted them to weigh the blowback from targeting a top Karzai aide. General Petraeus told members of the war cabinet that corruption cases against senior members of Karzai's government needed to be resolved with face-saving compromises behind closed doors instead of public prosecutions. Bob Gates argued for a diminished American role in fighting graft, saying the effort needed to be led by Afghans. Although embassy officials insisted that the FBI and DEA had just begun to develop extensive corruption investigations that could potentially sideline several top Karzai officials, the Pentagon didn't want to spend the precious months before the drawdown began trying to remake the Afghan government. The Karzai establishment was what it was, and they'd simply have to work with it.

The back-down found favor among National Security Council officials who had long been dubious about counterinsurgency. They saw in the military's push for a weaker policy an implicit admission that the grand COIN plan was not working. Instead of saying "I told you so," the White House quietly agreed to the change.

A month later, the Afghan government dropped all charges against Salehi.

The next time I saw Razziq, he was a general not just in name only. Appointed by Karzai to be police chief for all of Kandahar province, he had traveled to Zhari district for a community meeting to discuss the creation of armed village defense forces in the area. He still wore his black, gray, and white border patrol uniform, but he traveled with a larger retinue of Achekzai bodyguards. His predecessor had been killed by a suicide bomber dressed as a police officer, and he wasn't about to take chances.

Because of Karzai's concern that the local forces could morph into militias, he required the Interior Ministry to assess every district before the U.S. military could arm its villagers. The process involved asking elders whether they supported the idea. At the meeting, a parade of officials from Kabul and Kandahar city rose to speak. Each urged residents to back the effort. They promised improved security and additional development assistance.

Razziq employed a different approach. "If you don't help us, we will force you to help," he told the crowd. "It is your responsibility to defend this area."

I couldn't be sure whether Razziq was joking. But when it came time for the elders to speak, nobody objected.

15

A Fresh Can of Whoop-ass

KILO COMPANY'S VERY FIRST PATROL introduced its men to the horrors of Sangin.

It began as an early afternoon visit to meet their new neighbors. First Platoon left Patrol Base Fires, a rustic outpost in a belt of farmland between the Helmand River and Route 611, the district's main north–south road. Walking single file, scanning the shoulder-high cornfields for signs of insurgents, the platoon set out for the nearest village. The day before, four Marines from a different company had been killed when their armored all-terrain vehicle had struck a massive roadside bomb. The members of First Platoon figured they would be safer on foot.

The platoon had not traveled more than 250 meters when the shooting started. First a few pops. Then a volley. And then a fusillade—not just from handheld AK-47 rifles but from high-powered, belt-fed machine guns too. Pinned down amid the cornstalks, the platoon radioed for help. A machine-gun squad from Second Platoon threw on their gear and hustled out of Fires to set up a blocking position so their buddies could withdraw. But as soon as the backup squad neared the scene, it was ambushed by a dozen more insurgents. Within minutes, the squad's leader was shot in the leg. The only place they could take cover was an adobe compound to the southwest marked on their maps as Building Three. They hustled for protection.

Moments later, the Marines would come to understand why more than a hundred British soldiers had been killed in Sangin from 2006 to 2010; why Larry Nicholson had been loath to put it on his plate; why it was, without a doubt, the most dangerous place in Afghanistan.

As the squad rushed toward the compound, a machine gunner, Lance Corporal Alec Catherwood, stepped on a homemade mine and was blown into a nearby canal. On the other side of the building, Lance Corporal Joseph Lopez triggered another bomb as he sought cover behind a wall. When the squad's medic rushed over to help Lopez, he took a path that had not been swept for mines. He too stepped on a pressure-triggered bomb. The medic lost his legs. Lopez and Catherwood died before the medical evacuation helicopters arrived.

There were so many explosions, so close together, that others in the platoon assumed that fellow Marines were firing mortars at the Taliban. It was not until later that they understood that the booms they heard were their buddies stepping on mine after mine. "Nobody move!" screamed Sergeant Joel Bailey, who had jumped into the canal and tried to save Catherwood. Bailey had served on two combat deployments in Iraq before coming to Afghanistan. "Stay the fuck where you are!"

The Marines would soon learn that Building Three was no anomaly. Scores of other compounds had been similarly rigged with mines, as had canal embankments and treelines. In the years during which British forces had stuck close to their bases, the Taliban had painstakingly prepared their battlefield defenses. When Marines pushed through the fields, squads of a dozen or more insurgents would open fire, forcing the Americans to seek cover in embankments, treelines, and compounds—the very places that had been seeded with bombs.

When First Platoon and the response squad from Second Platoon made it back to Fires, they were desperate for more bullets and grenades. But the Taliban had dammed up nearby irrigation canals, flooding the sole dirt road leading to the outpost and rendering it impassable to American armored vehicles. The Marines eventually waded through the muck on foot, hoisting ammunition on combat stretchers under the cover of darkness. To the commander of Kilo Company, Captain Nikolai Johnson, it appeared that the Taliban were seeking a return to the status quo that had existed when British troops were responsible for Sangin. "They wanted to isolate us," he said. "They didn't want us to patrol."

Once the outpost was resupplied, Johnson spoke to his men. Two of their comrades had been killed and another gravely wounded. But he couldn't allow them to dwell on their loss. He believed his Marines needed to send a message to the insurgents the following day—and every day thereafter.

Marines revel in their history. Every Leatherneck learns the story of how his Korean War brethren who were encircled by Chinese forces at the Chosin Reservoir managed to break out and inflict crippling losses on the enemy. The Third Battalion of the Fifth Marine Regiment—of which Kilo was a part—had been among the units at Chosin. Johnson urged his Marines to emulate the bravery of their predecessors. "This is your breakout," he told them. "This is your opportunity to write history for the Marine Corps."

It was October 14, 2010—the first night of Kilo Company's seven-month tour in Sangin. Johnson wondered if every day would be like their first. *This is going to be a long deployment,* he thought. But he didn't betray any concern to his men. He told his Marines they were the strongest tribe in the valley.

First and Second platoons pushed out of Fires early the next morning. Their destination was the closest mud-walled building flying a white Taliban flag. "Follow them to where they are sleeping," Johnson exhorted. The platoons got into another firefight and Kilo lost another man, but they kept advancing. The insurgents near the building eventually retreated, and the Marines seized their first flag.

The following weeks would bring more fallen angels, more double amputees, and more ripped-down Taliban flags. The battalion pursued the Taliban with relentless ferocity. Almost every day, Kilo Company conducted missions in areas long deemed enemy territory, even if doing so meant that one or two of their number stepped on a mine. Their goal was to get into fights and kill as many insurgents as they could. "We developed a hunter mentality," Johnson said. "This was a great place to be if you're a Marine infantryman."

Johnson's men unleashed a blistering volume of ordnance

during their deployment. His company requested more than eighty air strikes. He lost count of the total number of mortars his men fired after a day during which they lobbed sixty. The 3/5's commander, Lieutenant Colonel Jason Morris, encouraged the punishment. After losing ten Marines within a week of their arrival, he realized that much of the battalion's predeployment training, which had focused on the soft side of COIN—engaging with tribal leaders and rebuilding infrastructure—didn't apply. "Sangin was a minefield," he said, "and you can't do COIN in a minefield." He told his men to one-up the insurgents. If they were receiving fire from rifles and machine guns, he wanted his Marines to respond with rockets. "We need to make a statement," he said.

The exclamation point on his message was delivered on Route 611. When Kilo Company had arrived in Sangin, it had taken them eight hours to travel from the battalion's headquarters in the district's main town to their forward operating base. The encampments were just six miles apart, but the road had been mined with so many bombs that the Marines had had no choice but to thread a circuitous path through the desert. Later that autumn, the battalion received two tanklike machines with giant steel claws. The fearsome contraptions were called Assault Breacher Vehicles, and they looked like something that had rolled off a *Mad Max* movie set. The vehicles could launch line charges—small rockets that pull a wire embedded with C4 explosive that can clear a path as wide as a truck for a hundred meters, pulverizing everything in the way and ringing ears miles away. The 3/5 fired two dozen of them to tear up a 1,500-meter stretch of Route 611 that was embedded with fifty-two bombs. In another part of the district, they employed multiple line charges to raze tall compound walls that insurgent snipers and bomb layers hid behind. When residents returned to the rubble, Marine officers told them that if they wanted to rebuild, their walls would have to be lower than four feet.

Morris had no qualms about demolishing property. A quarter of the British troops who had perished in Sangin had died along the high-walled road. "We threw out the COIN playbook and treated this like a conventional battlefield," he told me.

"You can only take so many killed and wounded before you say, 'This cannot continue.' We didn't want to destroy Sangin to save it, but there were places that we had to flatten. We had no choice."

The Marines used similarly aggressive tactics to stanch the bleeding ulcer in Marja after they established their own NATO regional command at Camp Leatherneck. That meant they no longer had to report to Nick Carter, the British major general at the Kandahar Airfield who had been criticized by McChrystal for not devoting more troops to the initial invasion. Carter had wanted the Marines to concentrate in central Marja and focus on protecting the population. But Marine commanders believed they couldn't secure Marja until they attacked Taliban enclaves in the desert to the east and west. As soon as they were freed from Carter's grip, the Marines swept into the desert. The result was almost immediate: Acts of violence inside Marja plummeted.

In Kandahar province, newly arrived Army surge units also began to forsake elements of COIN strategy in the autumn of 2010. When Lieutenant Colonel David Flynn had brought his battalion from the Army's 101st Airborne Division to the northern fringe of Arghandab district, he had planned to win over the locals by building schools and clinics, handing out seeds to farmers, and sipping tea in weekly *shuras* with village elders. But as soon as his soldiers arrived, they faced the same reception as the Marines in Sangin had. Mines fashioned from plastic jugs of homemade explosive and crude, pressure-sensitive triggers were everywhere—on dirt paths, under culverts, in the branches of pomegranate trees. Sometimes the bomb-sniffing dogs caught them. Sometimes the soldiers spotted them. And sometimes they stepped on them. Blown-off limbs quickly became the signature injury for America's surge troops in the south. In the battalion's first hundred days on the ground, it lost seven soldiers. Seventy more were wounded, many of them double-leg amputees.

Like Sangin, Arghandab had become a command-and-control node for the Taliban. Because it ran along the northern fringe of Kandahar city, it was an ideal staging area for attacks. The local population was ripe for recruitment; President Karzai's decision in 2007 to anoint an inexperienced young man as leader of the Alikozai tribe had created fissures that the Taliban quickly exploited. And coalition forces had never flexed their muscle there. Canadian troops, and the American Stryker soldiers who had followed them, lacked the strength to stay in areas long enough to prevent insurgents from returning. The Taliban turned bunkers used during the Soviet occupation into weapons caches. Abandoned homes became hideaways and crude labs where they transformed ammonium nitrate fertilizer into explosives. "When we came out there, we were fully bought into the idea of protecting the population," Flynn told me. "But we were surprised to find there was nobody in most of these villages."

Instead of sipping tea, Flynn struck back. An initial target was the village of Tarok Kolache, a collection of about a dozen mud-brick, multifamily housing compounds surrounded by pomegranate orchards. Video from surveillance aircraft indicated that the village had been vacated, save for insurgents who were manufacturing homemade explosives in the walled-off courtyards. Officers in Flynn's battalion had the aircraft fly overhead for a few weeks—to ensure that there were no signs that civilians had returned. He also consulted a local leader, who confirmed that all the residents had left Tarok Kolache.

Then Flynn flattened the village.

U.S. B-1B Lancer and A-10 Warthog jets conducted repeated bombing runs in early October. A new ground-launched artillery rocket system also pelted the enclave. All told, almost twenty-five tons of ordnance was dropped on Tarok Kolache. When it was over, the village was a giant patch of dirt, except for a few mud walls that had survived the onslaught. Flynn went on to flatten parts of three nearby villages. The air strikes in Arghandab helped set a record: U.S. and NATO aircraft unleashed more than one thousand bombs and missiles that October, the highest tally in any single month since 2001.

The tactics did not fuel a groundswell of anger. The destroyed compounds were largely empty, and no civilians were killed. The military also doled out compensation, either in the form of cash payments or, in the case of Tarok Kolache, a U.S.-supervised rebuilding of the village. Flynn's battalion established an outpost in the village and hired contractors to resurrect the structures. The local mosque, once a mud-walled edifice, was rebuilt with brick and concrete—it featured colorful minarets and a large prayer room—and a series of long brick buildings replaced the adobe housing compounds. The cost of the reconstruction, including compensation for damaged fields and culverts, was about $1.3 million. But Flynn regarded it as a small price to pay to evict the Taliban and save the limbs of his soldiers. In the months after the village was razed, there was almost no insurgent activity in the area. The presence of U.S. troops made it an inhospitable place to reestablish bomb factories. Residents also pledged to provide the Americans with information about Taliban infiltration. "People understand that if the Taliban come back again," Flynn said, "that could happen again."

For the Marines in Helmand, the postapocalyptic Assault Breacher Vehicles whetted their appetite for more muscle. Eager to employ every tool in the Marine arsenal—the everyone-gets-to-play attitude of elementary school kickball games—Major General Richard Mills, who succeeded Larry Nicholson as the top Marine commander in Helmand, asked General Petraeus for permission to field a company of sixteen M1A1 Abrams battle tanks. Originally developed to defend Western Europe from a Soviet invasion, the sixty-eight-ton beasts were equipped with 120 mm main guns and powered by jet engines. They certainly weren't a COIN tool. When Kael Weston heard of the tank request, he was incredulous. No other American unit had used tanks in Afghanistan. Weston feared the tanks would remind the locals of the Soviets, whose rusting armored vehicles still littered the landscape. "What kind of message are we sending to the Average Omars of Helmand?" he fumed. But there was little he could do from southwestern Utah other than write exasperated e-mails to his Marine friends. Petraeus eventually approved the tanks, and Mills sent them on missions in the desert south of Sangin. When I asked the Marines what the tanks could do, officers held forth about the precision of the 120-mm gun, which would strike targets a mile away with frightening accuracy. It was faster and better, they insisted, than relying on air strikes or artillery. What about the psychological impact? I wondered. "Fuck this nice-guy shit," one of them said. "We're opening a fresh can of whoop-ass."

The get-tough tactics were not confined to razing roads and villages. Soon after Petraeus replaced McChrystal in July 2010, U.S. Special Operations forces more than tripled the pace of their nighttime missions to snatch Taliban commanders and financiers. In the wee hours of almost every morning, black helicopters would lift off from the Kandahar Airfield and other large bases, ferrying Army Special Forces soldiers, Navy SEALs, and Marine commandos. The troops would swoop into villages, descend by rope from hovering aircraft, and surround the homes of their targets. The suspected insurgents would often be given an opportunity to surrender. If they didn't, it usually didn't end well for them. In the last three months of 2010, Special Operations teams conducted an average of fifteen raids a night, killing more than a thousand insurgents—about a third of them were classified as midlevel leaders—and capturing almost three thousand others.

The raids incensed President Karzai, who exploded in anger at every report of a civilian casualty resulting from a nighttime mission. McChrystal, who had led the Joint Special Operations Command and knew how valuable it had been to get insurgent leaders off the battlefield in Iraq, had limited night raids when he was in charge of the Afghanistan campaign, in part to appease Karzai and to avoid the perception that he was not sufficiently supportive of counterinsurgency strategy. But he had also faced a practical constraint: Many of the military's special operators were still in Iraq, as were the critical "enablers" that allowed them to conduct their operations—eavesdropping aircraft, intelligence analysts, and specially configured helicopters. Those assets began flowing into Afghanistan as Petraeus arrived.

As they learned of their brethren being hooded and handcuffed or pocked with bullets, many midlevel Talibs disobeyed orders from their Pakistan-based leaders to stay put. Some fled into the mountains; others retreated to Pakistan. Either way, they lost the ability to fund and coordinate their foot soldiers. Recruitment of new fighters slowed, and desertions increased. Homemade bombs were still planted, and snipers still shot at American patrols, but overall insurgent efforts became far less intense and organized. Mines were laid in the wrong places. Bunkers were abandoned. Ambushes fell apart. Top American officers were thrilled. The uptick in night raids had become their most effective tactic in beating back the Taliban in Kandahar province and across southern Afghanistan. The irony within the NATO headquarters that fall was thicker than the smoky dust clouds that settle upon Kabul in the cold months: The counterterrorism policy of raids and air strikes that Petraeus and other commanders had derided in the 2009 White House strategy review had become the military's principal tool to weaken the insurgency.

Petraeus, of course, bristled at that conclusion. He insisted that counterterrorism operations were merely part of his counterinsurgency strategy. When I posed a skeptical question during a conversation in his wood-paneled office, he pulled out a sheet with his Anaconda slide—the one that had become a joke at the White House—and pointed to the words "counterterrorist operations." It seemed to me that he was defining COIN to include every military tactic in his arsenal except the use of nuclear weapons.

He maintained that successful CT (what the acronym-loving military called counterterrorism) required COIN, because good relations with the locals generated good intelligence. But the vast majority of the night raids conducted in Afghanistan during the second half of 2010 were based on signals intelligence—mobile phone calls, text messages, and conversations on walkie-talkies that were vacuumed up by the National Security Agency and the U.S. military eavesdropping aircraft that continuously circled over the country—not on information provided by villagers who suddenly felt safer because American troops were around. The intelligence analysts who assembled "target packets"—the material given to Special Operations teams that identified where individual insurgent leaders were hiding—had a bias against tips from Afghans who walked up to U.S. bases. More often than not, the supposed bad guy was simply a member of a rival tribe or someone who had a dispute with the tipster. It was a lesson the Americans had learned the hard way: Too often, in the early years of the war, U.S. troops had unwittingly been pulled into local conflicts. By relying on phones and radios, they avoided that problem, though that approach led to other challenges. Once the Taliban understood that their calls were being monitored, they began to switch SIM cards every few days. The old ones were sometimes handed off to unsuspecting villagers, who would then receive a nighttime visit from the special operators. Sometimes they were killed trying to defend their homes. Sometimes they were arrested before the Americans realized they had picked up the wrong man. As 2010 drew to a close, I was struck by the discrepancy between the large number of Afghans arrested in night raids and the country's stagnant prison population. It appeared that for every insurgent commander who was killed or captured, a few innocent Afghans were rounded up as well and then let go. The practice did not trouble American officials so long as they were netting big fish.

At the White House, the effectiveness of signals intelligence–driven CT operations did not go unnoticed among COIN skeptics. A few chuckled to themselves during monthly strategy meetings when Petraeus detailed the increase in night raids. "It became clear to us that CT could work without full-blown COIN," one official who attended war cabinet meetings told me. "It was a vindication of the vice president's hybrid approach."

Although many in the military believed Biden had sought to limit the U.S. involvement to raids and little more—a misperception that was fueled, in part, by the vice president's conflicting statements on television—his plan envisioned a limited surge: counterterrorism plus more troops on the ground in key areas. Obviously he was not in favor of sending as many troops as McChrystal or Petraeus wanted, and not to places such as Taghaz and Now Zad. But the three principal districts around Kandahar city—Arghandab, Zhari, and Panjwai—were different. Evicting the insurgents from those areas would deny them the ability to seize the city and assert a claim to the entire nation. They were the strategic prize, and saving them required a combination of Special Operations night raids and conventional boots on the ground during the day.

Many of the Americans required to secure those districts

could have been drawn from the first 21,000 troops Obama approved in the spring of 2009—had the Marines not insisted upon limiting themselves to Helmand and had commanders in the field at the time grasped the importance of protecting Kandahar city. When McChrystal arrived, he understood it, and he earmarked for Kandahar one of the three infantry brigades that would arrive under Obama's 30,000-troop West Point surge. He wanted to devote more resources to Kandahar, but the other two surge brigades were otherwise committed. One had to go north, to Kunduz province, to take over from German troops, who had been unwilling to employ aggressive measures to tamp down Taliban advances. The third was headed to Helmand. It comprised the Marines who would head into Marja, Musa Qala, and Sangin. Had Larry Nicholson's brigade been allowed to take Marja in the summer of 2009, and had Marine commanders been willing to deploy some of their battalions outside Helmand, McChrystal could have had more firepower in Kandahar, and he could have had it sooner. Instead, he felt compelled to finish what had been started in Helmand, and he could not ignore the Taliban's metastasis in the north. That left him with just one additional Army brigade for Kandahar.

Although the Second Brigade of the storied 101st Airborne Division arrived in Kandahar in May 2010, it did not commence operations until that July—a full year after Nicholson's Marine brigade moved into Nawa, Garmser, and Khan Neshin. Any incoming unit required a few weeks to set up camp before it could begin conducting combat missions. By the summer of 2010, the preparations had become even more complicated. Because of the improvised-bomb threat, soldiers needed to learn how to drive mine-resistant trucks and employ new explosives-detection technologies, including ground-penetrating radar units. Much of that training had to be performed in Afghanistan because bases in the United States didn't have the equipment. But the NATO regional headquarters at Kandahar Airfield, which was run at the time by a British Army division staff, lacked the resources to speedily prepare the newly arrived Americans. As a consequence, the 101st soldiers were delayed by six weeks in the middle of summer—right at the peak season of Taliban activity.

The leadership team of the Tenth Mountain Division, which was scheduled to replace the British division staff that fall, offered to come earlier so the deployment of U.S. troops could be accelerated, but top American commanders refused. With the British leaving Musa Qala and Sangin, they didn't want to embarrass their coalition partner. Once again, deference to a NATO ally was impeding the war effort.

When soldiers from the Second Brigade of the 101st finally got to Zhari district, nothing seemed to break their way. The Taliban had mined the dirt paths through the district's agricultural belt, forcing the troops to scale row after row of the chest-high mud mounds farmers used to grow grapes. The terrain was similar to the hedgerows in Normandy that had so challenged American soldiers in the weeks after D-Day. The Afghan army battalion assigned to fight with the American brigade was fresh out of basic training. Only one of the five hundred soldiers was from Kandahar province. But the most vexing problem was the local government in Zhari. It consisted of one man, Karim Jan, the district governor. He rarely left the district's main town, and he had little interest in convening assemblies of village elders. He steered jobs and resources to his fellow Alizai tribesmen, and he seemed beholden to the local power broker, Haji Lala.

The Americans wanted Karim Jan out, but there was little they could do about him. His presence in the district was the direct result of political deals made by President Karzai. In 2004, Karzai had created Zhari by carving it out of two neighboring districts as a reward for Habibullah Jan, an Alizai warlord who had helped liberate Kandahar from the Taliban. The president even gave him a forty-member police detachment as a personal security detail. But his rule was so corrupt that many residents urged the Taliban to return. After he died, his brother, Haji Lala, anointed Karim Jan to do the family's bidding.

Then the Americans got lucky. When they learned that Karim Jan was trying to spring two men from police custody who had been implicated in the deaths of three U.S. soldiers, they urged the governor of Kandahar province to move him to another district. The new district leader, a well-regarded Zhari resident, built a staff of two dozen municipal employees, including education and agriculture officials. He convened regular community meetings and traveled through the district. And he persuaded Zhari residents who had fled to Kandahar city to return.

That helped. So did the brigade's approach to quashing the Taliban. Instead of confining their activities to patrolling villages and waiting for insurgents to attack, they assaulted enemy strongholds every few days, often using helicopters to drop behind Taliban front lines. The military's map of the district, once shaded entirely red to denote full insurgent control, began to turn pink. Splotches of yellow emerged. Then spots of green appeared and started to expand.

In the upper Sangin Valley, elders of the Alikozai tribe decided in December that they had had enough of the Marines. Although Alikozai leaders had talked earlier in the year to Afghan government officials about a peace deal that would involve development assistance and prisoner releases if the tribe turned its back on the insurgency, the discussions never progressed beyond preliminaries. The Alikozai were scarred by a previous attempt to oppose the Taliban, in 2007, that had collapsed when they had failed to receive assistance from Afghan and coalition forces. The Taliban had tied one Alikozai elder to the back of a pickup truck and dragged him out of the district. Furthermore, the Alikozai were involved in large-scale opium processing in the valley. The tribe did not seem ready to give up its stake in the lucrative drug trade.

Then an elite Marine reconnaissance battalion had pushed into the Alikozai area, about five miles north of where Kilo Company had been operating in Sangin. Attacked by young Alikozai fighters who had been egged on and paid off by Taliban commanders, the Marines battled back, killing about two hundred of them in October and November. The 3/5 killed several hundred more insurgents to the south over the same period, many of them Alikozai as well. "We started stacking bodies like cordwood," an officer in Sangin told me. "And they came to a point where they said, 'Holy shit, there aren't that many of us left.'"

On New Year's Day 2011, Alikozai elders agreed to a security pact with the governor of Helmand province that called for the tribe to forsake the Taliban and rein in their young men. In exchange, the Afghan, U.S., and British governments would fund development projects in the fifteen-mile-long Alikozai area, and the Marines would consider releasing some Alikozai detainees. Although Afghan officials and U.S. diplomats hailed the deal as a sign of how the promised carrot of reconstruction aid could lead to reintegration, Marine officers saw in the change of heart the power of the stick.

"You can't just convince them through projects and goodwill," one senior Marine officer said. "You have to show up at their door with two companies of Marines and start killing people."

The surge forces and the hard-edged tactics began to shift the momentum of the war, and by the spring of 2011, unprecedented signs of change were evident amid the lush fields and mud-brick villages of the south. In Sangin, the demining of Route 611 and security improvements along the way reduced the travel time from the district center to Kilo Company's headquarters from eight hours to eighteen minutes. In Zhari, when Taliban henchmen threatened residents who were working U.S.-funded day-labor jobs, they were met with a volley of stones from the workers and shouts of "Go away!" And in Arghandab, three gray-bearded village elders walked up to Lieutenant Colonel Flynn's base to attend a memorial service for an Army staff sergeant killed by a roadside bomb.

Although all three districts remained dangerous, more residents were attending *shuras*. People began telling American and Afghan troops where the Taliban had buried bombs. In some cases they dug them up and carried them to the gates of U.S. bases for disposal—an act of bravery that always unnerved the privates on guard duty. Intelligence reports indicated that the insurgents had begun to run out of money and munitions because so many of their commanders and facilitators had been taken out by special operators. But nothing made American officers happier than listening to Talibs expressing their desperation over walkie-talkies.

"We don't know what to do," one insurgent in Sangin told his commander. "The Marines keep running at our bullets."

"You have to do something," the commander replied. "We're losing."

American officers maintained to me that the shift across the south was different from earlier proclamations of success. Even if the Taliban planted a bomb here and there, they argued, the destruction of numerous bunkers, the seizure of tons of munitions, and the removal of thousands of homemade bombs over the winter had put the insurgents at an unprecedented disadvantage. "We've changed the battlefield," said Lieutenant Colonel Morris, the 3/5's commander. "They're not going to be able to fight the way they used to."

The cost of the progress was steep. In Sangin, twenty-nine Marines from the 3/5 were killed, and thirty others lost both legs. In Zhari and Arghandab, the Second Brigade of the 101st lost sixty-three soldiers. But those places weren't Taghaz. They were vital to protecting Kandahar city and marginalizing the insurgency. Zhari, once home to Taliban leader Mullah Omar, sat to the city's east. Arghandab protected the northern fringe. Sangin was off in northern Helmand, but securing it was a critical step in pacifying the next district to the north—Kajaki—which housed the dam built by Morrison-Knudsen during the Little America days. If the Taliban could be evicted from Kajaki, USAID could install a third turbine at the hydropower plant next to the dam. When that day came, USAID officials promised, power-strapped Kandahar would receive more electricity.

As I traveled through Sangin, Arghandab, and Zhari in April 2011, I was struck by the transformation. In Zhari, I drove with the Second Brigade's deputy commander, Lieutenant Colonel Joseph Krebs, to a village three miles south of his base for a gathering of elders. The trip there took fifteen minutes—and not a shot was fired. A few months earlier, we would have been pelted with gunfire and rocket-propelled grenades within minutes of heading south from the base.

At the meeting, held in an Army tent, forty-five elders sat in a circle, munching on apples provided by the soldiers. They did a lot of grousing about the lack of a doctor, the poor flow of water in irrigation canals, and the need for a new school. But Krebs and his fellow officers deemed the session a success. The fact that residents were willing to gather, even if to complain, was a major step forward. Before the participants left, the Afghan army battalion commander in the area implored them to seize the opportunity afforded by the American surge. He urged them to stand up to the insurgency by reporting any suspicious behavior, and he told them to take advantage of U.S.-funded day-labor programs. He did not delve into the politics of the war playing out in Washington, but it was clear that he understood the slim prospects of the U.S. military expending so much blood and treasure over another year if residents once again acquiesced to the Taliban. "This is a golden chance," he told the crowd. "You'll never get it again."

But would the Afghans seize the opportunity? Would the Afghan government fulfill its obligation by providing residents of those districts with basic public services—schools, a health clinic, and some agricultural assistance? Would Afghan soldiers and policemen become capable enough to take control of those places when the Americans pulled out in a few years? Was the grand experiment sustainable? Was it worth the cost—in lives, limbs, and dollars?

There was also the question of the Taliban's response. Although the insurgents had been hammered across the south, they were far from defeated. They soon found new ways to demonstrate their resilience to their fellow Afghans—and to the Americans.

16

There Was No Escaping Him

IN EARLY FEBRUARY 2010, days before the Marines stormed into Marja, Taliban commanders in the American-built farming community received a surprise visit in the late evening from a tall, fit thirty-seven-year-old with a close-cropped beard and intense brown eyes. Most of the men in the mud-walled house did not recognize their parka-clad guest, who had driven through the desert from Pakistan on a motorcycle. But those who did were stunned. In their midst was the Taliban's new military leader, Mullah Abdul Qayyum Zakir. He dispensed with pleasantries. He was near the top of the military's kill-or-capture list, and every minute he stayed in Afghanistan, especially in an area crawling with Special Operations troops, his chances of winding up as an American "jackpot" increased.

He had traveled to Marja to rally his lieutenants and plot strategy. He asked about supplies and the morale of their foot soldiers. He and his men talked about where they expected the Marines to attack and the most effective tactics to protect their weapons caches. They discussed snipers, roadside bombs, and rearguard assaults. Then he mounted his motorcycle, wrapped a scarf around his face, and rode into the chilly night.

For the Americans, Zakir was an adversary unlike any other in Afghanistan. He was responsible for more U.S. and British troop deaths than any of his fellow insurgent commanders. He possessed a rare willingness to leave the safety of Pakistan to meet with ground commanders in Afghanistan. And he won over tribal leaders by purging lieutenants who sought personal enrichment, demonstrating that he would tackle corruption in ways the government never would. But it was the six years he had spent locked up at the Guantánamo Bay military prison that put him in a league of his own. His time at the maximum-security detention center on the southeastern coast of Cuba had helped vault him up the Taliban's leadership ranks, and it had hardened his extreme, uncompromising views. "I have a strong feeling of revenge in my heart," he once told a Taliban subcommander in Helmand province. "Until this fire of revenge is quenched, the jihad will continue."

Abdul Qayyum was born to a modest Pashtun family in Helmand's Kajaki district but grew up in an enclave in the country's north populated by ethnic Tajiks and Uzbeks. Because he was too young to join the mujahideen when the Soviets invaded, he was sent to study at a madrassa in Quetta, where he befriended an influential mullah, Abdul Raouf, who was a fellow member of the Alizai tribe from Helmand. By the mid-1990s, he adopted Zakir as his nom de guerre and returned to Afghanistan to serve as a deputy to Raouf, who had become a senior leader in the Taliban army. Zakir's military prowess so impressed Raouf that he gave Zakir command of a thousand-man brigade that was sent to battle the Tajik- and Uzbek-dominated Northern Alliance. His daring battlefield tactics—he attacked behind enemy lines and once managed to extricate Taliban troops who had been surrounded—eventually attracted the attention of the Taliban's supreme leader, Mullah Omar, and top officials of the radical Islamist movement. They conferred special status upon Zakir's fear-inspiring unit, which he called the Helmandi Brigade, reserving it as a commando force for critical missions.

After the September 11 attacks, Zakir took his brigade to the city of Kunduz to defend the northern gateway to Kabul against an onslaught of Northern Alliance fighters, but soon his men were hammered by U.S. air strikes. In late November 2001, as thousands of Northern Alliance troops besieged the city, Zakir met with a group of senior Taliban officials that included Raouf and Mullah Dadullah Akhund, the fearsome one-legged commander who had murdered scores of ethnic

Hazaras. All of them, save for Dadullah, voted to surrender. On November 28, five days after his soldiers gave up, Zakir turned himself in to Northern Alliance forces with four other Taliban leaders, including the regime's army chief. In early December, General Abdul Rashid Dostum, a top Northern Alliance leader, gave Zakir and the four others to U.S. soldiers. (Dostum's men caught Dadullah but inexplicably released him.) Zakir supplied his American interrogators with a false name—Abdullah Gulam Rasoul—and described himself as a mere foot soldier in the Taliban army. The Americans did not know who he was, but the fact that he had surrendered with the Taliban's army chief suggested he was someone of importance. He was flown to a makeshift prison aboard an amphibious assault ship in the Arabian Sea and then back to Afghanistan's Bagram Airfield, which had become a giant American base that housed a CIA-run prison and interrogation center. But he didn't stay there long. On January 11, 2002, he was among the first wave of prisoners to arrive at Guantánamo. Declared an enemy combatant, he was shackled and clad in an orange jumpsuit. His possessions, which had been seized and placed in a plastic bag, included three Casio wristwatches, 2,000 Pakistani rupees, 160 U.S. dollars, 2,100 Saudi riyals, 60 German marks, and a notebook with blue and black writing.

During repeated interrogation sessions at Guantánamo, Zakir stuck to his false name and his cover story. He claimed that he had traveled to Kabul after the Taliban seized it in the late 1990s, "just to see the city." He insisted that he had gone to Kunduz in September 2001 to earn money and that he harbored no animus toward the Americans.

He eventually admitted that he had fought with the Taliban and that he believed it was acceptable to wage jihad against Americans in his country, but transcripts of his three Administrative Review Board hearings indicate that his captors had no idea how significant a role he played in the Taliban military hierarchy. U.S. intelligence analysts and interrogators never pieced together an accurate portrait of his life or even ascertained his real name. As a consequence, board members resorted to inane questions in determining whether he should be kept at Guantánamo:

BOARD MEMBER: Do you like what the United States is
    doing in Afghanistan now?
DETAINEE: Yes, I am very happy. I am very pleased, like I
    told you before. They are building my country.

On Christmas Day 2006, the commander of the military's
Guantánamo task force, U.S. Navy Rear Admiral Harry B. Harris, Jr., recommended that Zakir be transferred out of U.S. military control. In a SECRET/NOFORN memorandum to the head
of the U.S. Southern Command, Harris wrote that Zakir was
believed to be no more than "a bodyguard for a high-ranking
member of the Taliban." According to Harris, the task force
had determined that he was of medium intelligence value and
posed only a medium risk to the United States, its interests,
and its allies.

Zakir was sent back to Afghanistan on December 12, 2007,
along with twelve other Guantánamo detainees, including
Raouf, who had insisted to his interrogators that he was only
a bread deliveryman in the Taliban army. Hamid Karzai's
government promised that all thirteen would remain incarcerated unless compelling evidence proved their innocence.
But less than six months later, Zakir was freed from prison.
Although the Karzai government never explained why he had
been released, some Afghan officials suspected the president
had been asked to do so by former Helmand governor Sher
Mohammed Akhundzada and other influential Alizai elders.

Zakir quickly made his way to his old stomping grounds in
Quetta. The city was the capital of Pakistan's Baluchistan province, where senior Taliban leaders operated with impunity. The
Pakistani military had declared the entire province off limits
to U.S. drone strikes, in part because officials from the country's spy agency, the Inter-Services Intelligence Directorate,
frequently met there with members of the Taliban high command. The ISI's relationship with many Taliban leaders dated
to the early 1980s, when they had been mujahideen and the
United States had funneled arms to them via Pakistani spies.

With Mullah Dadullah Akhund dead—he had been killed by
British special forces in 2007—Mullah Omar gave Zakir control
of insurgent forces in Helmand. Zakir's military acumen once

again impressed Omar and other Taliban leaders, and his writ
was soon expanded to include Kandahar and the rest of southern Afghanistan. Zakir called his fighters the Mullah Dadullah
Front, and they continued their namesake's bloodthirsty tactics
by expanding the ranks of suicide bombers and training munitions teams to develop ever-more-lethal improvised explosive
devices. In 2009, the vast majority of U.S. military fatalities and
injuries occurred in areas under Zakir's authority.

He had become the Taliban's military commander—the
movement's number two leader—soon after the previous second in command, Mullah Abdul Ghani Baradar, had sought to
communicate with an emissary for President Karzai about possible ways to involve the Taliban in the Afghan government
in exchange for a cessation of hostilities. Upon learning of his
contacts, the ISI had him arrested in January 2010. He had vio-
lated a cardinal rule of Taliban life in Pakistan: no pursuing
deals of any sort unless the ISI serves as the agent. Omar's
decision to replace him with Zakir helped appease the ISI. "He
will never agree to a peace deal," a senior Taliban official told
me. "All he wants to do is fight."

His ascension occurred at the Taliban's most challenging
moment. The arrival of 20,000 American surge troops in the
south during 2010 halted, and then reversed, the insurgency's
momentum in Helmand and Kandahar. Zakir lost thousands
of fighters and hundreds of weapons caches. His foot soldiers
and subcommanders grew demoralized, and his logisticians
faced new difficulties in transporting bomb-making supplies
to those tasked with planting them along roads and footpaths.
Key districts that his men had owned a year earlier—including
Marja, Sangin, Arghandab, and Zhari—slipped out of their
grasp, and their efforts to capture Kandahar city seemed
ever more unlikely. But Zakir and his fellow Taliban leaders
had sanctuary in Pakistan, and the Americans couldn't pressure them there, no matter how many troops they sent into
Afghanistan.

Zakir and the rest of the Taliban leadership had free rein in
Quetta and its environs. They visited madrassas where a new
crop of Afghan and Pakistani boys were being initiated into
the radical fold. They zipped around on motorcycles to meet

with lieutenants who had come over for money, rest, and strategic guidance. And they often drove over the Kojak Pass to the rough-and-tumble town of Chaman, just across the border from Spin Boldak, where their operations chiefs used Afghan mobile phones, two-way radios, and human couriers to send orders and receive battlefield updates. By 2010, Chaman had turned into the Taliban's forward operating base. Fighters lived in fly-infested roadhouses along the highway. Buildings on the outskirts of town housed bags of ammonium nitrate. Triggering components could be acquired from several stores in the teeming bazaar.

In the spring of 2011, as the snowy mountain passes between Pakistan and Afghanistan became passable and the Taliban's annual fighting season started, Zakir worked at a frenetic pace, crisscrossing Baluchistan to hold as many as ten meetings a day with his lieutenants, often working late into the night to plot strategy. At one session described to an American journalist by a senior Taliban intelligence official, Zakir rode up on his Honda motorcycle to a dirt-floored house in the crowded Quetta suburb of Pashtunabad.

> Zakir walked in and quickly got down to business, asking what the men needed to make their forces more lethal. More money for weapons, ammunition, and roadside bombs, they told him—and more suicide bombers. A major ambush, the kind that involves IEDs, RPGs, automatic weapons, and suicide bombers, costs some 200,000 Pakistani rupees, they said: the equivalent of $2,300. Zakir's secretary took notes, wielding a big, ledger-like agenda, while Zakir promised the cash and help they wanted. "This will be the year of bombs and fedayeen [suicide bombers]," he vowed.

After the Taliban leadership relocated to Pakistan in late 2001, they were provided safe harbor by the ISI. They were allowed to meet and reorganize and even reestablish networks inside Afghanistan, but the Pakistani spies refrained from giving them overt assistance. Although ISI officials regularly met with a handful of senior Talib mullahs, Taliban commanders had to raise their own capital from drug trafficking and foreign donations, and they had to acquire their own munitions, which wasn't all that difficult in Pakistan. Dealers sold tons of ammonium nitrate to Taliban middlemen with the full knowledge of the ISI. But in mid-2009, as American surge forces began flooding into southern Afghanistan, the ISI adopted a far more hands-on strategy. Concerned that U.S. gains on the battlefield would hobble the Afghan insurgency, ISI spymasters began interacting with far more Taliban commanders, often providing them arms and intelligence via civilian intermediaries. According to one assessment, at least half of all insurgent commanders were working closely with ISI operatives by the spring of 2011. The operatives provided some of them with sophisticated explosives that were almost seven times more powerful than conventional bombs mixed from ammonium nitrate.

Such perfidy had never been factored into the American plan. In his initial assessment, Stan McChrystal wrote that success in Afghanistan required "Pakistani cooperation and action against violent militancy." Even if the Pakistanis didn't crack down, McChrystal predicted he could strengthen Afghanistan against insurgent penetration by implementing a counterinsurgency strategy—if Afghans began to trust their government, the argument went, they'd be more willing to report Talibs in their midst. For that logic to hold, the sanctuaries could not expand or turn into ISI support centers. But that was exactly what had started to happen, and it had little to do with a lack of money or manpower or any of the other lies Pakistani leaders told their American counterparts. It came down to Pakistan's core national security interests: If Afghanistan was left alone, its government—which would likely be run by moderate Pashtuns working with Tajiks, Uzbeks, and Hazaras—would be able to beat down the Taliban with American assistance so that the insurgency no longer posed a threat to the state. At that point, the Afghan government would almost certainly forge a stronger relationship with India than with Pakistan. The northern Afghans were predisposed to ally with the Indians because of support they had received from New Delhi during their civil war with the Taliban in the late 1990s, and they hated Pakistan for backing their enemies. Even many moderate Pashtun Afghans respected India for offering them educational and

commercial opportunities, and they resented Pakistan for stir-
ring up trouble in their landlocked nation. The suspicion ran so
deep that Afghan children were reminded in school that their
nation had been the only one to oppose Pakistan's member-
ship in the United Nations in September 1947. For Islamabad,
the risk of a hostile Afghanistan in league with India was simply unacceptable. If Pakistan had to fight a war with India, it
could not afford trouble on its rear flank. Some in the ISI went
a step further: They hoped the Taliban could one day serve as a
proxy force to seize India's half of the Kashmir region.

But greater support from the ISI wasn't enough for the Taliban to hold its ground against tens of thousands more American forces in the south. As conventional U.S. troops flooded
into districts that had long been insurgent strongholds and
special operators snatched field commanders at night, Zakir
shifted strategy. Instead of trying to control large swaths of
territory, he began to play a long-term game. Obama had promised to start withdrawing U.S. troops by July 2011, and NATO
members had agreed to wrap up the alliance's combat mission
in 2014. All Zakir and his men had to do was hold out for a
few more years, to recruit enough foot soldiers and scrounge
enough funds to keep their insurgency alive until the day the
battle for Afghanistan would once again become Afghan on
Afghan, or until they could extract a good enough deal across
the negotiating table. In the interim, his fighters reminded
Afghans from time to time that the Taliban remained a potent
force, even if they did not control as much turf as they once
had. In early 2011, they blew up Kandahar's police chief; a few
months later, they killed the city's mayor. U.S. commanders
might have thought they had Zakir's men on the ropes, but ordi-
nary Afghans saw a different message in the assassinations:
The American achievements in Helmand and Kandahar were
far from a decisive victory against the tenacious insurgents.

The Pakistanis looked for points of American weakness. With
the bulk of surge forces tied up in the south, the ISI ramped
up its support of the Taliban faction in eastern Afghanistan.
Led by former mujahideen commander Jalaluddin Haqqani
and his son, Sirajuddin, who enjoyed ISI protection in Pakistan's North Waziristan area, the group seized dozens of dis-

tricts that U.S. commanders thought they had pacified. The
Haqqani network also managed to infiltrate Kabul's security
ring and conduct spectacular attacks in the capital, including
several suicide bombings and an assassination attempt against
President Karzai.

By mid-2011, the security improvements across the south
because of the troop surge were profound, but it was still not
certain that they could be sustained with the continued sanctuary in Pakistan and the ISI's increasing support for the insurgents. U.S. military commanders argued that the gains could
be cemented with a few more years of comprehensive counterinsurgency operations. Some also privately called for a green
light to whack a few bad guys in Baluchistan, just as a team of
Navy SEALs had done with Osama bin Laden on the outskirts
of Islamabad. But civilians in the White House and the State
Department opposed the idea of staying longer and expanding
the war across the border. It would be too costly, too risky, too
politically untenable. Moderating Pakistan's behavior would
require sustained, patient engagement by the United States
and its allies.

Zakir eventually got another nom de guerre, courtesy of the
U.S. military. He became Objective Nidhogg, after the dragon
in Norse mythology who gnaws at the root of the World Tree.
American intelligence analysts occasionally got a bead on him,
but every time they did, he was in Baluchistan. And as long as
he was there, he was untouchable.

Many American commanders tended to view the Taliban as a
band of simpleton zealots. Many of them were. Foot soldiers
fired their AK-47s indiscriminately, and they tended to wage
foolhardy, one-in-a-million attacks on heavily fortified NATO
bases. But Mullah Zakir also had a cadre of field operatives
who could plan and execute complex missions. Their most
stunning achievement occurred in April 2011, when they tun-
neled under Kandahar's Sarposa prison and freed almost five
hundred fellow insurgents, several of whom were hard-core
fighters, under the feet of unsuspecting U.S. soldiers stationed
on the prison grounds.

A month later, the Taliban published a long narrative account of the escape in its Arabic-language magazine, *Al-Samood*. The piece, titled "The Prison Break Story: How Fiction Became Reality," provided a remarkable account of how the Taliban had pulled it off:

> Six months ago, these committed mujahideen rented a house opposite the south corner of the Kandahar prison. The rooms of the old house were in disrepair. They initially built a new room. They brought in all necessary [equipment] and machines to make concrete, hiring a number of workers who worked during the day. But in the afternoon, when the workers left, the mujahideen stayed under the pretence of guarding the house. It was during that time that they proceeded to dig the tunnel from within the room they had just built.
>
> At first, four mujahideen were plodding through this operation. Their work method was the following: One was to hit with the pickaxe, digging the tunnel, while the other three were to move the soil. The soil could not be moved out by wheelbarrows because the tunnel was narrow, so some of the planners of the operation went to the market and bought a number of children's bicycles. They removed the small wheels and fixed barrows on them. Those wheelbarrows suited their task. They filled those barrows with soil, pulling them by a rope to the tunnel opening. Then they moved the collected soil to a truck. In the morning, when other soil trucks headed to the city, the mujahideen would bring in their soil-filled truck and sell it, thus getting rid of it.
>
> For two months, four mujahideen dug in the tunnel. Then their number increased to eight. By then, they were digging four meters every night. When their work reached 100 meters, they faced the issue of ventilation and lack of oxygen. Nevertheless, they carried on until cutting a distance of 150 meters. At that point it was terminally difficult to continue working. The work carried on no further. At first, they tried a ground fan; it resolved the ventilation issue, but it was winter and the cold weather caused headaches. Then they made an

air-pumping machine, delivering air by a pipe from the outside to the inside of the tunnel. That was the best method to resolve the ventilation problem and the lack of oxygen. The machine worked quietly with a charged battery.

Then they realized the risk of digging a tunnel under the road that carried heavy enemy vehicles to the inside of the prison: There was a possibility of a tunnel collapse under intense vehicle pressure. The question was how deep the tunnel was to be dug to exclude that possibility. As an experiment, they parked a truck atop the tunnel. It suffered no damage, assuring them that it would not suffer because of enemy vehicles. The tunnel was 2.5 meters deep between the house and the public road, but as a precaution they deepened it further.

After four months, the tunnel went on for 220 meters. Then they saw an iron pipe. They realized it was not a prison pipe but a pipe to a village south of the prison. The tunnel diggers, having no map, realized they had deviated from the correct path. . . . The diggers downloaded the prison map off the Internet, which they used to pinpoint the prison location. Using earth measurement tools, they redug for a distance of 100 meters directly toward the prison.

When the diggers reached the prison grounds, they had to figure out where to tunnel upward. Their ingenious solution was to use an iron blade to poke through the subterranean layer; a prisoner who knew of the scheme would get word to them if the blade was hitting the concrete floor in the correct area. But that raised two more hurdles. How would they angle a 2.5-meter-long blade into a vertical position in a tunnel that was just 70 centimeters high? And how would their collaborator on the inside hear the faint tap with fellow prisoners milling about? The blade was cut into segments, which were reattached as it was driven upward. And the collaborator arranged a Koran-reading session in a different part of the prison to distract his fellow inmates.

On the night of the escape, the tunnel crew dug additional

ventilation holes and strung forty-five lamps to illuminate the passageway. A team of ready-to-die insurgents was sent to a nearby neighborhood in case a diversionary attack was needed.

For operational security, only six members of the digging team were involved in the final stage. They got word to three collaborators on the inside at 9 a.m. on April 24. They in turn informed a small number of fellow inmates. At 10 p.m., the diggers punched a hole through the floor of the prison's intake room and started funneling out prisoners. The next destination was the prison's political wing—home to the most senior incarcerated Taliban members—but that proved more difficult to breach than expected because of the thickness of its concrete floor. Finally, at 1:30 a.m., they got through and began freeing inmates. The organizers, communicating among themselves with a phone line they had strung in the tunnel, sought to manage the flow of escapees so they would not congregate on the outside and draw attention. They also inspected each prisoner to ensure that he was not carrying luggage that might delay his progress. And those who had more than 3,000 Pakistani rupees were told to share money with those who were penniless.

By 3 a.m., Sarposa had been emptied of prisoners. Although U.S. and Afghan forces would round up a few of the escapees over the next few weeks, most evaded capture by melting back into their villages or heading across the border to Pakistan. Afghan authorities did make one quick arrest: the warden. He was accused of gross negligence, investigated for complicity, and locked in the prison.

The escape, according to *Al-Samood,* cost 900,000 Afghanis, or about $20,000—roughly the amount required to keep one American soldier in Afghanistan for one week. The Taliban also managed to offset some of its expenses. During the five-month excavation, the digging crew manufactured and sold 150 concrete blocks, the magazine noted, "making much profit."

The breakout was an unmistakable demonstration to the Afghans that, despite enormous American battlefield gains, the insurgents were neither a spent force nor a bunch of two-bit pikers.

. . .

Richard Holbrooke rushed into Hillary Clinton's ornate office on the State Department's seventh floor. He was late, as usual, and although he hated to keep Clinton waiting, she always seemed to tolerate his tardiness. When fellow members of her senior staff questioned his idiosyncrasies, she would usually smile and say, "It's just Richard being Richard."

He doffed his coat and plopped into a chair. Suddenly his chest began to heave and his face turned scarlet. He put his hands over his eyes.

"Richard, what's wrong?" Clinton asked.

"I don't know," Holbrooke said. "I've never felt like this before."

Holbrooke said he thought the feeling would pass and urged the meeting to proceed, but Clinton insisted that he see the department's in-house doctor. Holbrooke said he was able to walk and shuffled into the secretary's private elevator, but when he got downstairs, he collapsed. Clinton told her personal physician at the George Washington University Hospital to alert the emergency room that Holbrooke was on the way.

Holbrooke's aorta had torn. When he arrived at the hospital, he was in severe pain. Clinton's internist urged him to stay calm as they prepared him for tests and then surgery. The doctor told him to think of a beach. Holbrooke had a better idea. "Ending the war in Afghanistan—that would relax me!" he said.

He was wheeled into the operating room, where one of Washington's top thoracic surgeons tried to patch the artery. The rip was too severe. Holbrooke died three days later, on December 13, 2010.

When I reported his words in a *Washington Post* obituary, initially relayed to me by family members as "Stop this war," many interpreted it as a deathbed wish for the United States to lay down arms. But the fuller statement, which was conveyed the following day by a person who was in the room, was far from a confession. He believed, to his dying breath, that America needed to negotiate an end to the war.

His memorial service in Washington was held on a chilly January afternoon in the packed opera house of the John F. Kennedy Center for the Performing Arts. Pakistan's corrupt and ineffectual president, Asif Ali Zardari, flew in for it. Every Democratic Party foreign policy bigwig was there, as were dozens of members of Congress and scores of journalists. Obama delivered a eulogy. So did Bill and Hillary Clinton and former U.N. secretary-general Kofi Annan.

The differences in their speeches revealed just how distant and difficult Holbrooke's relationship with Obama had been. The sitting president spoke with eloquence, but his remarks sounded stiff, and they were devoid of a single personal anecdote.

Hillary Clinton, by contrast, celebrated the very traits that Jim Jones, Doug Lute, and others in the White House had derided:

> There are many of us in this audience who've had the experience of Richard calling ten times a day if he had to say something urgent, and of course, he believed everything he had to say was urgent. And if he couldn't reach you, he would call your staff. He'd wait outside your office. He'd walk into meetings to which he was not invited, act like he was meant to be there, and just start talking.
>
> I personally received the Richard Holbrooke treatment many times. He would give me homework. He would declare that I had to take one more meeting, make one more stop. There was no escaping him. He would follow me onto a stage as I was about to give a speech, or into my hotel room, or, on at least one occasion, into a ladies' room—in Pakistan.
>
> When he had an idea, he would pitch it to me. If I said no—"Richard, no"—he would wait a few days, and then he would try again. Finally I would say, "Richard, I've said no. Why do you keep asking me?" And he would look at me so innocently and he would reply, "I just assumed at some point you would recognize that you were wrong and I was right." And you know, sometimes that did happen.

Had he been alive, Holbrooke would have smiled. But it wasn't until the following month, at a memorial event for him at the Asia Society in New York, that Clinton said what he really would have wanted to hear: "The security and governance gains produced by the military and civilian surges have created an opportunity to get serious about a responsible reconciliation process." The United States finally had indicated a clear desire to negotiate with the Taliban.

Clinton also revealed a crucial shift in U.S. policy. The three core American requirements—that the Taliban renounce violence, abandon its alliance with al-Qaeda, and abide by Afghanistan's constitution—were no longer preconditions for engagement but "necessary outcomes of any negotiation." That meant the Taliban could come as they were.

It was the speech that Holbrooke had sought to deliver for a year. Although military gains across the south had put the United States into a slightly better negotiating position by that February, nothing had changed fundamentally since his last push to persuade others in the Obama administration to embrace a peace plan. Nothing except his death.

Ironically, the only man in the administration to negotiate an end to a war had been an impediment to ending this war. That was due not to his policies or his strategies but to personal antagonisms. Too many high-ranking colleagues did not bother to get to know him, let alone trust him. They homed in on his flaws and were determined not to let him hog the glory.

With Holbrooke gone, Doug Lute stopped insisting upon an envoy from outside the State Department. Others at the White House dropped their objections to proposals from Holbrooke's team and empowered his successor, the veteran diplomat Marc Grossman, to pursue negotiations. That shift prompted Pentagon and CIA officials to cease their opposition to the prospect of talks with the Taliban.

By then Obama's surge was fourteen months old. It was just five months before the president would outline his drawdown plans. Although Grossman quickly sought to kindle negotiations, initially through a Taliban contact whom Holbrooke and his German counterpart had cultivated, America had wasted crucial time and squandered its moment of greatest leverage to hammer out a peace deal.

17

My Heart Is Broken

IN THE 1950S AND 1960S, when the residents of Little America wanted to escape the stifling summer heat, they headed north along narrow, rutted dirt roads into the foothills of the Hindu Kush. The Morrison-Knudsen dam in Kajaki, near the chilly headwaters of the Helmand River, was a popular destination. Families spent long weekends in stone-walled cottages that had been constructed for American engineers when they erected the dam. An Italian caretaker and his wife had transformed the buildings into holiday villas with trellised gardens, gazebos, and sidewalks inlaid with elaborate designs fashioned out of colored pebbles. During the day, the children frolicked in the dam's reservoir, their mothers read or knitted, and their fathers tromped through the hills, rifles in hand, to hunt gazelle. Dinner was served in a common dining room, after which visitors sang songs and gazed at the stars through the clear, crisp mountain air. To Rebecca Pettys, who spent six years of her childhood in Helmand, the cottage resort seemed like a fairyland.

The dam, which had been completed in 1953, was a great feat of American engineering and logistics. Morrison-Knudsen had had to import cement, steel beams, and construction equipment and then transport all of it on countless lumbering convoys to the project site, where an army of laborers toiled away through the summer heat and wintertime chill, driven by the single-minded pursuit of modernizing their nation. The entire development effort along the valley—the irrigation canals, the new farms and villages—depended on regulating the river's torrential waters. Although soil and drainage problems would bedevil the overall project, the dam stood as a symbol of American ingenuity and commitment.

In 1975, USAID installed two 16.5-megawatt hydropower generators at the dam and strung transmission lines to Lashkar Gah and Kandahar, providing the first jolt of reliable electricity to the inhabitants of southern Afghanistan's two principal cities as well as to those who lived along the way. Residents purchased lights and fans and refrigerators. The farms along the Helmand were foundering, but thanks to the Americans, they finally had power.

There was more to be done. The dam needed to be raised and a new spillway constructed. A third turbine had to be installed in the generating house. But before any of that could be accomplished, Communists toppled the government in Kabul. American efforts at the dam, and along the Helmand Valley, halted. Although the Soviets wanted little to do with the hydropower project—they were more interested in killing the mujahideen who had holed up in the mountains of Kajaki—the dam's indefatigable chief engineer, Rasul Baqi, refused to leave, even as fighting raged around him. He single-handedly kept the generators running throughout the 1980s, cobbling together spare parts with scrap metal and using barbed wire to splice transmission lines. The generators limped along through the civil war and the Taliban takeover in the 1990s. When U.S. experts returned to the dam in 2002, Baqi was still there. But the lack of equipment and proper maintenance had taken a toll. The turbines were barely eking out 3 megawatts.

In 2003, USAID hired the Louis Berger Group, a Washington-based engineering firm, to rehabilitate the two turbines. But the agency failed to take advantage of the relative calm at the time to install the third turbine and string new utility lines to Kandahar, despite the city's need for more power than the existing units could provide. The bureaucrats squandered time. They rejected a proposal from the German engineering firm Siemens to install the third turbine, which would generate an additional 18 megawatts, eventually hiring a state-owned Chinese firm that submitted a lower bid. The Chinese didn't start on the project in earnest until 2007, and by then it was too dangerous to move the necessary parts up Route 611 through Sangin, a road USAID officials began to call "Hell's Canyon."

USAID eventually turned to British troops for help. In September 2008, 4,000 British soldiers were pulled off their assignments elsewhere to escort a massive convoy of trucks bearing parts for the turbine. USAID officials hailed the operation as a major success and promised that more electricity would soon hum toward Kandahar. The convoy, however, failed to include the seven hundred tons of cement necessary to emplace the turbine in the generating house. (The plan was to bring it up later.) But the British forces were soon transferred elsewhere, and security along Route 611 deteriorated. Before long, the Chinese contractors packed up and left. The Chinese didn't want to antagonize the Taliban and jeopardize their other, larger investments in the country, including a $3 billion copper mine south of Kabul. USAID could not find another firm to take on such a perilous job.

Although the Louis Berger engineers finished their repairs to the other two turbines by relying on costly helicopter flights to transport employees and equipment, the uninstalled components of the third turbine cast a dark shadow over the dam. What had once been a manifestation of America's initiative and generosity now stood as a monument to its incompetence. USAID officials in Kabul and Washington sought to divert attention from the failure, drawing the attention of journalists and visiting members of Congress to the schools and clinics the agency was building. USAID planned to return to the dam when the violence ebbed, but nobody knew when that would be.

By the spring of 2010, the military's focus had shifted to securing Kandahar city. Commanders planned to use surge troops to conduct large-scale clearing operations in Arghandab and Zhari districts, but they did not plan a significant troop presence inside the city, save a battalion of military police officers who would work with the local police and a battalion of 82nd Airborne paratroopers who would search vehicles on inbound roads. That meant commanders would have to rely on the Afghan government and its security forces to pacify the city. The Americans hoped an Afghan government push

to improve public services would help, but that effort quickly
foundered. Worried that the military campaign would be for
naught if they were unable to build support for the Afghan
government and sap Taliban influence inside the city, coalition commanders cast about for other ways to win over the
population.

When soldiers asked residents what they wanted, increased
security was always the first response. Electricity was usually a
strong second. Although Kajaki was producing 33 megawatts
(enough to power about 33,000 homes), much of it was going
to Lashkar Gah, Musa Qala, Sangin, and other towns in Helmand. Some of the consumption was sanctioned, but much of
it was the result of theft, often by the Taliban, which ran a far
more effective distribution and billing system than the government. By the time the lines got to Kandahar, only 9 megawatts
were left. The city had two banks of old diesel generators that
could produce an additional 16 megawatts, but the Finance
Ministry in Kabul was not giving the city enough money to
buy fuel for them to run continuously. The result was a dire
shortage. Residents fortunate enough to have had their homes
and shops connected to the city's rickety network of electricity
wires received about six hours of power a day. But there were
days and nights without a flicker of light, the whir of a fan,
or the distraction of television. Frequent blackouts shut down
factories and kept people locked indoors after sunset. "We keep
praying for some light at night," Mohammed Jan, a carpet merchant in the main bazaar, told me. "If there was more electricity, there would be more security."

Military engineers at the Kandahar Airfield suggested
spending $225 million to buy two new 10-megawatt diesel
generators and enough fuel to power them for a year. The 20
additional megawatts would almost double Kandahar's power
supply, although it wouldn't come close to meeting demand,
which was estimated at 200 megawatts. The top NATO commander in southern Afghanistan, British Major General Nick
Carter, endorsed the plan, arguing that increasing power in the
city would produce a "head-turning moment" among residents.
But Carter didn't have that kind of money at his disposal. He

turned to American commanders for help. They, in turn, asked USAID to foot the bill.

By then the USAID officials responsible for the mistakes with the third turbine had left the country. The new team in Kabul had little incentive to atone for their colleagues' sins. To them, the military's plan involved a huge expenditure for questionable gain: Would 20 more megawatts really make a difference? Would it lead Kandahar residents to view their government more favorably? Furthermore, there was no way the Afghan government would be able to cover the diesel costs once American support ended. USAID enlisted the support of Karl Eikenberry, who cabled his objections to the State Department. He told Stan McChrystal that USAID would not pay.

Undaunted, McChrystal dug into the military's own deep pockets. American officers had a seemingly limitless fund called the Commander's Emergency Response Program that had been designed in the early years of the Iraq and Afghan wars to allow troops to pay for small projects—repairing a school or digging a well—to build goodwill in the months before USAID could begin larger reconstruction and development work. Before long, commanders began using CERP for larger projects: roads, police stations, tiny factories. It was an ATM that never ran out of cash, although nobody had ever spent $225 million on a CERP project before. The generator proposal was so costly that it required approval from Dave Petraeus, who was then head of the Central Command, and other officials at the Pentagon. They all signed off on it.

When USAID officials learned of the military's plans, they were determined not to lose the spending game to the Pentagon. Agency staffers concocted a nearly $5 billion proposal to increase the country's overall electricity supply by building a national power grid, constructing new generating plants, and expanding distribution networks. USAID assumed that the U.S. government would cover about $3.4 billion of the cost. "It was an asinine, unrealistic plan," a USAID official told me. "It was all about trying to spend money and stick a finger in the Pentagon's eye."

A key element of the USAID plan was to install the third

turbine at Kajaki. USAID officials pledged to commence construction as soon as the area was secure. It was just the sort of
incentive the Marines needed to hear.

"There's a dam up that road," Lieutenant Colonel Jason Morris told me as we walked along Route 611 in Sangin. "The
Marines are going to get up there and help get the electricity
flowing to Kandahar."

It sounded like a noble mission, but Afghan officials questioned the wisdom of Marines charging up to the dam. In 2010,
before Morris's battalion began pushing north on 611, Eikenberry paid a visit to Kajaki. While he was there, he was asked
by an Afghan engineer who worked at the site to sign a document certifying that he was employed at the dam. The engineer said he intended to use the paper to pass through Taliban
checkpoints. Eikenberry was incredulous. "Why do you want
the U.S. ambassador to sign this?" he asked the engineer. "This
would seem like your death sentence."

No, said the engineer. "The Taliban is benefiting from Kajaki.
They're siphoning power from the transmission lines and providing it to the people for a fee," Eikenberry recalled the engineer telling him. "If I could get the U.S. ambassador to sign,
that's proof positive that I am the right guy."

Eikenberry turned to Gulham Faruq Qarizada, the deputy
minister of energy and water. Both men had traveled together
from Kabul. Eikenberry asked him what he thought of the
Marine operation to secure the dam.

"I just don't understand what you're doing," Qarizada said.
"Who are you fighting up here? This isn't al-Qaeda. These are
tribes that don't like each other. I would sit down with these
tribes and tell them that you want to put another turbine in.
Everyone will get richer, there will be no battles, and everyone
will be happier."

"How does this end?" Eikenberry asked Qarizada.

"In about ten or fifteen years," he replied. "Eventually it
won't pay to fight anymore."

"If you try to fight your way here," Qarizada warned, "you're
going to lose a lot of Marines and I don't know what for."

· · ·

Brigadier General Ken Dahl thought he had seen the worst of the dysfunctional relationship between civilians and the military in Baghdad. He had spent a year, starting in the summer of 2005, as the top military officer in charge of the Green Zone. The security of the sprawling enclave had fallen to him, as had refereeing disputes among soldiers, diplomats, aid workers, and contractors. By then the State Department had assumed control of the Republican Palace—and responsibility for the reconstruction effort—from the Coalition Provisional Authority, which had been filled with young Republican Party members, some of whom were so dismissive of the military that they treated full-bird colonels as drivers and errand boys. The professional diplomats were no better. Many of the military officers in the Green Zone had worked to rebuild shattered societies during stints in the Balkans, Somalia, and Haiti, but the State guys couldn't have cared less. The soldiers were there to play guard and fight the bad guys. The diplomats—many of them, at least—believed they had a monopoly on setting policy.

Before Dahl went to Iraq, he had studied for a year at Harvard's John F. Kennedy School of Government, where he had written a paper about the importance of civilian-military cooperation. When he had returned from Baghdad, he had received another prestigious fellowship outside the military bubble—at the Brookings Institution in Washington. He had decided to use his year in the nation's capital to try to fix the disconnects he had experienced in the Green Zone. His model was the Goldwater-Nichols Act of 1986, which had reorganized the Defense Department and forced the services to share bases and assignments. Dahl, compact and bald, put on a suit and spent day after day knocking on doors on Capitol Hill, talking to any legislator or staffer who would listen about the need for similar legislation to integrate civilian and military operations. He received a polite reception, but few people had any interest in upending the current bureaucracy. They told him it would be too difficult and too costly.

When Dahl learned in early 2010 that he would become a deputy commanding general of the Tenth Mountain Division, which would be taking charge of the NATO regional headquarters in Kandahar that November, he decided to give civilian-military integration another shot. If initial American gains were to be expanded and sustained, he reasoned, diplomats and soldiers would need to forge a much closer relationship. He and his boss, Major General James Terry, brought the Tenth Mountain's command staff to Washington to meet with State Department officials, including members of its reconstruction and stabilization office. Dahl and Terry offered to let members of the office help draft the division's campaign plan. The generals even said they'd be willing to transform the document into a joint civilian-military plan. State officials were astounded. No other incoming division command team had offered them such an influential seat at the table.

When it came time to deploy to Afghanistan, Dahl asked State officials how many of the reconstruction and stabilization staffers who had helped plan the campaign would be coming with the division leadership to Kandahar. None, the officials said. They told him that five staffers had agreed to go but that the U.S. Embassy in Kabul had nixed the request; it had other plans for them. Dahl later discovered that the embassy had assigned all of them to a planning office in Kabul, where they worked on projects unrelated to the Tenth Mountain's mission.

That turned out to be the least of Dahl's staffing woes. In early 2011, as the Canadians began to reduce their presence at the reconstruction team office in Kandahar city in advance of a July deadline for the country's military to cease combat operations in Afghanistan, Dahl waited for the State Department to fill the vacant positions. The U.S. Embassy had assured Dahl's superiors that fifty-seven American civilians would replace the Canadians. When nobody showed, Dahl went to the top State Department official in Kandahar, who told him to "expect nothing" from the embassy. Dahl was dumbfounded. A few weeks later, Dahl saw Karl Eikenberry on one of the ambassador's visits to Kandahar and asked about staffing.

"General Dahl, the civilians are at the high-water mark right now," Eikenberry said.

"That's great," Dahl responded. "I can feel it lapping at my ankles."

Dahl eventually asked higher-ranking commanders to send him a contingent of military personnel to fill positions at the reconstruction office. The embassy howled, but Dahl stood firm. As far as he was concerned, the embassy had had its chance.

He didn't expect the State Department to match the Army's force levels. He knew that State possessed only a fraction of the Pentagon's budget and staff. (There were more members of military bands than there were Foreign Service officers.) What riled Dahl were broken promises—none more than USAID's plans for agriculture in Kandahar. Before the Tenth Mountain's departure to Afghanistan, USAID had assured the division's command staff that it would start a massive new agriculture initiative in the spring to succeed the troubled AVIPA program. Dahl and Terry knew that more than 80 percent of working-age males in Kandahar province were involved in farming, and they made the large program an element of their overall campaign. But when spring arrived, and Dahl inquired about the status of the $350 million program, USAID officials sheepishly told him that it had not yet even been put out for bids from prospective contractors. That meant the new effort was months away. AVIPA was due to end soon. Unless USAID moved with alacrity, there would be no U.S. assistance for farmers in Kandahar at the height of the summer fighting season.

The problem had begun in the summer of 2010. As reports of AVIPA's shortcomings had begun to filter back to USAID's headquarters in Washington, agency officials had resolved to design a new program that would involve fewer handouts. USAID had initially aimed to have the new effort operational by October 2010, when the one-year AVIPA program finished. The winning bidder for the new program was none other than International Relief & Development—the firm that had made such a mess of AVIPA. When senior agency officials learned of the decision, they canceled the project altogether. USAID then set out to redesign the program, hoping that another firm would win the contract. But the agency was paralyzed by a dispute over whether to play a short or long game. Some agency officials wanted to continue to emphasize day-labor projects, which the military favored because of their immediate impact. Others wanted to skew their efforts toward long-term agriculture development work.

By the time Dahl made his inquiry, USAID had reached an untenable position: The agency did not have a new program ready. With AVIPA's extensive cash-for-work projects set to end, Dahl feared he would lose a critical tool to lure away disaffected unemployed young men from Taliban recruiters. "Our flank is exposed," he groused to me during a visit to Kandahar.

USAID eventually caved in on all fronts. It extended AVIPA for another three months. It gave the military extensive day-labor projects. And it awarded a contract for the new agriculture program—worth $65 million for one year's work in just Kandahar and Helmand provinces—to none other than International Relief & Development.

The agency had also intended to begin a $140 million initiative in the spring of 2011 to help stabilize areas in the south that had recently been cleared of insurgents. The new program was supposed to bankroll local governments and fund small reconstruction projects in and around Kandahar city. USAID had released an outline of the new program the previous November and solicited bids from contractors. Then it went to the Afghan government's Ministry of Rural Rehabilitation and Development and asked for one person to participate on the evaluation team—in a nonvoting capacity. The Afghans balked. They had not been consulted in a substantive way during the design of the program, despite repeated promises from USAID officials that they would work as partners with the Afghans. Fearful of an angry reaction from President Karzai, the agency withdrew the solicitation and spent weeks working with the ministry to revise it. The job of listening to Afghan objections and rewriting the program fell to USAID staffer Summer Coish. The do-over postponed the start of the initiative by at least four months. "If you're looking at this in terms of counterinsurgency and trying to partner and plan with the military," she said, "the civilians aren't doing their jobs properly."

After six months in Kandahar, Dahl gave up on civilian-military integration. The relationship, as he saw it, was beyond repair. Despite his determined efforts, the embassy didn't seem to understand that 2011 was the last real chance for the United States in southern Afghanistan. Dahl began to wonder if all he had tried to do at Harvard and Brookings had been a waste of time. "I want the last ten years of my life back," he told me in April 2011. "My heart is broken."

From then on Dahl decided to go it alone. When he had arrived in Kandahar, he had been astounded by the embassy's obsession with district-level government. "Did they need judges and prosecutors in Zhari? No," he said. "There's no history of that. It's unnatural." Instead, he believed, what rural residents needed was a *hukook,* a government-funded mediator to adjudicate small disputes; if residents had larger grievances, they could drive to Kandahar city to see a judge. He felt the same way about many other services the embassy wanted the Karzai administration to provide in each district. When Kandaharis failed to embrace the local-government initiative, the embassy assumed the problem was a lack of security and trained civil servants. But Dahl saw a different reason: Southern Afghans didn't want Kabul telling them what to do.

In the south, people often referred to the government by the Pashto word for "burden." For centuries, the population had paid taxes in exchange for security, but that was it. Public services such as education and health care had never been part of the social contract, nor had governance at the district level. The U.S. counterinsurgency strategy was predicated on the belief that people would cast their lot with the government if it could provide services that the Taliban couldn't. But what the people wanted was order—and that was all they wanted. If the Americans focused their military and civilian resources on that goal—by mounting aggressive operations to flush out insurgents, empowering traditional leaders, and training the Afghan army—they'd prevail.

As he grasped the folly of the embassy's district-government efforts, Dahl began to recognize the extent of Ahmed Wali Karzai's influence across the south. To Dahl, the president's brother "was the don of Kandahar," a man who possessed the political and tribal clout to rally grassroots opposition to the Taliban as security improved. Ahmed Wali chaired the Kandahar provincial council, but his real power came from his family ties and his leadership of the Populzai tribe. More Kandaharis considered him their leader and problem solver than they did the governor, Tooryalai Wesa, an introverted agricultural economist. Although Wesa received extensive support from the embassy and regularly met with State Department personnel in Kandahar, it did not escape Dahl's notice that Wesa's office was usually empty, while Ahmed Wali's office at the provincial council had a hundred people waiting outside. "All the governance was taking place there," Dahl said. "We were kidding ourselves if we thought filling the *tashkeel*"—the list of positions on the governor's staff—"would fix the government."

But Ahmed Wali remained a pariah to American commanders and diplomats. Unlike Abdul Razziq and other power brokers whom Stan McChrystal had initially tried to sideline, Ahmed Wali had not been rehabilitated and embraced in the quest for expedient solutions to security as the U.S. troop drawdown neared. Dahl once asked a senior American diplomat at the Kandahar Airfield when he had last touched base with Ahmed Wali. "We don't talk to him," the diplomat said. Dahl was amazed. *If we're going to have an impact here*, he thought, *we need to work with the people who make shit happen.*

Dahl's first meeting with Ahmed Wali was cordial. Ahmed Wali's initial reaction, as Dahl remembered it, was along the lines of "Where have you been?" His willingness to work with the Americans, despite their earlier efforts to remove him, suggested to Dahl that Ahmed Wali had grasped the new balance of power in the south. An American Army division was headquartered at the Kandahar Airfield, and thousands more U.S. troops were stationed in Arghandab and Zhari. He had quickly concluded that he was better off with the Americans than against them.

It was more than realpolitik. Ahmed Wali wanted the Taliban defeated. He wanted order. And he thought American efforts to micromanage in the districts would fail. Dahl concluded that U.S. and NATO objectives "were not all that different from what he wanted."

Dahl knew he couldn't tell the embassy about his desire to collaborate with Ahmed Wali; it would probably oppose him.

He concluded that the military would have to do it on its own. Before deploying, he and Jim Terry had read an insightful book on the history of Afghanistan by the Boston University anthropologist Thomas Barfield. It described how southern Afghans had traditionally looked to Kandahar, not Kabul, for leadership. An idea came to them: What if they resurrected that concept—it used to be called *Loy* (Greater) Kandahar—as a way of fostering unity among prominent tribal chiefs and encouraging them to band together against the Taliban? The generals consulted with two of their most gifted political advisers: Neamat Nojumi, an Afghan American working for the U.S. Central Command's intelligence fusion center; and Todd Greentree, a retired Foreign Service officer who had lived through insurgencies in Central America and Angola before spending a frustrating year as political adviser to Harry Tunnell's Stryker brigade. The four of them cooked up a strategy to re-create Loy Kandahar. It began with asking Ahmed Wali to lead the effort. He required no persuasion.

They also enlisted another Karzai brother, Qayum, a former member of parliament who split his time between Kandahar and Baltimore, where he owned an Afghan restaurant. Qayum lacked Ahmed Wali's rough edges, allowing him to reach out to a broader collection of elders. He too signed on right away. "The concept of Loy Kandahar was a unifying slogan that had immediate meaning for every southern Pashtun," said Greentree, a lanky, gray-haired strategist who hung film posters over his desk at the Kandahar Airfield for *Chinatown, The Godfather,* and *Groundhog Day,* the movie in which a television weatherman must relive the same day over and over until he gets it right. It mirrored the rough-and-tumble world of America in Afghanistan, where fresh teams of diplomats and officers often repeated the mistakes of their predecessors.

Greentree and Dahl figured Ahmed Wali was probably mobbed up in the drug trade, but they saw no saints among the other influential men vying for power in Kandahar. If they were going to build a viable political order in the little time remaining, they would have to work with unsavory characters.

In early May 2011, Greentree and Nojumi spent four days meeting with Ahmed Wali, Qayum, and a small group of tribal chiefs to forge a plan to reclaim the lost glory of Kandahar. They identified a series of steps to build regional unity, strike deals to reintegrate Taliban fighters, and lobby for greater resources from Kabul. The subversion they were plotting was not lost on anyone in the room: They were rejecting the American model of governance and seeking to co-opt the Taliban's goal of southern Pashtun empowerment.

In the following weeks, Ahmed Wali expanded the provincial council so that marginalized constituencies would be represented. He convened a meeting among southern governors and organized two delegations to travel to Kabul, where they lobbied his brother Hamid to devolve more authority to regional leaders. Tribal chiefs who had long shunned the government said they were willing to stand against the Taliban. Those who had been active in the Kandahar and Helmand governments told me they had not felt so optimistic since the Taliban regime had been routed in late 2001.

Although State Department officials belittled the effort, it was one of the most significant breakthroughs of the decade-long war. Finally, in the waning months of Obama's surge, Dahl, Greentree, and others on the Tenth Mountain team had developed a realistic and sensible attempt to govern the most important part of Afghanistan. And it had occurred only because they were willing to strike their own path and ignore the embassy.

After he grew tired of fighting USAID, Dahl decided to focus his energy on the military's reconstruction programs. He wanted to trim waste. He didn't believe his tenure would be judged by the number of dollars disbursed, and he worried that overspending from the Commander's Emergency Response Program account was exacerbating the corruption and inefficiency the Americans were trying to address.

His first target was a $150 million project to construct a new highway for military vehicles to bypass Kandahar city. It had seemed like a good idea when his predecessor had approved it: The road would prevent long supply convoys from creating traffic jams and infuriating residents. Petraeus and other senior commanders enthusiastically supported the idea. But the need had evaporated by the spring of 2011, when most convoys ran through the nearly empty streets of the city at night. And with all the surge troops deployed, the volume of traffic was on the wane. When Dahl proposed terminating the project, other officers thought it unwise to torpedo something Petraeus had endorsed. Dahl figured Petraeus wanted him to be smart about spending money.

After killing the road, Dahl set his sights on Kajaki. When he first read through USAID's reports on the hydropower project and he examined the diesel generators in Kandahar city, he thought he had misread the numbers. Once the third turbine was installed, the plant would generate only 18 more megawatts. Assuming all of it made its way to Kandahar—which was highly unlikely—it would not be nearly enough to meet the city's demand. USAID mentioned a possible second-stage project to install three more turbines at the dam to produce an additional 50 megawatts, but that was years away. It would also require a whole new set of transmission lines from the dam and security along the way to prevent them from being tapped or toppled by the Taliban. Dahl wondered why USAID was so gung ho about a project that, in its initial years, wouldn't meet the city's needs. He also wondered if the Marines, who were devoting so much blood and treasure to securing the road to the dam, understood just how insignificant the third turbine was. "Everyone was blindly supporting it, but it made no sense," he said.

His view of Kajaki also led him to reexamine the military's $225 million diesel generator project, billed as a "bridging solution" until the turbine was installed. Once again, the math didn't add up: The generators were producing far more power—around 20 megawatts—than the city would receive once the third turbine was installed, according to the USAID reports he had read. Something was screwy. Dahl also couldn't find any evidence that the additional electricity was yielding greater employment, stability, or support for the government. "This is a bridge to nowhere," he declared to his staff.

Dahl proposed pulling the plug on the generators. Senior officers reminded him that increasing electricity supply was another Petraeus pet project, and some warned that there would be riots in the streets if the power supply dropped. Dahl scoffed at the alarmist predictions, but other obstacles were thrown in his way. Fellow generals stood to be embarrassed if an initiative they had so loudly supported—over the objections of the embassy and USAID—was deemed a failure. They protected their interests. When Dahl boarded his flight back to the United States, nothing had changed.

He had arrived in Kandahar the previous autumn with the idea that electricity needed to be the top nonmilitary priority for the Tenth Mountain team. He left thinking that the military and USAID had overstated the importance of turning on a few more lights and televisions. He had come to believe that American ambition needed to be focused on assisting farmers and making modest improvements to residents' lives, not on the massive infrastructure projects that had been America's obsession for much of the last six decades. "Frankly, in southern Afghanistan, when the sun goes down, it gets dark," he said, "and that's fine."

Two months after Dahl returned home to Fort Drum in upstate New York, USAID decided to cut funding for the Kajaki project. USAID's budget had been slashed by Congress, and agency officials concluded that installing the third turbine was not worth the cost. Sixty years later, the United States still did not have the time or the money to realize the dream of Little America.

18

What We Have Is Folly

TWO YEARS AFTER LARRY NICHOLSON thrust his Marines into the central Helmand River Valley, the grunts stationed there longed for a gunfight, "just to get off a few rounds," said one, "so we can feel like Marines." The battalion in Garmser had not suffered a single fatality from a roadside bomb in three months. Only one rocket-propelled grenade and a few scattered bullets had been fired their way.

The turnaround in Garmser was the product of arduous combat operations by four successive infantry battalions, each one pushing a little farther down the river during its seven-month tour to seize a few more miles of territory from the Taliban. Part of the mission involved by-the-book counterinsurgency tactics—protecting the good people of the district so they'd feel confident enough to rat out the bad guys in their midst—but a key reason for the improvement was a gloves-off thrashing. The Marines had fanned out in the desert, searching for a fight. When they found one, the insurgents usually wound up dead. The expanding Marine presence had spurred many of the remaining militants to flee, and it had encouraged the local police to return to their posts. By the spring of 2011, Garmser's cops were leading the way against the last bands of foolhardy Talibs, raiding safe houses and unearthing vast caches of explosives, as Marines looked on in amazement. As violence ebbed, tribal leaders who had fled to Lashkar Gah came home to Garmser. Schools and bazaars reopened. Farmers grabbed their shovels and headed back to their fields. Life resumed in the simple rhythms of the past few centuries.

Although the Marines had transformed one of the most Taliban-infested corners of the country, they believed the district remained too fragile to turn over to Afghan security forces. There was still at least one insurgent cell operating in the area. The Afghan army battalion in the district was lazy. And the Afghan government was still missing in action. Garmser had had a skilled and respected district governor, but he had been sacked on orders from President Karzai in 2010 and replaced with a twenty-two-year-old from Kabul who lacked any interest in rural politics. Even the police needed continued oversight, lest they revert to their old, venal ways. "Don't let the lack of violence deceive you," the battalion commander, Lieutenant Colonel Sean Riordan, warned me when I visited him at the two-year mark in early July 2011. "Our job here isn't done."

I accompanied Riordan as he met with the crafty police chief, Omar Jan, in a bid to improve communication between the police and the Marines. A week earlier, Omar's cops had conducted a daring raid, dressing in civilian clothes and closing in on a Taliban safe house on tractors. They killed a few bad guys and apprehended two teenage insurgents trying to escape clad as women. The chief insisted they keep their dresses on as they stewed in the station's lockup. The teens were paraded before us while we sat in Omar's office. We suspected that his men forced the boys to dance and perform sexual favors in the evenings—a common custom among police officers in southern Afghanistan—but Riordan lacked proof, so he didn't broach the matter. Instead he chided Omar for not informing the Marines about the raid ahead of time. Warning of such operations, Riordan said, would reduce the chance of a friendly-fire incident, and it would allow the Marines to provide medical and bomb-disposal assistance if the police required it. "All I ask is that you coordinate with us," he said.

Omar, a stout man who beckoned his deputies with a hand, was noncommittal. He described how his extensive network of informers had provided a tip about where the insurgents were hiding. "You are blind in this area," Omar said to Riordan. "If the enemy shows up without their weapons, you guys won't recognize them, but we will."

Then Omar revealed the real reason he didn't want the Marines to tag along. He was worried that the Americans would hear complaints from residents. "If we search and we don't find anything, people will sometimes accuse us of stealing," he said. "When the Marines arrive, they will think we are misbehaving." That was the opening Riordan needed. He was concerned that Omar's proclivity for graft would cause history to repeat itself: The people of Garmser would once again welcome the Taliban as corruption fighters. He implored Omar to focus not just on apprehending insurgents but on winning the trust of the people.

Riordan and his State Department political adviser, the indefatigable Carter Malkasian, were not trying to create a model district in Garmser. They knew that most of the municipal positions would remain unfilled and the district governor would never earn the respect of the people. Instead of waiting for a miracle, as the U.S. Embassy seemed to be doing, they pursued a far more sensible plan: Malkasian reached out to tribal and religious leaders, enlisting them to exercise more authority in the district. Riordan and Malkasian also recognized that the police, the most effective local security force, would have to be a little more unorthodox than bureaucrats in Kabul might like. They tolerated Omar's antics, and they even agreed to give him money to hire a few trusted buddies who could provide valuable tips about insurgent activities. America's ticket home, they reasoned, depended on encouraging Afghans to take charge, even if their methods sometimes made outsiders cringe.

When military commanders looked at the before and after in Garmser, they saw success. But the inability to hand off the district to the Afghans after two years raised fundamental questions about America's war strategy. In selling the troop surge to Obama during the 2009 White House strategy review, military leaders had assured the president that they could clear areas of Talibs and transfer responsibility to the Afghans after eighteen to twenty-four months of counterinsurgency operations.

Garmser wasn't the only area whose progress lagged behind

the Americans' time line. The Marines weren't ready to hand over Nawa or Khan Neshin, the other two districts where COIN operations had commenced two years earlier. Had the commanders made a false promise to the president?

"Anyone who said you can go from full-on combat to transition in two years wasn't being realistic," a field-grade military officer in Afghanistan told me. "The lesson is that these things are going to take a lot of time and a lot of treasure."

Even the few bright spots turned out not to be all that glowing. Three days before my arrival in Garmser, Ken Dahl and I were supposed to meet Ahmed Wali Karzai for lunch in Kandahar. As Dahl and I were walking to an armored vehicle that would ferry us to the meal, his aide's mobile phone rang. It was the NATO regional operations center, with an urgent message: Ahmed Wali had just been assassinated by one of his guards. Without Ahmed Wali to corral the tribes and reallocate the spoils, what would happen to the crucial Loy Kandahar initiative? The United States had finally forged a plan for a political breakthrough in southern Afghanistan, but it lost the man to lead the charge.

In Garmser, the progress had come at a steep cost: Twenty-five Marines were dead and more than a hundred seriously wounded. The United States had spent roughly $2 billion. Sticking around through the following summer, which Marine commanders believed was necessary to cement their gains, would require almost another billion dollars—and perhaps a few more body bags. All this for a district of 150,000 peasants who lived in mud-walled homes. Was it worth it? Garmser was far from Kabul. Its poppy harvest was not the insurgency's lifeblood. It had never been home to an al-Qaeda training camp. Was this what America had gone to Afghanistan to accomplish?

Three weeks earlier, President Obama had commenced the American endgame in Afghanistan. In announcing the 30,000-troop surge at West Point, he had pledged to begin drawing down forces in July 2011, but how many he would withdraw, and how quickly, remained an open question. It was going to be "conditions-based," but that didn't stop rival camps within the war cabinet from offering their own interpretations. Vice President Biden had said that the troops should be removed as quickly as they had been added, while Defense Secretary Gates maintained that the initial reductions would involve only a handful of personnel. In the months that followed, those battle positions became entrenched.

By the spring of 2011, top commanders believed they had a winning argument to forestall the drawdown. They pointed to Nawa, Garmser, Arghandab, and Zhari to argue that the surge was working. Letting up too soon, they maintained, would sacrifice all they had achieved.

The president's civilian advisers were unconvinced. They focused on President Karzai's erratic behavior, Pakistan's failure to tackle the insurgent sanctuaries, and the Afghan army's rank incompetence. The advisers questioned how long it would take for Afghans to assume responsibility for districts the U.S. military had pacified. Garmser had proved that two years was a pipe dream. Would it be three years? Four? If the Afghan government lacked the capacity and political will to provide security and civil administration in the districts, counterinsurgency seemed to be the wrong strategy.

A majority of Americans no longer believed the war was worth fighting. Afghan patience was also wearing thin. Many Afghans had welcomed the Americans as liberators in 2001, but a decade later, the presence of so many foreign troops was stoking frustration and anger. Although McChrystal and Petraeus had sought to avoid civilian casualties and cultural affronts, almost every month brought news of another set of villagers mistakenly killed in an air strike or a night raid. Afghans even took to blaming U.S. and NATO forces for civilians blown apart by Taliban bombs. To the American military, more troops meant more security. To many Afghans, it was just the opposite: More troops meant more insecurity. If the foreign forces weren't here, they maintained, the insurgents wouldn't be seeding the roads with explosives.

In 2002, people in Helmand told Elisabeth Kvitashvili, one of the first USAID field officers to visit the province since the Little America days, that they welcomed U.S. assistance. But they warned that they would be watching carefully and that at some point, as with all foreign powers that had entered

Afghanistan, they would ask the Americans to leave. "The test of our success, they said then, was whether their request for us to leave was violent or not," she recalled a decade later. "Many would say we've blown the test."

Obama's civilian advisers thought that if the United States had a lighter footprint, if local leaders were weaned off American largesse, perhaps they would have a greater incentive to make peace with tribal rivals who were supporting the insurgency. Karzai might even be compelled to strike a deal with Mullah Omar. So what if the Taliban took over a few more remote districts? It was hard to imagine they could roll into Kabul in pickup trucks with the same ease as they had in 1996. The Afghan security forces, bungling as they were, appeared capable enough to hold on to major cities if they received a few more years of training. That was good enough for the White House.

Military leaders believed that approach was too risky and presaged a messy outcome. Did Washington want Arghandab and Zhari to slide back to anarchy? Did it want to allow the Talibs to stalk the gates of Kabul? And if Washington truly wanted to strike a peace deal with the Taliban, it made more sense to do it from a position of strength, not when planeloads of Americans were heading home. Petraeus's campaign plan called for a major offensive against the Haqqani network in the east in 2012, an aggressive effort to expand the Afghan army, and intensive operations in the south to solidify the gains there. Although Karzai and Pakistan were wild cards, the general believed his plan would improve the odds of security and stability in Afghanistan.

The military vision was far more expansive than what the president had outlined in the six-page terms sheet he had given Petraeus, Stan McChrystal, and Admiral Mullen when he had approved the surge in late 2009. "This approach is not fully resourced counterinsurgency or nation building," Obama had written, "but a narrower approach tied more tightly to the core goal of disrupting, dismantling, and eventually defeating Al Qaeda." Several months later, I asked one of Petraeus's aides how he had reconciled the general's plan with the president's goal. "We didn't pay much attention to that memo," he said.

In weighing the drawdown, Obama was willing to hear others' opinions, but he did not want the decision process to become as protracted and acrimonious as the surge debate in 2009. Some of his discussions were limited to one-on-one sessions with Gates, Hillary Clinton, and Tom Donilon, who had replaced Jim Jones as national security advisor, and though the president was willing to consider Petraeus's recommendation, he was not going to permit the military to constrain his options as it had done before.

The president convened the first session to discuss the drawdown in the Situation Room on Wednesday, June 15, 2011. Gone was the feeling of a graduate school seminar on South Asia, with history lessons and questions of grand strategy. The focus of the meeting was on Petraeus, who had flown in from Kabul. There were 33,000 troops at issue because Gates had given Petraeus the 3,000 additional discretionary troops Obama had put at Gates's disposal.

The general, working with a small team of senior officers in Kabul, had come up with five drawdown options. All of them proposed a token reduction of 3,000 to 5,000 troops at the end of 2011. The most conservative option called for the rest of the surge forces to remain for two years beyond July 2011; that plan, Petraeus maintained, involved the best chance of achieving a scenario in which Afghanistan's government and security forces had control over the majority of the country. The most radical option called for all the surge forces to leave by July 2012; that alternative, he said, carried the greatest risk of a Taliban takeover. He recommended a middle-ground option: Keeping the remainder of the surge troops—totaling 28,000 or more—in Afghanistan through the end of 2012. He said that approach would give him a good chance to achieve his campaign plan.

After listening to Petraeus, Obama made it clear that he favored a faster effort to "recover" the surge forces than Petraeus advocated. He asked Petraeus to assess the impact of removing 15,000 troops by the end of 2011 and the remaining 18,000 by July 2012. "How would that change the strategy?" Obama asked Petraeus. The president wanted the general's answer in two days, when the group would meet again.

For Obama, the decision hinged on more than whether the surge was working. The world had changed since he had announced the 30,000-troop deployment on December 1, 2009. With the nation in the throes of economic stagnation, the price tag of the war had become a major factor in his thinking. It cost $1 million to keep one American service member in Afghanistan for a year. That meant the annual bill for the war was more than $100 billion. Was achieving a marginally less bad outcome in Afghanistan worth the expense? With other pressing security challenges—Iran, North Korea, and the political upheaval in the Middle East—was it prudent to be tying up so many forces and disbursing so many precious dollars in remote Afghan villages? The United States was spending more each year to keep Marine battalions in Nawa and Garmser than it was providing the entire nation of Egypt in military and development assistance. When I shared that math with one of Obama's senior advisers, he nodded. "It's totally out of whack," he said.

The death of Osama bin Laden at the hands of Navy SEALs in Pakistan a month earlier had also transformed the debate. Al-Qaeda looked to be on the ropes. The odds were slim that the terrorist group would return to Afghanistan and reestablish training camps. And if it did, the Americans could strike them with drones or Special Operations teams. But nobody in the White House, not even the most ardent surge skeptics, was in favor of pulling large numbers of American commandos out of Afghanistan.

On Friday morning, Petraeus presented a chart showing a revised set of options to Obama and the war cabinet. The new alternatives outlined a steeper troop reduction at the end of 2011 than Petraeus had initially proposed, along with a summary of the pitfalls associated with removing so many forces in that time frame. Because he was going to be leaving Kabul soon—Obama was planning to appoint him director of the CIA—Petraeus shared the matrix with his successor, Marine General John Allen, who sent a message to Petraeus and his staff suggesting that a note be added at the bottom of the chart stating that the options put the accomplishment of the campaign plan at risk. That was a point that Petraeus also emphasized to the president.

But Petraeus was willing to compromise. By reallocating forces and trimming positions in large headquarters bases, he said, he could remove 10,000 troops by the end of 2011 and still execute his campaign plan—so long as he could keep the remaining 23,000 until November 2012. Doing so would allow him to maintain pressure in the south and east through the Taliban fighting season, which typically ends in October so commanders can head back to Pakistan before mountain passes are blocked by snow.

That wasn't good enough for Obama. The president wanted all of the surge forces out by July 2012—two years from the arrival of the last brigade. Vice President Biden and Tom Donilon concurred. Obama asked for Petraeus's view of that timetable.

"That invalidates my campaign plan, Mr. President," Petraeus said.

"David, you shouldn't have assumed I wouldn't do what I told the American people I would," Obama replied.

The war cabinet met again the following Tuesday—six days after the initial session—to hear the president's decision. Obama began by reiterating his desire for the remaining 23,000 surge troops to be removed by July 2012. Mullen argued that a midsummer pullout would require the forces to begin departing by the late spring, before the peak of the fighting season. Clinton said she shared that concern, as did Gates, who sought to strike a compromise. He proposed that the 23,000 be withdrawn at the end of summer, in September. Clinton and Mullen said they could support that option. Biden was unmoved—he wanted July or sooner. Petraeus held his ground. He said the additional months were crucial to his plan. Obama said he could live with Gates's middle-ground approach. The defense secretary, who had crafted the 30,000 option during the 2009 surge debate, had once again brokered a deal among the rival factions within the war cabinet.

The following evening, in a televised speech from the East Room of the White House, Obama reminded the nation of the promise he had made at West Point. "Tonight," he said, "I can tell you that we are fulfilling that commitment." But he did not betray any of the skepticism he had voiced in the Situation Room. The surge, he said, had yielded profound changes:

> We've inflicted serious losses on the Taliban and taken a number of its strongholds. Along with our surge, our allies also increased their commitments, which helped stabilize more of the country. Afghan security forces have grown by over 100,000 troops, and in some provinces and municipalities we've already begun to transition responsibility for security to the Afghan people. In the face of violence and intimidation, Afghans are fighting and dying for their country, establishing local police forces, opening markets and schools, creating new opportunities for women and girls, and trying to turn the page on decades of war.

More than 1,500 Americans had been killed in Afghanistan since the war had begun almost ten years earlier. "Thousands more have been wounded," Obama said. "Some have lost limbs on the battlefield, and others still battle the demons that have followed them home. Yet tonight, we take comfort in knowing that the tide of war is receding."

As he ended his address, he alluded to another withdrawal— not of troops but of the ambition to remake Afghanistan. Massive reconstruction and development projects would soon draw to a close. There would be no more grand efforts to realize the dream of Little America.

"America," he said, "it is time to focus on nation building here at home."

As the president had been considering his drawdown options, the CIA had finished an assessment of each of Afghanistan's nearly four hundred districts. Agency analysts had conducted similar studies every six months or so since 2007. The last one had been done in October 2010, and the new evaluation measured changes in security, government presence, and development since then. Each district was graded on a four-level scale, ranging from government-controlled to Taliban-controlled. The assessment was based on statistics—among them the

number of insurgent attacks and the number of Afghan security forces in the area—as well as input from the CIA's network
of Afghan informants. White House officials regarded it as "the
report card on the surge."

The CIA's conclusion was that Afghanistan was "trending to
stalemate." The report, which was written before Petraeus took
over as the agency's director, showed that gains in the south
resulting from the additional troops were offset by losses to
the Taliban in the eastern and northern parts of the country. "There has been no net progress," I was told by a senior
White House official who had read the assessment. In asking
for the surge, military commanders had asserted that security
improvements in the districts where the new troops were initially concentrated would be like inkblots that would expand
across the map of Afghanistan. That hadn't occurred. "Where
we went, we made a difference. But not next door," the official
said. "The surge worked locally, but it did not have the nation-
wide effect that was advertised."

Senior military officials were outraged at the contention that
Afghanistan was headed for a stalemate. They insisted that the
CIA had overstated the impact of Taliban gains in the north
and east and underemphasized security improvements in the
south. The White House official said he and his colleagues were
unconvinced by the military's objections. The CIA, he noted,
had used the same methodology in earlier reports that the military had championed in arguing for more troops in 2009.

The CIA did find that the surge had arrested Taliban
momentum—a goal Obama articulated in announcing the
troop increase—but it also echoed what I had seen in Garmser: The Afghans did not appear to be ready to assume control
of districts where security had improved. "We're stuck," the
White House official said.

I asked him whether Obama had read the CIA assessment
before making his decision.

No, he said. "We didn't want it."

Although many in the White House believed the surge had
been a failure, he said, the president's top advisers "didn't want
a counternarrative inside the U.S. government that says it
wasn't successful."

"The president's announcement needed to be made on the basis of 'the surge worked,'" he added, "'and therefore we can bring 33,000 troops home as I promised the American people.'"

The day after I had sat in the office of Garmser's police chief, I accompanied Sean Riordan as he drove south along the Helmand River to visit one of his rifle companies. We alighted in Lakari, a dusty village next to a swiftly flowing irrigation canal. It consisted of one main drag—a trash-strewn dirt road—lined with mud-walled shops and stalls, most of which had been abandoned. A few donkeys and emaciated dogs wandered about, as did some scruffy children looking for candy from the American visitors. A sandstorm had just blown through the area, rendering the landscape a sepia hue. The place had the same end-of-the-earth feeling as many other hamlets in Helmand.

Riordan had 225 Marines stationed in and around the village. As Larry Nicholson had believed when he had gone to the remote village of Taghaz, where Rick Centanni had been killed, Riordan viewed planting a flag in Lakari as a rational decision. He had more than a thousand men in his battalion, and he had to find places for them to patrol. Although Obama's drawdown decision could have prompted Marine commanders to thin out the ranks in Helmand and address other hot spots before the clock ran out, they remained unwilling to move. They wanted to make Helmand a showcase. A few weeks later, over drinks with a Marine general in a still gentrifying Washington neighborhood, I compared Afghanistan to a run-down urban street. It seemed, I said, as if the United States were devoting a large share of its community redevelopment funds to transform one tenement at the end of the block into a swanky mansion. What happens, I asked the general, if we win Helmand but lose Afghanistan? "That would be just fine for the Corps," he said.

As I walked down the dirt road in Lakari, I contemplated how it was that more than two hundred Americans had found themselves in this strategically questionable patch of Afghanistan. Why weren't they in the districts abutting Kandahar or in parts of the east besieged by the Haqqani network? This wasn't an issue of grand strategy. Even if Karzai hadn't been a loose cannon and Pakistan hadn't provided sanctuary to Taliban commanders and the White House hadn't blanched at the hundred-billion-dollar annual tab, Obama's vast increase of American troops and reconstruction dollars would still have amounted to a missed opportunity in Afghanistan. The reason wasn't to be found in Kabul or Islamabad. It was in Washington: The American bureaucracy had become America's worst enemy.

The Pentagon was too tribal. If the Marines hadn't insisted on going it alone or the Army had been willing to send a bigger, better-led unit than the Strykers, the United States could have undertaken meaningful COIN operations in Kandahar a year earlier than it did. Either decision could have obviated the need for a full 30,000-troop surge, or granted Petraeus the flexibility to swing surge forces east much sooner, allowing him to meet Obama's drawdown targets without objection. Now Zad and Taghaz would have been written off, and there would have been only a handful of Marines in the Lakari bazaar, if any.

The generals were too rigid. It wasn't just the campaign plan, which was far grander than their commander in chief had ordered. They were designing a larger Afghan army than many of the president's civilian advisers favored, placing a massive ongoing financial burden on the United States, which had committed to paying much of the costs. (The meter had already reached $50 billion.) Some of the expense was to provide luxuries the Afghans did not need and could not sustain. Many of their bases featured air-conditioned buildings with networked computers, and each army corps was slated to get a modern hospital, even though the country didn't have enough trained doctors and nurses to staff the facilities. All that might have been excusable had the U.S. military wholeheartedly embraced the mission of training the Afghans and conducting joint operations with them. Some officers understood that partnering with the Afghans was a central element of their COIN mission, but too many treated it as an afterthought. Top commanders refused to break apart enough infantry units to create teams of mentors. For all of their talk about the importance of building an Afghan army, the American generals didn't act on their words.

The grunts committed too many unforced errors. Although

the vast majority of American soldiers and Marines served with honor and distinction, a handful of miscreants would soon tar America's "we're here to help" message with a series of egregious acts: murdering civilians, disrespecting the Koran, mistreating Taliban corpses. Afghans saw in them the telltale signs of a decadelong war turned toxic, and it fueled doubts about the sort of long-term partnership Afghanistan would seek to forge with the United States. When the surge began, most Afghans viewed the Americans as good guys, the Talibs as bad guys, and the Afghan government as somewhere in between. When the drawdown commenced, many Afghans no longer saw America as their ally.

The war cabinet was too often at war with itself. Richard Holbrooke, Doug Lute, and Karl Eikenberry were all honorable men who worked eighteen hours a day, seven days a week, to save Afghanistan. They could have accomplished so much more if they hadn't been consumed with one-upping one another.

Those rivalries were compounded by stubbornness and incompetence at the State Department and USAID. Why had the power plant at Kajaki been mismanaged and cotton neglected? Why did the embassy waste so much time and money on useless district governments? Why couldn't State and USAID find more people like Kael Weston and Carter Malkasian? After a year in Kandahar, Brigadier General Ken Dahl came to believe the military had set itself an impossible task by conceiving a COIN strategy that the State Department could not fulfill. "The main effort in COIN is civilians, but they never signed up for it," Dahl told me. "So what we have is folly: We have a counterinsurgency doctrine we can't execute."

Weston had been right all along: Afghanistan was a marathon, not a sprint; Obama should have gone long, not big. It would have forced the Afghans to do more for themselves, and it would have led the Americans to pursue more modest and sustainable initiatives. Fewer troops would also have meant fewer bureaucratic obstacles and turf battles. Less could have been more. But taking that path would have required a first-term Democratic president with no military experience, who had promised during his campaign to fix Afghanistan, to stand up to his troop-hungry generals. "Surging was the easy thing to do," Weston said. "It's much harder to say no."

Although far more Americans perished on the beaches of Normandy and in the jungles of Vietnam, Afghanistan stands alone in the annals of American warfare. It is the country's longest war. It is a forgotten war—with no draft, the fighting has been left to a small cadre of professional officers and volunteer grunts. And it is by far the most complicated war our nation has ever prosecuted. Troops have been told to befriend villagers and bombard insurgents with the same fervor, often in the same day. Commanders have been ordered to fight with fewer forces, and in less time, than they wanted. Diplomats and development experts have been required to work in environments that were more dangerous than they had signed up for.

All told, I spent three years observing Americans attempting to defeat the insurgency in Afghanistan. For a long time, I believed that we could pull it off if only we had enough people, money, and patience. But the real challenge wasn't head counts, budgets, or public opinion. For all the lofty pronouncements about waging a new kind of war, our nation was unable to adapt. Too few generals recognized that surging forces could be counterproductive, that the presence of more foreign troops in the Pashtun heartland would be a potent recruiting tool for the Taliban. Too few soldiers were ordered to leave their air-conditioned bases—with the siren call of Baskin-Robbins ice cream in the chow halls and big-screen televisions in the recreation rooms—and live among the people in fly-infested villages. Too few diplomats invested the effort to understand the languages and cultures of the places in which they were stationed. Too few development experts were interested in anything other than making a buck. Too few officials in Washington were willing to assume the risks necessary to forge a lasting peace. And nobody, it seemed, wanted to work together. The good war had turned bad.

I kept hearing promises of how it all would be fixed. New strategies. New teams of officers and diplomats. New requests for money. A new man in the White House. But none of it remedied the core problem: Our government was incapable of meeting the challenge. Our generals and diplomats were too

ambitious and arrogant. Our uniformed and civilian bureau-
cracies were rife with internal rivalries and go-it-alone agen-
das. Our development experts were inept. Our leaders were
distracted.

Afghanistan was Larry Nicholson and Kael Weston's war. It
was Dick Scott and Ken Dahl's war. It wasn't Obama's war, and
it wasn't America's war.

For years, we dwelled on the limitations of the Afghans. We
should have focused on ours.

On my final day in Garmser, I walked over to a salmon-colored
building across the street from the Marine battalion headquarters. Sixty years earlier, the grounds had been a
Morrison-Knudsen camp whose brick walls encircled a pool, a
tennis court, air-conditioned dormitories, and limitless American ambition. After the engineering company packed up, the
site housed an agricultural school, but, like so much else in the
south, it had fallen into disrepair during the Soviet occupation
and the Taliban reign. When the Marines had arrived, they had
resolved to refurbish the main building so a new generation of
farmers could receive the same basic lessons in planting, fertil-
izing, and irrigating that Americans had taught decades earlier.

The construction work had been completed the same week
President Obama announced his drawdown plan. When I
arrived, a few dozen turbaned men in dirty shalwar kameez
and slippers had just finished listening to Garmser's agriculture director explain the benefits of forming farming cooperatives. A small group of the farmers gathered around me, and
we began talking about their lives and livelihoods.

All of them were poor—even by the standards of rural
Afghanistan. Many were sharecroppers, and most cultivated
poppy on at least half of their land. They were pleased the
Marines were so bored, but they feared that the reduction in
violence meant an American exodus was imminent. "If they
leave, it will become very dangerous here," one man said, pointing at the Marine base. "Our army is not ready to provide us
with security."

I turned to a man standing to my right. A gray turban sat on
his head above a furrowed, sun-beaten face. Bits of soil flecked

his long, graying beard. His leathery hands gripped the handle of a rusty shovel. His name was Raz Mohammed, and his father had moved to Helmand in the mid-1950s, soon after Paul Jones had returned home to Northern California.

After his father settled in Garmser, the saline soil began to stunt his crops. As he struggled to sustain his family, he told young Raz about the promise that had drawn him to Helmand—of bountiful fields, new villages, modern schools. He had been dubious at first, but then he heard something that changed his mind: The Americans were building it.

When Raz took over the farm, he turned to poppy to pay off the family's debt. Although he planned to grow it for only a year, there were always new reasons he needed the money: a dowry, a motorcycle, a Taliban shakedown.

He had stopped a year earlier because he feared the Marines would chop down his poppy stalks. But the winter wheat and summer corn he planted earned him barely enough to put food into the bellies of his dozen family members. He coveted the lush and lucrative agrarian vision that had lured his father.

"We are waiting," he said as he hoisted his shovel to his shoulder, "for you Americans to finish what you started."

ACKNOWLEDGMENTS

This book would not have been possible without Kael Weston. He introduced me to Larry Nicholson and convinced him to grant me insider access to the Second Marine Expeditionary Brigade during its year in Helmand province. Kael and Larry spent countless hours talking to me, they took me with them on trips to frontline outposts, and they ensured that I had an opportunity to visit every part of Marineistan. I am deeply grateful for their openness, hospitality, and willingness to allow a journalist in their midst to observe the good, bad, and ugly of the Afghan War. They are the gold standard in civilian-military cooperation. Our nation needs more generals and political commissars who can work together as closely, honestly, and respectfully as they did.

Larry's deputies, his successors, and their staff officers went to great lengths to help me observe and understand Marine operations. They include Richard Mills, Mike Killion, Paul Kennedy, Curtis Lee, Wes Harris, Carter Malkasian, Pat Carroll, Nina D'Amato, George Saenz, Bill Pelletier, Abe Sipe, Chris Hughes, and Gabby Chapin. In Kandahar and Kabul, I benefited from the generosity and assistance of Mick Nicholson, Ken Dahl, Ben Hodges, Scott Miller, Kim Field, Mark Jacobson, Erik Gunhus, Tim Nye, Todd Greentree, Web Wright, Bill Harris, Fred Tanner, Josh Welle, Jen Reynolds, J. D. Stevens, Tim Graczewski, Marie-Noelle Blanchet, Tadd Sholtis, Duncan Boothby, Mark Ward, and Alex Strick van Linschoten. In Washington, Vali Nasr and Vikram Singh explained the diplomatic side of the war. I'm also deeply appreciative of the time Stan McChrystal, Dave Petraeus, Karl Eikenberry, Bill Caldwell, and Dave Rodriguez spent meeting with me.

Others provided more than time and a seat on a helicopter: The witty and irreverent Marc Chretien, a raconteur par excellence, offered his leg as bait to a scorpion crawling between our cots in Marja. I'm still repaying the debt with bottles of red wine.

Many in Washington and Afghanistan, including senior officials at the White House, the Pentagon, and the State Department, as well as at the NATO headquarters and U.S. Embassy in Kabul, provided essential information that helped me develop a deeper, more nuanced understanding of the American effort to stabilize Afghanistan. Most of them spoke to me on the condition that they not be named. I am, nonetheless, tremendously grateful for their cooperation.

I owe the genesis of this book, just as I did with my previous one, to my friend and former editor Phil Bennett. In 2003, he exhorted me to focus my reporting on the American attempt to govern and rebuild Iraq; in 2009, he urged me to set my sights on how Obama would oversee the war in Afghanistan.

My employer, *The Washington Post,* remains one of the few American newspapers with a genuine commitment to covering the war. The desire for original journalism from the field begins with Don Graham, whose interest in the war has spurred me to make trip after trip to Afghanistan. I am also indebted to the *Post*'s publisher, Katharine Weymouth, and executive editor, Marcus Brauchli, for supporting my work, and to editors Liz Spayd, Cameron Barr, Kevin Merida, Carlos Lozada, Tim Curran, Doug Jehl, Griff Witte, and Jason Ukman for making my stories smarter and sharper. I've benefited from excellent reporting by several colleagues at the newspaper: Josh Partlow, Karen DeYoung, Greg Jaffe, and Scott Wilson.

Carlos, Greg, Scott, and Bill Hamilton—first-rate journalists and friends—read early drafts and provided wise counsel, and all four spent hours ministering to me during moments of doubt along the way.

My agent, Rafe Sagalyn, championed this book when it was an amorphous idea and wisely helped me find its focus. It was a privilege once again to write for Jonathan Segal and Sonny Mehta at Knopf. Jon wielded his pencil with grace and precision, and his sage guidance helped me see the story within my box of sand-encrusted notebooks. Many others at Knopf, particularly Maria Massey and Joey McGarvey, provided invaluable assistance in getting me across the finish line.

I wrote much of the book at the Woodrow Wilson International Center for Scholars in Washington, where Jane Harman, Mike Van Dusen, Rob Litwak, and Sam Wells have created an oasis of thoughtful research amid the partisan rancor of our capital. I finished the manuscript across Pennsylvania Avenue at the Center for a New American Security, thanks to the collegiality and generosity of Nate Fick, John Nagl, Kristin Lord, Shannon O'Reilly, and Ellen McHugh, who gave me a precious office when I needed it most. They have built a remarkable institution that has produced some of the smartest analyses of the Afghan War.

Three talented research assistants—Britta Ellwanger, Marissa Brogger, and Michael Boyce—helped me transcribe interviews and pore through documents. Britta worked countless nights and weekends on the book, even after her internship finished and she returned to her studies at Stanford University.

The brilliant Sarah Courteau took her pen to draft chapters and again to the entire manuscript, improving each paragraph and page with her incisive questions and deft suggestions. I'm deeply thankful for all that she did, particularly her willingness to work through a nasty illness as I sought to meet my final deadline.

This project afforded me few diversions, but those I did enjoy were often in the company of Meena and Liaquat Ahamed, whose enthusiasm and advice propelled me through the project. I'm also grateful for the friendship of Peter Baker and Susan Glasser, Hilliard and Kate Zola, Karen Dunn and Brian Netter, Spencer Hsu and Lori Aratani, Amanda Kosonen and David Schleicher, Anne Kornblut and Jon Cohen, Catherine Philp, Jon Finer, Theo Baker, Carrie Camillo, Omar Fekeiki, and Naseer Nouri.

My parents, my brother and his family, and my in-laws were a constant source of support, even though each visit to southern Afghanistan prompted a new round of stress for my mother.

My deepest appreciation is reserved for my wife and son. Julie's love and encouragement sustained me through long trips and nights in front of the computer. Max entered our world in early 2011. His smiles, laughter, and babbles of "Dada" were the ideal antidote to arduous days of writing. I couldn't have started this book without Kael and Larry; I couldn't have finished it without Julie and Max.

NOTES

I reported on the Afghan War for *The Washington Post* from February 2009 to July 2011. In that time, I made more than a dozen trips to southern Afghanistan. Although some of the material in this book appeared in different form in the *Post*, much of my account is based on more than seventy original interviews conducted exclusively for this book. Because of fears of retribution, several of my sources requested not to be identified by name; in those cases, I have tried to be as specific as possible about their role in the U.S. government without compromising their identity.

I have benefited greatly from the reporting of my *Post* colleagues, in particular Joshua Partlow, Karen DeYoung, Greg Jaffe, Scott Wilson, Craig Whitlock, Pamela Constable, Ernesto Londono, Karin Brulliard, and Bob Woodward.

Unless cited below, all of the material in this book is a result of my reporting and all statements quoted in the book are from interviews I conducted, documents and e-mail messages I obtained, or public sources. The principal exceptions are the sections about the history of southern Afghanistan in chapters 1 and 2; for those, I relied on numerous sources listed in the bibliography. I also benefited from descriptions of White House meetings in books by Bob Woodward and Paula Broadwell and in stories that appeared in *The Washington Post* and *The New York Times*. However, with the exception of specific quotes noted in the following pages, my accounts of those sessions are based on my own reporting.

I have chosen not to cite my interviews, the documents and e-mails I received, and public comments of senior officials. I do, however, indicate where I have used details gleaned from specific State Department cables and other government documents that were released on the Internet by the antisecrecy group WikiLeaks.

Where statements or conversations are recounted, it is on the basis of at least one person who could hear what was said. Although memories do slip and recollections differ even among eyewitnesses, I have attempted to describe past events as accurately as possible.

1 An Enchanting Time

15 *Paul Jones arrived:* All information about Paul Jones in this chapter is drawn from his memoir, *Afghanistan Venture.*

17 *The development of the valley:* My description of the history of the Helmand Valley development project is drawn from numerous sources listed in the bibliography. Dupree's book and Cullather's paper were important resources and valuable starting points for my research. I also relied on many reports and documents posted in Dick Scott's electronic archive at http://scottshelmandvalleyar chives.org.

20 *"In a country where":* The Em-Kayan, August 1949.

21 *"only tangible returns":* U.S. State Department, "Ambassador in Afghanistan Dreyfus," p. 1778.

21 *"there should have been":* Franck, *Obtaining Financial Aid for a Development Plan,* p. 34, fn. 64.

22 *"seriously undermining U.S. prestige":* U.S. State Department, "Ambassador in Afghanistan Dreyfus," p. 1778.

23 *The team eventually:* U.S. Technical Cooperation Service to Afghanistan, *Report on the Site Selection,* p. 15.

26 *"a piece of America":* Toynbee, *Between Oxus and Jumna,* p. 68.

27 *"A jeep full":* Ansary, *West of Kabul,* p. 69.

28 *"with a very strange":* U.S. State Department, "Religious Conservatism in Southern Afghanistan."

28 *"exaggerated the dangers":* Ibid.

29 *In 1956, it issued:* International Cooperation Administration, *Report on Development of Helmand Valley.*

31 *"the birds got fat":* Clapp-Wincek, *A.I.D. Special Study No. 18,* p. 25.

2 Stop the Slide

40 *The Communist revolution:* My descriptions of Nasim Akhundzada and Helmand province in the 1980s are drawn from works by Coghlan, Giustozzi and Ullah, Hafvenstein, and Rubin.

43 *ARJ was a leading member:* Dressler, "Counterinsurgency in Helmand," p. 44, fn. 268.

46 *"If we came for":* House of Commons, *Foreign Affairs Committee: Eighth Report, Global Security: Afghanistan and Pakistan,* para. 218.

47 *"I sent 3,000 of them":* McElroy, "Afghan Governor Turned 3,000 Men over to Taliban."

47 *SMA's decision coincided:* Coghlan, "The Taliban in Helmand."

48 *"We need you":* House of Commons, *Defence Committee: Fourth Report, Operations in Afghanistan,* sec. 2, para. 46.

49 *But the Brits were:* Ferguson, *A Million Bullets,* p. 47.

3 Marineistan

60 *He revolutionized the command's:* Priest and Arkin, "Top Secret America."

4 The Wrong Man

82 *"You must give":* U.S. State Department cable, "Helmand Governor Mangal Upbeat, Hopeful in Meeting," U.S. Embassy Kabul, June 27, 2009.

82 *"The question is why":* U.S. State Department cable, "Boucher and Karzai, Spanta on Jirgas, Drugs, Econ Cooperation, Governance, Iran," U.S. Embassy Kabul, September 8, 2007.

6 The Surge

115 *"does not presently measure":* U.S. State Department cable, "Helmand's Now Zad Challenge: What's Next?," U.S. Embassy Kabul, July 26, 2009.

116 *The next afternoon:* Although most information in this section is based on my reporting, some details were gleaned from Woodward, *Obama's Wars,* pp. 222–33.

123 *"Of course, 40,000 more":* U.S. State Department cable, "Helmand Views on U.S. Troop Levels in Afghanistan," U.S. Embassy Kabul, November 16, 2009.

123 *"I am concerned":* U.S. State Department cable, "COIN Strategy: Civilian Concerns," U.S. Embassy Kabul, November 6, 2009.

128 *The surge came:* Woodward, *Obama's Wars,* pp. 385–90.

7 Bleeding Ulcer

138 *"We have government":* Filkins, "Afghan Offensive Is New War Model," p. A1.

143 *"We will tell you":* Rahimi and Oppel, "Afghanistan's President Receives a Mixed Reception," p. A4.

145 *"You've got to be":* Nissenbaum, "McChrystal Calls Marja a 'Bleeding Ulcer' in Afghan Campaign."

8 Search and Destroy

153 *"Military leaders must":* Tunnell, "Red Devils: Tactical Perspectives from Iraq," p. 53.

159 *"sporadically moving into":* Naylor, "Stryker Soldiers Say Commanders Failed Them," p. 6.

163 *"the kingpin of Kandahar":* U.S. State Department cable, "Kandahar Politics Complicate U.S. Objectives in Afghanistan," U.S. Embassy Kabul, November 6, 2009.

11 Allies at War

205 *In Musa Qala:* Ferguson, *A Million Bullets,* pp. 266–92.

206 *"made a mess":* U.S. State Department cable, "ONDCP Director Walters' March 17–20 Visit to Afghanistan," U.S. Embassy Kabul, April 6, 2007.

207 *"Stop calling it":* U.S. State Department cable, "Frustrations Continue in Sangin District," U.S. Embassy Kabul, January 14, 2009.

207 *"take the British":* U.S. State Department cable, "Karzai Urges CODEL McCain to Support Zardari and Welcome Increase in U.S. Forces," U.S. Embassy Kabul, December 21, 2008.

207 *"We and Karzai agree":* U.S. State Department cable, "Scenesetter for December 10–11, 2008 Visit to Afghanistan by SecDef Robert M. Gates," U.S. Embassy Kabul, December 9, 2008.

213 *"The cupboard is bare":* U.S. State Department cable, "Afghanistan: UK Will Say No to a Request for More Troops Beyond the 1,200 Already Promised," U.S. Embassy London, November 24, 2009.

213 *"spread too thinly":* McVeigh, "Cameron in Afghanistan Says Tories Are 'Unlikely' to Reduce UK Troop Levels."

12 Odd Man Out

219 *An article appeared:* All quotes from the *Rolling Stone* article appear in Hastings, "The Runaway General," pp. 92–121.

14 The Boss of the Border

258 *The master of the racket:* This chapter is based on multiple conversations with Razziq and several days of reporting in Spin Boldak. Matthieu Aikins's article in *Harper's* provided valuable background information and biographical details about Razziq.

260 *"After that, everyone":* Aikins, "The Master of Spin Boldak."

264 *"That fall, another NATO officer":* Trofimov, Yarolsav and Rosenberg, Matthew. "In Afghanistan, U.S. Turns 'Malignant Actor' Into Ally." *The Wall Street Journal,* November 18, 2010.

16 There Was No Escaping Him

286 *In early February 2010:* Gopal, "Qayyum Zakir: The Taliban's Rising Mastermind."

287 *"I have a strong feeling":* Moreau, "The Taliban After Bin Laden."

288 *During repeated interrogation sessions:* U.S. Department of Defense, "Combatant Status Review Tribunal Statement of Abdullah Gulam Rasoul."

288 *but transcripts of:* U.S. Department of Defense, "Summary of Administrative Review Board Proceedings for Abdullah Gulam Rasoul."

291 *"Zakir walked in":* Moreau, "The Taliban After Bin Laden."

295 *"Six months ago":* Hikma, "The Prison Break Story: How Fiction Became Reality."

18 What We Have Is Folly

322 *"This approach is not":* Woodward, *Obama's Wars,* p. 387.

323 *"How would that":* Broadwell, *All In,* p. 292.

BIBLIOGRAPHY

BOOKS

Ansary, Tamim. *West of Kabul, East of New York: An Afghan American Story*. New York: Picador, 2002.

Barfield, Thomas. *Afghanistan: A Cultural and Political History*. Princeton, N.J.: Princeton University Press, 2010.

Beardsley, Charles. *The Naked Hills: Some Tales of Afghanistan*. London: Peter Davies, 1959.

Broadwell, Paula. *All In: The Education of General David Petraeus*. New York: Penguin, 2012.

Chayes, Sarah. *The Punishment of Virtue: Inside Afghanistan After the Taliban*. New York: Penguin, 2006.

Coll, Steve. *Ghost Wars: The Secret History of the CIA, Afghanistan, and bin Laden, from the Soviet Invasion to September 10, 2001*. New York: Penguin Press, 2004.

Dupree, Louis. *Afghanistan*. Oxford, England: Oxford University Press, 1973.

Ferguson, James. *A Million Bullets: The Real Story of the British Army in Afghanistan*. London: Transworld, 2008.

Giustozzi, Antonio. *Koran, Kalashnikov, and Laptop: The Neo-Taliban Insurgency in Afghanistan 2002–2007*. London: Hurst, 2007.

Hafvenstein, Joel. *Opium Season: A Year on the Afghan Frontier*. Guilford, Conn.: Lyons Press, 2007.

Jones, Paul S. *Afghanistan Venture*. San Antonio, Tex.: Naylor Company, 1956.

Jones, Seth. *The Graveyard of Empires: America's War in Afghanistan.* New York: W. W. Norton, 2010.

Kilcullen, David. *Counterinsurgency.* New York: Oxford University Press, 2010.

Michener, James A. *Caravans.* New York: Random House, 1963.

Neumann, Ronald E. *The Other War: Winning and Losing in Afghanistan.* Dulles, Va.: Potomac Books, 2009.

Rashid, Ahmed. *Descent into Chaos: The U.S. and the Disaster in Pakistan, Afghanistan, and Central Asia.* New York: Penguin, 2008.

Rubin, Barnett. *The Fragmentation of Afghanistan: State Formation and Collapse in the International System.* New Haven, Conn.: Yale University Press, 2002.

Stewart, Rory. *The Places in Between.* London: Picador, 2004.

Toynbee, Arnold J. *Between Oxus and Jumna: A Journey in India and Afghanistan.* New York: Oxford University Press, 1961.

U.S. Army/U.S. Marine Corps. *Counterinsurgency Field Manual.* Chicago: University of Chicago Press, 2007.

West, Bing. *The Wrong War: Grit, Strategy and the Way Out of Afghanistan.* New York: Random House, 2011.

Woodward, Bob. *Obama's Wars.* New York: Simon & Schuster, 2010.

ARTICLES, CHAPTERS OF BOOKS, AND PAMPHLETS

"Afghanistan Sets a Pace of Progress," *The Em-Kayan,* August 1949.

Aikins, Matthieu. "The Master of Spin Boldak: Undercover with Afghanistan's Drug-Trafficking Border Police." *Harper's,* December 2009.

Coghlan, Tom. "The Taliban in Helmand: An Oral History." In *Decoding the New Taliban,* ed. Antonio Giustozzi. New York: Columbia University Press, 2009.

Cullather, Nick. "From New Deal to New Frontier in Afghanistan: Modernization in a Buffer State." Working Paper 6, Indiana University, 2002.

Dressler, Jeffrey. "Counterinsurgency in Helmand: Progress and Remaining Challenges." Afghanistan Report 8, Institute for the Study of War, Washington, D.C., January 2011.

Filkins, Dexter. "Afghan Offensive Is New War Model." *The New York Times,* February 12, 2010.

Franck, Peter G. "Economic Progress in an Encircled Land." *Middle East Journal* 10 (1949): 43–59.

———."Problems of Economic Development in Afghanistan." *Middle East Journal* 3 (1949): 293–314.

Giustozzi, Antonio, and Noor Ullah. "Tribes and Warlords in Southern Afghanistan, 1980–2005." Working Paper no. 7, Crisis States Research Centre, London School of Economics, 2006.

Gopal, Anand. "Qayyum Zakir: The Taliban's Rising Mastermind." *The Christian Science Monitor,* April 30, 2010.

Hastings, Michael. "The Runaway General." *Rolling Stone,* July 8, 2010.

Hikma, Abd al-Rauf. Trans. Alex Strick van Linschoten. "The Prison Break Story: How Fiction Became Reality." *Al-Samood,* May–June 2011.

McElroy, Damien. "Afghan Governor Turned 3,000 Men over to Taliban." *The Telegraph,* November 20, 2009.

McVeigh, Tracy. "Cameron in Afghanistan Says Tories Are 'Unlikely' to Reduce UK Troop Levels." *The Observer,* December 5, 2009.

Moreau, Ron. "The Taliban After Bin Laden." *Newsweek,* May 15, 2011.

Naylor, Sean. "Stryker Soldiers Say Commanders Failed Them." *Army Times,* December 21, 2009.

Nissenbaum, Dion. "McChrystal Calls Marja a 'Bleeding Ulcer' in Afghan Campaign." McClatchy Newspapers, May 24, 2010.

Priest, Dana, and William M. Arkin. "Top Secret America: A Look at the Military's Joint Special Operations Command." *The Washington Post,* September 2, 2011.

Rahimi, Sangar, and Richard A. Oppel, Jr. "Afghanistan's President Receives a Mixed Reception in a Visit to Newly Won Marja." *The New York Times,* March 8, 2010.

Tunnell, Harry D., IV. "Red Devils: Tactical Perspectives from Iraq." Fort Leavenworth, Kans.: Combat Studies Institute Press, 2010.

GOVERNMENT REPORTS AND DIPLOMATIC CABLES

Clapp-Wincek, Cynthia. *A.I.D. Special Study No. 18: The Helmand Valley Project in Afghanistan.* Washington, D.C.: U.S. Agency for International Development, 1983.

Franck, Peter G. *Obtaining Financial Aid for a Development Plan: The Export-Import Bank of Washington Loan to Afghanistan.* Washington, D.C.: U.S. Senate Committee on Banking and Currency, 1953.

Harris, Harry B. *Recommendation for Transfer Out of DoD Control (TRO) for Guantanamo Detainee. ISN: US9AF-000008D.* Department of Defense memorandum for Commander, U.S. Southern Command, December 25, 2006. http://wikileaks.org/gitmo/pdf/af/us9af 000008dp.pdf.

House of Commons of the Parliament of the United Kingdom. *Defence*

Committee: Fourth Report, Operations in Afghanistan. London, July 6, 2011.

House of Commons of the Parliament of the United Kingdom. *Foreign Affairs Committee: Eighth Report, Global Security: Afghanistan and Pakistan.* London, July 21, 2009.

International Cooperation Administration. *Report on Development of Helmand Valley, Afghanistan.* Prepared by the Tudor Engineering Company, 1956.

Michel, Aloys Arthur. *The Kabul, Kunduz and Helmand Valleys and The National Economy of Afghanistan.* Washington, D.C.: National Academy of Science, Foreign Field Research Program, 1959.

U.S. Department of Defense. Summary of Administrative Review Board proceedings for Abdullah Gulam Rasoul. 2005. Declassified in 2007. http://humanrights.ucdavis.edu/projects/the-guantanamo-tes timonials-project/testimonies/testimonies-of-the-defense-department/arb1s/arb1_isn_008.pdf.

U.S. Department of Defense. Combatant Status Review Tribunal statement of Abdullah Gulam Rasoul. Precise date unavailable. Declassified in 2007. http://humanrights.ucdavis.edu/projects/the-guanta namo-testimonials-project/testimonies/testimonies-of-the-defense -department/csrts-1/csrt_statement_008.pdf.

U.S. State Department cable. "The Ambassador in Afghanistan Dreyfus to the Secretary of State." *Foreign Relations of the United States* 6 (1949): 1777–79.

U.S. State Department cable. "Religious Conservatism in Southern Afghanistan." U.S. Embassy Kabul, January 2, 1963.

U.S. State Department cables. "United States Policies with Respect to Afghanistan." *Foreign Relations of the United States* 11 (1952–1954): 1447–98.

U.S. Technical Cooperation Service to Afghanistan. *Report on the Site Selection for the Permanent Administrative Center of the Helmand Valley Authority.* 1953.

INDEX

Numbers in *italics* refer to the map.

A NOTE ABOUT THE AUTHOR

Rajiv Chandrasekaran is an assisting managing editor of the *Washington Post,* where he has worked since 1994. He previously served the Post as a bureau chief in Baghdad, Cairo and Southeast Asia, and as a correspondent covering the war in Afghanistan. He recently completed a term as journalist-in-residence at the International Reporting Project at the Johns Hopkins School for Advanced International Studies, and was a public policy scholar at the Woodrow Wilson International Center. He is the author of *Imperial Life in the Emerald City,* which won the 2007 Samuel Johnson Prize. He lives in Washington, D.C.

A NOTE ON THE TYPE

This book was set in Celeste, a typeface created in 1994 by the designer Chris Burke. He describes it as a modern, humanistic face having less contrast between thick and thin strokes than other modern types such as Bodoni, Didot, and Walbaum. Tempered by some old-style traits and with a contemporary, slightly modular letterspacing, Celeste is highly readable and especially adapted for current digital printing processes that render an increasingly exacting letterform.